Frequently Asked Questions in Corporate Finance

Frequently Asked Questions in Corporate Finance

Pierre Vernimmen, Pascal Quiry,
Antonio Salvi, Maurizio Dallocchio
and Yann LeFur

A John Wiley & Sons, Ltd., Publication

This edition first published in 2011

Registered office
John Wiley & Sons Ltd, The Atrium, Southern Gate, Chichester, West Sussex, PO19 8SQ, United Kingdom

For details of our global editorial offices, for customer services and for information about how to apply for permission to reuse the copyright material in this book please see our website at www.wiley.com

Library of Congress Cataloging-in-Publication Data

Frequently asked questions in corporate finance / Pierre Vernimmen … [et al.].
p. cm.
ISBN 978-1-119-97755-1 (pbk.)
1. Corporation–Finance. I. Vernimmen, Pierre.
HG4026.F747 2011
658.15 – dc23

2011031090

ISBN 978-1-119-97755-1 (pbk), ISBN 978-1-119-96069-0 (ebk),
ISBN 978-1-119-96066-9 (ebk), ISBN 978-1-119-96065-2 (ebk)

A catalogue record for this book is available from the British Library.

Typeset in 9/10.5pt Cheltenham-Book by Laserwords Private Limited, Chennai, India
Printed in Great Britain by TJ International Ltd, Padstow, Cornwall, UK

Contents

Frequently Asked Questions

About the Authors

Pascal Quiry is a professor of finance at the leading European business school HEC Paris, and a managing director in the Corporate Finance arm of BNP Paribas specialising in M&A.

Maurizio Dallocchio is Bocconi University Nomura Chair of Corporate Finance and Past Dean of SDA Bocconi, School of Management. He is also a board member of international and Italian institutions and is one of the most distinguished Italian authorities in finance.

Yann Le Fur is a corporate finance teacher at HEC Paris business school and an investment banker with Mediobanca in Paris after several years with Schroders and Citi.

Antonio Salvi is Full Professor of Corporate Finance at "Jean Monnet" University, Italy. He also teaches corporate finance at EM Lyon Business School and SDA Bocconi School of Management.

Pierre Vernimmen who died in 1996, was both an M&A dealmaker (he advised Louis Vuitton on its merger with Moët Henessy to create LVMH, the world luxury goods leader) and a finance teacher at HEC Paris. His book, *Finance d'Entreprise*, was and still is the top-selling financial textbook in French-speaking countries and is the forebear of *Corporate Finance: Theory and Practice*.

Chapter 1

Frequently Asked Questions

1. What is Corporate Finance?

Short Answer

Corporate finance describes the financial decisions of corporations. Its main objective is to maximize corporate value while reducing financial risk. The financial manager has responsibility for corporate finance decisions.

Long Answer

In order to understand what corporate finance is, we need to understand who the financial manager is and what his or her responsibilities are.

The financial manager is responsible for financing the firm and acts as an intermediary between the financial system's institutions and markets, on the one hand, and the enterprise, on the other. He or she has two main roles:

1. To ensure the company has enough funds to finance its expansion and meet its obligations. In order to do this, the company issues securities (equity and debt) which the financial manager sells to financial investors at the highest possible price. In today's capital market economy, the role of the financial manager is less a buyer of funds, with an objective to minimize cost, but more a seller of financial securities. By emphasizing the financial security, we focus on its value, which combines the notions of return and risk. We thereby reduce the importance of minimizing the cost of financial resources, because this approach ignores the risk factor. Casting the financial manager in the role of salesman also underlines the marketing aspect of the job. Financial managers have customers (investors) whom they must persuade to buy the securities of their company. The

better financial managers understand their needs, the more successful they will be.

2. To ensure that, over the long term, the company uses the resources provided by investors to generate a rate of return at least equal to the rate of return the investors require. If it does, the company creates value. If it does not, it destroys value. If it continues to destroy value, investors will turn their backs on the company and the value of its securities will decline.

The company's real assets are transformed into financial assets in the financial manager's first role. The financial manager must maximize the value of these financial assets, while selling them to the various categories of investors. The second role is a thankless one. The financial manager must be a 'party-pooper', a 'Mr. No' who examines every proposed investment project under the microscope of expected returns and advises on whether to reject those that fall below the cost of funds available to the company.

References and Further Reading

Quiry, P., Dallocchio, M., Le Fur, Y. and Salvi, A., *Corporate Finance*, 3rd ed. John Wiley & Sons, 2011.

2. What are cash flows?

Short Answer

Cash flows refer to the excess of cash revenues over cash outlays. They are usually measured during a specified period of time.

Example

Let's take the example of a greengrocer, who is 'cashing up' one evening. What does she find? First, she sees how much she spent in cash at the wholesale market in the morning and then the cash proceeds from fruit and vegetable sales during the day. If we assume that the greengrocer sold all the products she bought in the morning at a mark-up, the balance of receipts and payments for the day will be a cash surplus. If the greengrocer decides to add frozen food to her business, the operating cycle will no longer be the same. The greengrocer may, for instance, begin receiving deliveries only once a week and will therefore have to run much larger inventories. The impact of the longer operating cycle due to much larger inventories may be offset by larger credit from her suppliers. However, most importantly, before she can start up this new activity, our greengrocer needs to invest in a freezer chest. All these activities produce cash flows.

Example – Let's also take an example of a real company (Table 1.1), Indesit

Table 1.1: Cash flow statement for Indesit (€m)

		2006	2007	2008	2009
	OPERATING ACTIVITIES				
	Net income	77	105	56	34
+	Depreciation and amortization	143	141	130	141

Table 1.1: (*continued*)

		2006	2007	2008	2009
+	Other non-cash items	(16)	2	(75)	(15)
=	**CASH FLOW**	**204**	**248**	**111**	**160**
−	Change in working capital	(40)	(20)	61	(173)
=	**CASH FLOW FROM OPERATING ACTIVITIES (A)**	**244**	**268**	**50**	**333**
	INVESTING ACTIVITIES				
	Capital expenditure	136	172	145	83
−	Disposal of fixed assets	5	20	8	7
+/−	Acquisition (disposal) of financial assets	(9)	(12)	0	0
+/−	Acquisition (disposal) of other LT assets	(6)	(2)	0	0
=	**CASH FLOW FROM INVESTING ACTIVITIES (B)**	**116**	**139**	**136**	**76**
=	**FREE CASH FLOW AFTER FINANCIAL EXPENSE (A − B)**	**128**	**129**	**(87)**	**257**
	FINANCING ACTIVITIES				
	Proceeds from share issues (C)	3	2	0	0
	Dividends paid (D)	37	40	53	0
	A − B + C − D = DECREASE/(INCREASE) IN NET DEBT	**94**	**92**	**(139)**	**0**
	Decrease in net debt can be broken down as follows:				
	Repayment of short-, medium- and long-term borrowings	110	113	(316)	272
−	New short-, medium- and long-term borrowings	5	0	200	0

(*continued overleaf*)

Table 1.1: *(continued)*

	2006	2007	2008	2009
+ Change in marketable securities (short-term investments)	(6)	(23)	(15)	(27)
+ Change in cash and equivalents	(15)	2	(8)	13
= **DECREASE/(INCREASE) IN NET DEBT**	**94**	**92**	**(139)**	**257**

Long Answer

The cash flows of a company can be divided into four categories: *operating* and *investment* flows, which are generated as part of its business activities, and *debt* and *equity* flows, which finance these activities.

The operating cycle is characterized by a time lag between the positive and negative cash flows deriving from the length of the production process (which varies from business to business) and the commercial policy (customer and supplier credit). Operating cash flow (the balance of funds generated by the various operating cycles in progress) comprises the cash flows generated by a company's operations during a given period. It represents the (usually positive) difference between operating receipts and payments. Operating cash flow is independent of any accounting policies, which makes sense since it relates only to cash flows. More specifically:

- the company's depreciation and provisioning policy
- its inventory valuation method
- the techniques used to defer costs over several periods

have no impact on the figure.

From a cash flow standpoint, capital expenditures must alter the operating cycle in such a way as to generate higher operating inflows going forward than would otherwise have been the case. Capital expenditures are intended to enhance the operating cycle by enabling it to achieve a higher level of profitability in the long term. This profitability can be measured only over several operating cycles, unlike operating payments which belong to a single cycle. As a result, investors forgo immediate use of their funds in return for higher cash flows over several operating cycles (see Table 1.2 for a cash flow statement).

Table 1.2: A simplified cash flow statement

	2008	**2009**	**2010**
Operating receipts			
– Operating payments			
= **Operating cash flow**			
– Capital expenditure			
+ Fixed asset disposals			
= **Free cash flow (before tax)**			
– Financial expense net of financial income			
– Corporate income tax			
+ Proceeds from share issue			
– Dividends paid and share buybacks			
= **Net decrease in debt**			
With:			
Repayments of borrowings			
– New bank and other borrowings			
+ Change in marketable securities			
+ Change in cash and cash equivalents			
= **Net decrease in debt**			

Free cash flow can be defined as operating cash flow less capital expenditure (investment outlays).

When a company's free cash flow is *negative*, it must cover its funding shortfall by raising equity and debt capital.

Where a business rounds out its financing with debt capital, it undertakes to make capital repayments and interest payments (financial expense) to its lenders regardless of the success of the venture. Accordingly, debt represents an advance on the operating receipts generated by the investment that is guaranteed by the company's shareholders' equity.

Short-term financial investment, the rationale for which differs from investment, and cash should be considered in conjunction with debt. We prefer reasoning in terms of *net debt* (i.e. net of cash and of marketable securities, which are short-term financial investments) and net financial expense (i.e. net of financial income).

3. What alternative formats of the balance sheet may companies use?

Short Answer

A balance sheet can be analyzed either from a *capital-employed* perspective or from a *solvency-and-liquidity* perspective.

Example

Table 1.3: Capital-employed balance sheet for Indesit*

€ mln	2005	2006	2007	2008	2009
Goodwill	319	326	298	208	223
+ Other intangible fixed assets	107	115	108	124	109
+Tangible fixed assets	777	751	763	693	630
+ Equity in associated companies	22	13	1	1	1
+ Deferred tax asset	43	48	38	55	71
+ Other noncurrent assets	8	2	1	1	1
= NONCURRENT ASSETS (FIXED ASSETS)	**1275**	**1254**	**1208**	**1080**	**1035**
Inventories of goods for resale	0	0	0	0	0
+ Inventories of raw materials and semi-finished parts	93	121	119	112	92
+ Finished goods inventories	250	232	216	262	189
+ Trade receivables	555	573	523	456	392
+ Other operating receivables	97	116	141	138	87

(continued overleaf)

Table 1.3: *(continued)*

€ mln	2005	2006	2007	2008	2009
– Trade payables	820	886	856	765	660
– Tax and social security liabilities	123	147	165	138	147
– Other operating payables	39	37	25	52	94
= OPERATING WORKING CAPITAL (1)	**12**	**–28**	**–48**	**13**	**–141**
Nonoperating receivables	0	0	0	0	0
– Nonoperating payables	0	0	0	0	19
= NONOPERATING WORKING CAPITAL (2)	0	0	0	0	–19
= WORKING CAPITAL (1+2)	**12**	**–28**	**–48**	**13**	**–160**
CAPITAL EMPLOYED = NONCURRENT ASSETS + WORKING CAPITAL	**1288**	**1226**	**1160**	**1093**	**875**
Share capital	92	93	93	93	93
+ Reserves and retained earnings	412	453	485	327	374
+ Other reserves	73	74	58	46	40
= SHAREHOLDERS' EQUITY GROUP SHARE	577	620	636	466	507
+ Minority interests in consolidated subsidiaries	14	7	2	3	1
= TOTAL GROUP EQUITY	**592**	**626**	**638**	**469**	**508**
PROVISIONS	178	176	191	155	77
Medium and long term borrowings and liabilities	494	403	309	452	337
+ Bank overdrafts and short-term borrowings	319	296	276	250	170
– Marketable securities	96	90	68	53	26
– Cash and equivalents	200	185	187	178	191
= **NET DEBT**	518	424	331	470	290

Table 1.3: *(continued)*

€ mln	2005	2006	2007	2008	2009
= ADJUSTED NET DEBT	696	600	522	625	367
INVESTED CAPITAL = (GROUP EQUITY + NET DEBT) = CAPITAL EMPLOYED	**1288**	**1226**	**1160**	**1093**	**875**

*Indesit is one of Europe's leading manufacturers and distributors of major domestic appliances (washing machines, dryers, dishwashers, fridges, freezers, cookers, hoods, ovens and hobs). It is a lead player in major markets such as Italy, UK, Russia and France.

Long Answer

A *capital-employed analysis* of the balance sheet shows all the uses of funds by a company as part of the operating cycle and analyzes the origin of the sources of a company's funds at a given point in time.

On the asset side, the capital-employed balance sheet has the following main headings:

- fixed assets, i.e. investments made by the company;
- operating working capital (inventories and trade receivables under deduction of trade payables). The size of the operating working capital depends on the operating cycle and the accounting methods used to determine earnings;
- non-operating working capital, a catch-all category for the rest.

The sum of fixed assets and working capital is called capital employed.

Capital employed is financed by the capital invested, i.e. shareholders' equity and net debt.

From a capital-employed standpoint, a company balance sheet can be analyzed as follows:

	2008	**2009**	**2010**
Fixed assets (**A**)			
Inventories			
+ Accounts receivable			
– Accounts payable			
= Operating working capital			
+ Non-operating working capital			
= Working capital (**B**)			
Capital employed (A + B)			
Shareholders' equity (**C**)			
Short-, medium- and long-term bank and other borrowings			
– Marketable securities			
– Cash and equivalents			
= Net debt (**D**)			
Invested capital (C+D) = Capital employed (A+B)			

A *solvency-and-liquidity analysis* lists everything the company owns (on the asset side) and everything that it owes (on the liabilities side), the balance being the book value of shareholders' equity or net asset value. It can be analyzed from either a solvency or liquidity perspective.

Liquidity measures a firm's ability to meet its commitments up to a certain date by monetizing assets in the ordinary course of business.

A classification of the balance sheet items needs to be carried out prior to the liquidity analysis.

Liabilities are classified in the order in which they fall due for repayment. Since balance sheets are published annually, a distinction between the short term and long term depends on whether a liability is due in less than or more than one year. Accordingly, liabilities are classified into those due in the short term (less than one year), in the medium and long term (i.e. in more than one year) and those that are not due for repayment.

Likewise, what the company owns can also be classified by duration as follows:

- Assets that will have disappeared from the balance sheet by the following year, which comprise current assets in the vast majority of cases;
- Assets that will still appear on the balance sheet the following year, which comprise fixed assets in the vast majority of cases.

Consequently, from a liquidity perspective, we classify liabilities by their due date, investments by their maturity date and assets as follows:

- Assets are regarded as liquid where, as part of the normal operating cycle, they will be monetized in the same year. Thus they comprise (unless the operating cycle is unusually long) inventories and trade receivables.
- Assets that, regardless of their nature (head office, plant, etc.), are not intended for sale during the normal course of business are regarded as fixed (noncurrent) and not liquid.

Solvency measures the company's ability to honor its commitments in the event of liquidation; a company may be regarded as insolvent once its shareholders' equity turns negative. This means that it owes more than it owns.

References and Further Reading

Friedlob, G. and Welton, R., *Keys to Reading an Annual Report*, Barrons Educational Series, 2008.

Stolowy, H., Lebas, M. and Ding, Y., *Financial Accounting and Reporting: A Global Perspective*, 3rd ed., Thomson, 2010.

4. What is the working capital and how do companies manage it?

Short Answer

The working capital *is the net balance of operating uses and sources of funds.*

If uses of funds exceed sources of funds, the balance is positive and working capital needs to be financed, if negative, it represents a source of funds generated by the operating cycle (see Table 1.4).

Example

Table 1.4: Indesit working capital analysis

In days of net sales	2005	2006	2007	2008	2009
$\frac{\textit{Operating working capital}}{\textit{Net sales}} \times 365$	1	−3	−5	2	−20
$\frac{\textit{Inventories and work in progress}}{\textit{Net sales}} \times 365$	41	40	35	43	39
$\frac{\textit{Receivables}}{\textit{Net sales}} \times 365$	66	64	55	53	55
$\frac{\textit{Payables}}{\textit{Net sales}} \times 365$	98	100	91	89	92

Source: Annual Reports.

Long Answer

Working capital can be divided between *operating* working capital and *non-operating* working capital.

Operating working capital includes the following accounting entries in Table 1.5:

Table 1.5: Operating working capital

	Inventories	Raw materials, goods for resale, products and work in progress, finished products.
+	Trade receivables	Amounts owed by customers, prepayments to suppliers and other trade receivables.
–	**Trade payables**	Amounts owed to **trade suppliers**, **social security** and **tax payables**, **prepayments by customers** and other trade payables.
=	**Operating working capital**	

The working capital calculated at the year-end is not necessarily representative of the company's permanent requirement. Therefore, you must look at how it has evolved over time.

All of the components of working capital at a given point in time disappear shortly thereafter. Inventories are consumed, suppliers are paid and receivables are collected. But even if these components are being consumed, paid and collected, they are being replaced by others. Working capital is therefore both liquid and permanent.

Working capital turnover ratios measure the average proportion of funds tied up in the operating cycle. The principal ratios are:

- Days of Sales Outstanding (DSO)
  accounts receivable/sales (incl. VAT) × 365.

- Days of Payables Outstanding (DPO)
  accounts payable/purchases (incl. VAT) × 365.
- Days of Inventories Outstanding (DIO)
  inventories and work in progress/sales (excl. VAT) × 365.
- Working capital turnover
  working capital/sales (excl. VAT) × 365.

When a company grows, its working capital has a tendency to grow, because inventories and accounts receivable (via payment terms) increase faster than sales. Paradoxically, working capital continues to grow during periods of recession because restrictive measures do not immediately deliver their desired effect. It is only at the end of the recession that working capital subsides and cash flow problems ease.

The operating cycles of companies with *negative* working capital are such that, thanks to a favorable timing mismatch, they collect funds prior to disbursing certain payments. There are two basic scenarios:

- supplier credit is much greater than inventory turnover, while at the same time, customers pay quickly, in some cases in cash;
- customers pay in advance.

A low or negative working capital is a boon to companies looking to expand.

The *level* of working capital is an indication of the strength of the company's strategic position, because it reflects the balance of power between the company and its customers and suppliers.

Working capital is totally independent of the methods used to value fixed assets, depreciation, amortization and impairment losses on fixed assets. However, it is influenced by:

- inventory valuation methods;
- deferred income and cost (over one or more years);
- the company's provisioning policy for current assets and operating liabilities and costs.

Non-operating working capital is a catch-all category for items that cannot be classified anywhere else. It includes amounts due on fixed assets, dividends to be paid, extraordinary items, etc.

References and Further Reading

Biais, B. and Grolier, C., Trade credit and credit rationing, *The Review of Financial Studies* **10**, 903–937, 1997.

Cunat, V., Inter-firm credit and industrial links, Mimeo, London School of Economics, 2000.

Deloof, M., Does working capital management affect profitability of Belgian firms, *Journal of Business Finance & Accounting*, 585, 2003.

Long, M., Malitz, I. and Ravid, A., Trade credit, quality guarantees, and product marketability, *Financial Management* **22**, 117–127, 1993.

Maxwell, C., Gitman, L. and Smith, S., Working capital management and financial-service consumption preferences of US and foreign firms: A comparison of 1979 & 1996 preferences, *Financial Management Association*, 46–52, Autumn–Winter 1998.

Mian, S. and Smith, C., Accounts receivable management policy: Theory and evidence, *Journal of Finance* **47**, 169–200, 1992.

Ng, J. and Smith, R., Evidence on the determinants of credit terms used in interfirm trade, *Journal of Finance* **54**, 1109–1129, June 1999.

Shin, H. and Soenen, L., Efficiency of working capital management and corporate profitability, *Financial Management Association*, 37–45, Autumn–Winter 1998.

5. What are the alternative formats of an income statement?

Short Answer

Two main formats of income statement are frequently used, which differ in the way they present revenues and expenses related to the operating and investment cycles. They may be presented either by *function* or by *nature* (see Figure 1.1).

Long Answer

The two main alternative formats for an income statement are:

- **By function**, i.e. according to the way revenues and charges are used in the operating and investing cycle. This format shows the cost of goods sold (COGS), selling and marketing costs (S&M), research and development costs (R&D) and general and administrative costs (G&A).
- **By nature**, i.e. by type of expenditure or revenue which shows the change in inventories of finished goods and in work in progress (closing less opening inventory), purchases of and changes in inventories (closing less opening inventory) of goods for resale and raw materials, other external charges, personnel expenses, taxes and other duties, depreciation and amortization.

The *by-function income statement* format is based on a management accounting approach, in which costs are allocated to the main corporate functions (Table 1.6).

As a result, *personnel expense* is allocated to each of these four categories (or three where selling, general and administrative costs are pooled into a single category) depending on

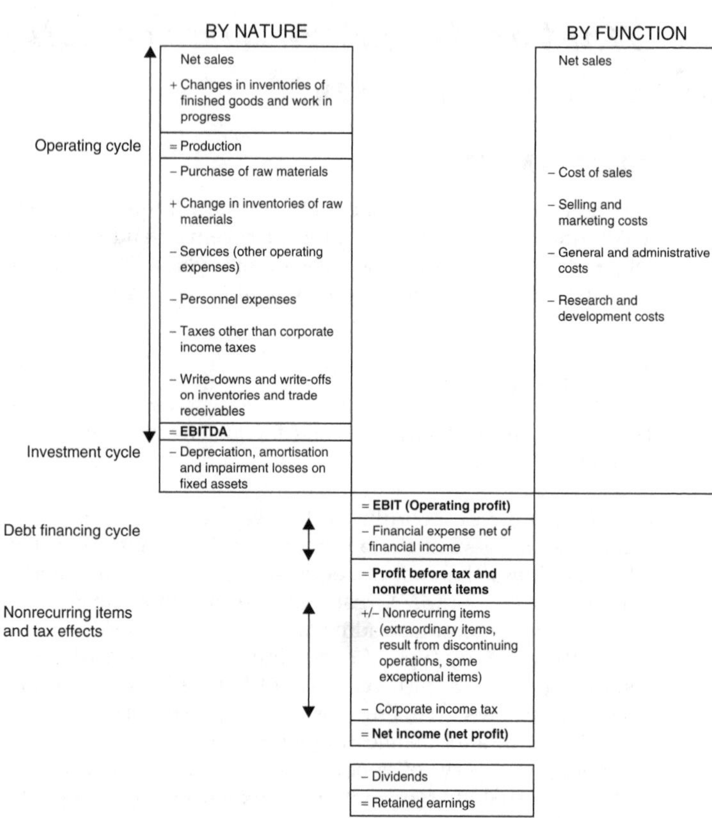

Figure 1.1: Two main formats of income statement by nature or by function

whether an individual employee works in production, sales, research or administration. Likewise, *depreciation expense* for a tangible fixed asset is allocated to production if it relates to production machinery, to selling and marketing costs if

Table 1.6: By-function income statement

Function	Corresponding cost
Production	Cost of Sales (or Cost of Goods Sold - COGS)
Commercial	Selling and marketing costs
Research and development	Research and Development costs (R&D)
Administration	General and Administrative costs (G&A)

it concerns a car used by the sales team, to research and development costs if it relates to laboratory equipment, or to general and administrative costs in the case of the accounting department's computers, for example.

The underlying principle is very simple indeed. This format clearly shows that operating profit is the difference between sales and the cost of sales irrespective of their nature (i.e. production, sales, research and development, administration).

On the other hand, it does not differentiate between the operating and investment processes since depreciation and amortization are not shown directly on the income statement (they are split up between the four main corporate functions), obliging analysts to track down the information in the cash flow statement or in the notes to the accounts.

Table 1.7 shows the Indesit by-function income statement:

The by-nature format is simple to apply, even for small companies, because no allocation of expenses is required. It offers a more detailed breakdown of costs.

Table 1.7: Indesit by-function income statement

	2005		2006		2007		2008		2009	
	in € m	%	in € m	%	in € m	%	in € m	%	in € m	%
NET SALES	3064	−1%	3249	6%	3438	6%	3155	−8%	2613	−17%
– Cost of sales	2276		2404		2543		2378		1939	
= GROSS MARGIN	788		845		895		777		674	
Selling and marketing costs	494		512		547		503		408	
– General and administrative costs	144		140		141		114		97	
+/– Other operating income and expense	7		6		13		0		0	
+ Income from associates	1		−2		4		0		0	
= RECURRING OPERATING PROFIT	158	5.2%	197	6.1%	224	6.9%	160	4.9%	169	6.5%
+/– nonrecurring items	−36		−39		−27		−19		−50	
= OPERATING PROFIT (EBIT)	122	4.0%	158	4.9%	197	6.0%	141	4.3%	119	4.6%
– Financial expense	43		41		46		58		53	
+ Financial income	13		14		16		13		2	
+ PROFIT BEFORE TAX	93	3.0%	132	4.1%	166	5.1%	95	2.9%	68	2.6%
– Income tax	42		55		61		39		33	
– Minority interests	0		0		0		1		1	
= NET PROFIT	50	1.6%	76	2.4%	105	3.2%	56	1.7%	34	1.3%

Naturally, as in the previous approach, operating profit is still the difference between sales and the cost of sales.

In this format, charges are recognized as they are incurred rather than when the corresponding items are used. Showing on the income statement all purchases made and all invoices sent to customers during the same period would not be comparing like with like.

A business may transfer to the inventory some of the purchases made during a given year. The transfer of these purchases to the inventory does not destroy any wealth. Instead, it represents the formation of an asset, albeit probably a temporary one, but one that has real value at a given point in time. Secondly, some of the end products produced by the company may not be sold during the year and yet the corresponding charges appear on the income statement.

To compare like with like, it is necessary to:

- eliminate changes in inventories of raw materials and goods for resale from purchases to get raw materials and goods for resale used rather than simply purchased;
- add changes in the inventory of finished products and work in progress back to sales. As a result, the income statement shows *production* rather than just sales.

The by-nature format shows the amount spent on production for the period and not the total expenses under the accruals convention. It has the logical disadvantage that it seems to imply that changes in inventory are revenues or expenses in their own right, which they are not. They are only an adjustment to purchases to obtain relevant costs.

Below in Table 1.8 is the model of a by-nature income statement.

Table 1.8: Model of a by-nature income statement

Periods	
	NET SALES
+	Changes in inventories of finished goods and work in progress
+	Production for own use
=	**PRODUCTION**
−	Raw materials used
−	Cost of goods for resale sold
=	Profit on raw materials used/goods for resale sold
−	Other purchases and external charges
=	**VALUE ADDED**
−	Personnel cost (incl. employee profit-sharing and incentives)
−	Taxes other than on income
+	Operating subsidies
−	Change in operating provisions[6]
+	Other operating income and cost
=	**EBITDA**
−	Depreciation and amortization
=	**EBIT (OPERATING PROFIT) (A)**
	Financial expense
−	Financial income
−	Net capital gains/(losses) on the disposal of marketable securities
+	Change in financial provisions
=	**NET FINANCIAL EXPENSE (B)**
(A) − (B) = PROFIT BEFORE TAX AND NONRECURRING ITEMS	
+/−	Nonrecurring items including impairment losses on fixed assets
−	Corporate income tax
=	**NET INCOME (net profit)**

References and Further Reading

Baker, C.R., Ding, Y. and Stolowy, H., The statement of intermediate balance: a tool for international financial statement analysis based on income statement 'by nature', an application to airline industry, *Advances in International Accounting*, **18**, 2005.

Stolowy, H. and Lebas, M., *Financial Accounting and Reporting: A Global Perspective*, 2nd ed., Thomson, 2006.

6. How can we perform the financial analysis of a company?

Short Answer

The aim of financial analysis is to explain how a company can create value in the medium term (shareholders' viewpoint) or to determine whether it is solvent (lenders' standpoint).

Either way, the techniques applied in financial analysis are the same.

Long Answer

First of all, financial analysis involves a detailed examination of the company's economics.

This study entails straightforward reasoning and a good deal of common sense. We can emphasize different aspects.

- **Company's market**, in other terms the niche or space in which the business has some industrial, commercial or service-oriented expertise, and understanding the company's position within its market. In particular:
  1. market growth;
  2. market risk;
  3. market share;
  4. competition;
  5. how the competition works (price-driven or product-driven).
- **Production model**, with specific focus on three aspects:
  1. value chain – when studying a value chain, analysts need to identify weaknesses where a particular category

of player has no or very little room for maneuver (scope for developing new activities, for selling operating assets with value independent of their current use, etc.);

2. production model – trying to detect any inconsistency between the product and the industrial organization adopted to produce it.
3. capital expenditure (CAPEX) – analysts should consider the relation between: time, product innovation and process innovation; as shown in the graph in Figure 1.2.

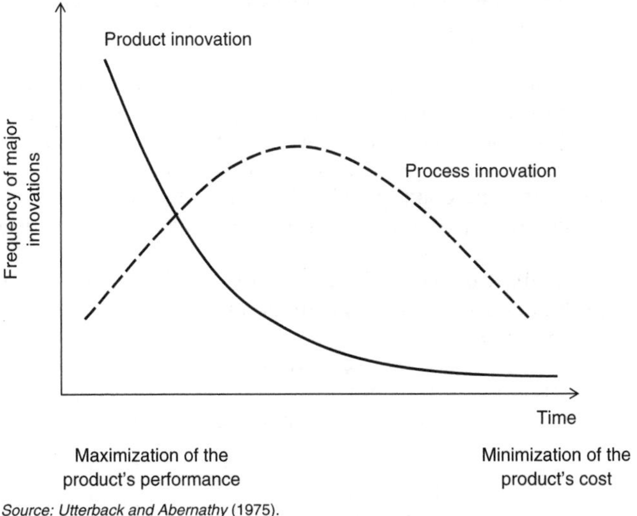

Source: Utterback and Abernathy (1975).

Figure 1.2: The relation between time, product innovation and process innovation

- **Distribution networks**. A distribution system usually plays three roles:
  1. *logistics* – displaying, delivering and storing products;

2. *advice and services* – providing details about and promoting the product, providing after-sales service and circulating information between the producer and consumers, and vice versa;
3. *financing* – making firm purchases of the product, i.e. assuming the risk of poor sales.

   The risk of a distribution network is that it does not perform its role properly and that it restricts the flow of information between the producer and consumers, and vice versa.

- **Motivations of the company's key people**, shareholders and managers, and the corporate culture.

Next, it entails a detailed analysis of the company's *accounting principles* to ensure that they reflect rather than distort the company's economic reality. Otherwise, there is no need to study the accounts, since they are not worth bothering with, and the company should be avoided like the plague, as far as shareholders, lenders and employees are concerned.

A standard financial analysis can be broken down into two preliminary tasks and four different stages:

Two preliminary tasks

GET TO KNOW THE BUSINESS WELL ...
• *The market(s)* • *The product(s)* • *Production model(s)* • *Distribution network* • *Human resources*

... AS WELL AS THE COMPANY'S ACCOUNTING POLICIES

Auditors' reports
Accounting principles

- *Consolidation techniques and scope*
- *Goodwill, brands, and other intangibles*
- *Provisions Inventories*
- *Unconsolidated subsidiaries*
- *Etc.*

Four-stage plan

WEALTH CREATION ...

- *Margin analysis:*
  – structure
  – scissors effect
  – operating leverage (breakeven point)

... REQUIRES INVESTMENTS ...

- *Working capital*
- *Capital expenditures*

... THAT MUST BE FINANCED ...

- *Cash flows*
- *Equity/debt*
- *Liquidity, interest rate and currency risk*

... AND PROVIDE A SUFFICIENT RETURN
• *Analysis of return on capital employed and return on equity: leverage effect* • *Comparison between ROCE /rate of return required by shareholders and lenders* → *Value* → *Solvency risk*

Only then can the analyst come to a conclusion about the solvency of the company and its ability to create value.

Analysts may use:

- *trend analysis*, which uses past trends to assess the present and predict the future;
- *comparative analysis*, which uses comparisons with similar companies operating in the same sector as a point of reference;
- *normative analysis*, which is based on financial rules of thumb.

References and Further Reading

AIMR, *Closing the Gap between Financial Reporting and Reality*, Association for Investment Management and Research, 2003.

Chopra, S. and Meindl, P., *Supply Chain Management*, Prentice Hall, 4th ed., 2009.

Kotler, P. and Keller, P., *Marketing Management*, Prentice Hall, 13th ed., 2008.

Moingeon, B. and Soenen, G., *Corporate and Organizational Identities*, Routledge, London, 2003.

Mulford, C. and Comiskey, K., *The Financial Number Game: Detecting Creative Accounting Practices*, John Wiley & Sons, 2002.

O'Glove, T., *Quality of Earnings*, Free Press, 1998.

Stevenson, W., *Operations Management*, McGraw-Hill/Irwin, 2004.

Utterback, J. and Abernathy, W., A dynamic model of process and product innovations, *Omega* **3**, 6, 1975.

7. What is the operating profit?

Short Answer

Operating profit or EBIT (earnings before interest and taxes) represents the earnings generated by investment and operating cycles for a given period.

Long Answer

Operating profit, which reflects the profits generated by the operating cycle, is a key figure in income statement analysis.

First of all, we look at how the figure is formed considering different factors.

- **Sales trends** are an essential factor in all financial analysis and company assessments. A company whose business activities are expanding rapidly, stagnating, growing slowly, turning lower or depressed will encounter different problems. An examination of sales trends sets the scene for an entire financial analysis. Sales growth forms the cornerstone for all financial analysis. Sales growth needs to be analyzed in terms of volume (quantities sold) and price trends, organic and acquisition-led growth.

  Key points and indicators:

  1. The rate of growth in sales is the key indicator that needs to be analyzed.
  2. It should be broken down into volume and price trends, as well as into product and regional trends.
  3. These different rates of growth should then be compared with those for the market at large and (general and sectoral) price indices. Currency effects should be taken into account.
  4. The impact of changes in the scope of consolidation on sales needs to be studied.

- **Production** represents what the company has produced during the year. It leads to an examination of the level of unsold products and the accounting method used to value inventories, with overproduction possibly heralding a serious crisis.

  Key points and indicators:

  1. The growth rate in production and the production/sales ratio are the two key indicators.
  2. They naturally require an analysis of production volumes and inventory valuation methods.
- **Raw materials** used and other external charges, which need to be broken down into their main components (i.e. raw materials, transportation, distribution costs, advertising, etc.) and analyzed in terms of their quantities and costs.

  Key questions:

  1. What are the main components of this item (raw materials, transportation costs, energy, advertising, etc.) and to what extent have they changed and are they forecast to change?
  2. Have there been any major changes in the price of each of these components?
- **Value added** is of interest only insofar as it provides valuable insight regarding the degree of a company's integration within its sector.
- **Personnel cost**, which can be used to assess the workforce's productivity: sales/average headcount and value-added/average headcount and the company's grip on costs: personnel cost/average headcount.
- **Depreciation and amortization**, which reflect the company's investment policy.

Further down the income statement, operating profit is allocated as follows:

- **Net financial expense**, which reflects the company's financial policy. Heavy financial expense is not sufficient to account for a company's problems, it merely indicates that its profitability is not sufficient to cover the risks it has taken.

- **Nonrecurring items** (extraordinary items, exceptional items and results from discontinuing operations) and the items specific to consolidated accounts (income or losses from associates, minority interests, impairment losses on fixed assets).
- **Corporate income tax**.

8. What is the scissors effect?

Short Answer

The *scissors effect* is what takes place when revenues and costs move in diverging directions. It accounts for trends in profits and margins.

Example

Figure 1.3 shows different examples of the scissors effect.

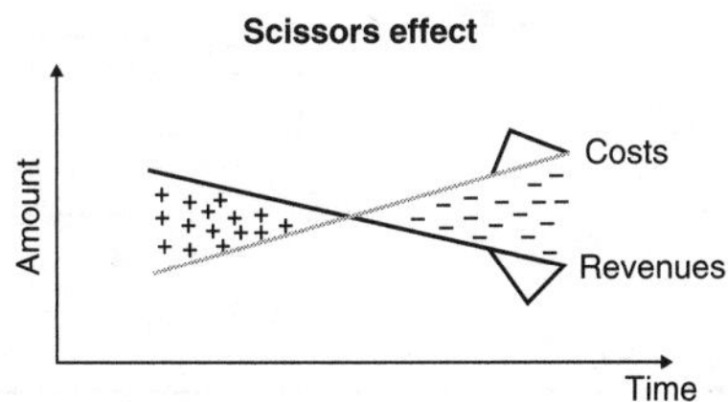

Ranging from carelessness ...

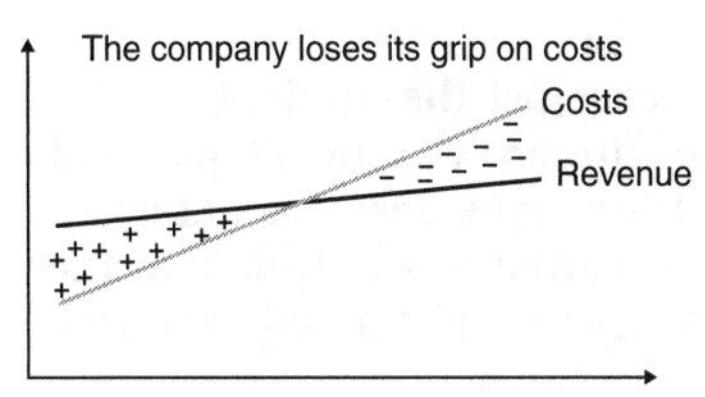

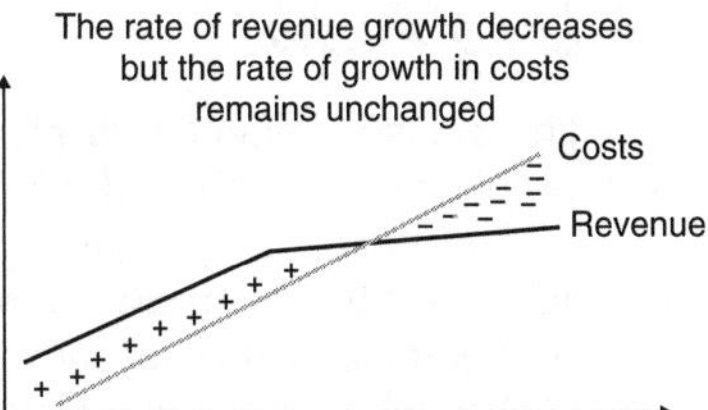

Figure 1.3: The scissors effect

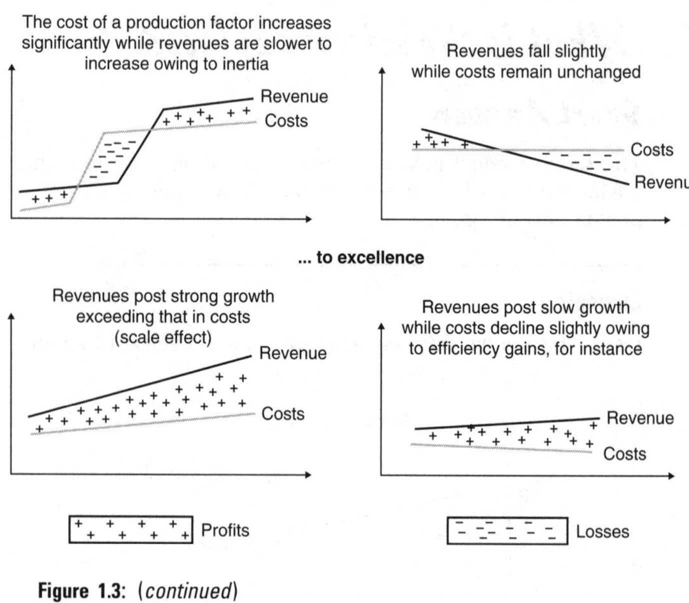

Figure 1.3: (*continued*)

Long Answer

The scissors effect is first and foremost the product of a simple phenomenon. If revenues are growing by 5% p.a. and certain costs are growing at a faster rate, earnings naturally decrease. If this trend continues, earnings will decline further each year and ultimately the company will sink into the red. This is what is known as the scissors effect.

Whether or not a scissors effect is identified matters little. **What really counts is establishing the causes of the phenomenon.** A scissors effect may occur for all kinds of reasons (regulatory developments, intense competition, mismanagement in a sector, etc.) that reflect the higher or lower quality of the company's strategic position in its market. If it has a strong position, it will be able to pass on any increase in its costs to its customers by raising its selling prices and thus gradually widening its margins.

A scissors effect may arise in different situations, some examples of which are given above. When it reduces profits, the effect may be attributable to:

- A statutory freeze on selling prices, making it impossible to pass on the rising cost of production factors.
- Psychological reluctance to put up prices. During the 1970s, the impact of higher interest rates was very slow to be reflected in selling prices in certain debt-laden sectors.
- Poor cost control, e.g. where a company does not have a tight grip on its cost base and may not be able to pass rising costs on in full to its selling prices. As a result, the company no longer grows, but its cost base continues to expand.

The impact of trends in the cost of production factors is especially important because these factors represent a key component of the cost price of products.

In such cases, analysts have to try to estimate the likely impact of a delayed adjustment in prices. This depends primarily on how the company and its rivals behave and on their relative strength within the marketplace.

But the scissors effect may also work to the company's benefit, as shown by the last two charts in the diagram above.

9. How does operating leverage work?

Short Answer

Operating leverage links variation in activity (measured by sales) with variations in result (either operating profit or net income). Operating leverage depends on the level and nature of the breakeven point.

Example

The higher a company's fixed costs, the greater the volatility of its earnings as illustrated in Table 1.9.

Table 1.9: Fixed costs and volatility of earnings

	Sales	Operating income
Tesco	£ 54.3bn (+9.3%)	£ 3.3bn (+10%)
SEB	€ 3,176mn (−2%)	€ 248mn (−11%)
Lufthansa	€ 22.3bn (−10%)	€ 96mn (−89%)

Tesco, the UK food retailer, has the lowest fixed costs of the three and the airline, Lufthansa, the highest. A 10% decrease in Lufthansa's turnover drives its earnings down by 89%, whereas a 9% increase in sales leads to a similar increase in Tesco's operating income (10%). The situation of SEB (small appliances) stands in between the two extremes of retail (very limited fixed costs) and airlines (almost all costs are fixed).

The purpose of the breakeven point analysis is to avoid extrapolating into the future the rate of earnings growth recorded in the past. Just because profits grew by 30% p.a. for two years as a result of a number of factors, does not mean they will necessarily keep growing at the same pace going forward.

Earnings and sales may not grow at the same pace owing to the following factors:

- structural changes in production;
- the scissors effect (see Question 8);
- **simply a cyclical effect accentuated by the company's cost structure. This is what can be examined using the breakeven point and the degree of operating leverage.**

The breakeven point is the level of business activity, measured in terms of production, sales or the quantity of goods sold, at which total revenues cover total charges. At this level of sales, a company makes zero profit.

The breakeven point can be presented graphically as shown in Figure 1.4.

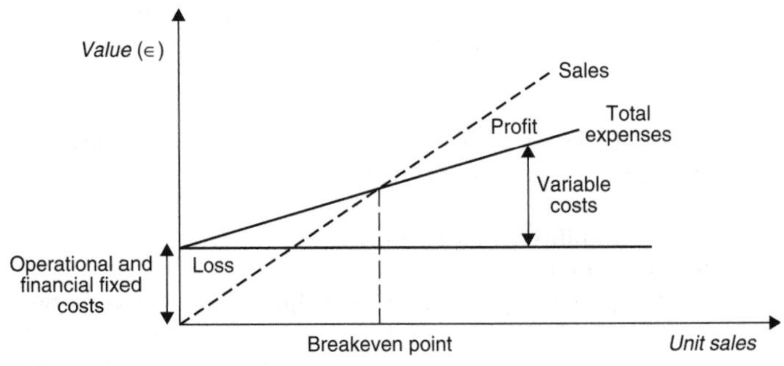

Figure 1.4: Breakeven point

The breakeven point is not an absolute measure – it depends on the length of period being considered because the distinction between fixed and variable costs can be justified only by a set of assumptions, and, sooner or later, any fixed cost can be made variable.

Three different breakeven points may be calculated:

- **Operating breakeven**, which is a function of the company's fixed and variable production costs. It determines the stability of operating activities, but may lead to financing costs being overlooked.
- **Financial breakeven**, which takes into account the interest expense incurred by the company, but not its cost of equity.
- **Total breakeven**, which takes into account both interest expense and the net profit required by shareholders. As a result, it takes into account all the returns required by all of the company's providers of funds.

Operating breakeven is calculated by dividing a company's fixed costs by its contribution margin ((sales – variable costs)/sales). Financial breakeven is calculated by adding interest expense to the fixed costs in the previous formula. Total breakeven is computed by adding the net income required to cover the cost of equity to fixed operating costs and interest costs.

The calculation and a static analysis of a company's breakeven point can be used to assess:

1. the stability of its earnings;
2. its normal earnings power;
3. the actual importance of the differences between budgeted and actual performance.

The further away a company lies from its breakeven point, the more stable its earnings and the more significant its earnings trends are.

The higher its fixed costs, as a share of total costs, the higher the breakeven point and the greater the operating leverage and the volatility of its earnings are.

The *degree of operating leverage* provides a useful measure of the link between the expected increase of sales and the increase of operating profit. This 'multiple' tells us *how many times* the operating profit will increase (or decrease) compared to the increase (or decrease) of sales:

$$\text{Degree of Operating Leverage (DOL)} = \frac{\text{Sales} - \text{Variable cost}}{\text{Operating profit}} = \frac{\text{Contribution margin}}{\text{Operating profit}}$$

References and Further Reading

Harvard Business School Press, *Breakeven Analysis and Operating Leverage*, 2008.

Marn, M., Roegner, E. and Zawada, C., The power of pricing, *McKinsey Quarterly* **1**, 27–36, 2003.

10. What is CAPEX?

Short Answer

CAPEX stands for 'Capital Expenditure' and represents the amount of money spent for investments carried out from a long-term perspective.

Long Answer

Through the production process, fixed assets are used up. The annual depreciation charge is supposed to reflect this wearing out. By **comparing capital expenditure with depreciation charges**, you can determine whether the company is:

- Expanding its industrial base by increasing production capacity. In this case, capital expenditure is higher than depreciation as the company invests more than simply to compensate for the annual wearing out of fixed assets.
- Maintaining its industrial base, replacing production capacity as necessary. In this case, capital expenditure approximately equals depreciation as the company invests just to compensate for the annual wearing out of fixed assets.
- Under investing or divesting (capital expenditure below depreciation). This situation can only be temporary or the company's future will be in danger, unless the objective is to liquidate the company.

Comparing capital expenditure with net fixed assets at the beginning of the period gives you an idea of the size of the investment program with respect to the company's existing production facilities. A company that invests an amount equal to 50% of its existing net fixed assets is building new facilities worth half what it has at the beginning of the year. This strategy carries certain risks:

- that economic conditions will take a turn for the worse;
- that production costs will be difficult to control (productivity deteriorates);
- technology risks, etc.

The theoretical relationship between capital expenditures and the cash flow from operating activities is not simple. New fixed assets are combined with those already on the balance sheet, and together they generate the cash flow of the period. Consequently, there is no direct link between operating cash flow and the capital expenditure of the period.

Thus, comparing cash flow from operating activities with capital expenditure makes sense only in the context of overall profitability and the dynamic equilibrium between sources and uses of funds.

The only reason to invest in fixed assets is to generate profits, i.e. positive cash flows. Any other objective turns finance on its head. You must therefore be very careful when comparing the trends in capital expenditure, cash flow, and cash flow from operating activities. This analysis can be done by examining the cash flow statement.

> *Any investment strategy must sooner or later result in an increase in cash flow from operating activities.*

If it doesn't, then the investments are not profitable enough.

Be on the lookout for companies that grossly overinvest, despite their cash flow from operating activities not growing at the same rate as their investments. Management has lost sight of the all-important criterion that is profitability.

All the above does not mean that capital expenditure should be financed by internal sources only. Our point is simply that a good investment policy grows cash flow at the same rate as capital expenditure. This leads to a virtuous circle of growth, a necessary condition for the company's financial equilibrium, as shown in graph (a) of Figure 1.5 below. Graphs (b), (c) and (d) of Figure 1.5 illustrate other corporate situations. In (d), investment is far below the company's cash flow from operations.

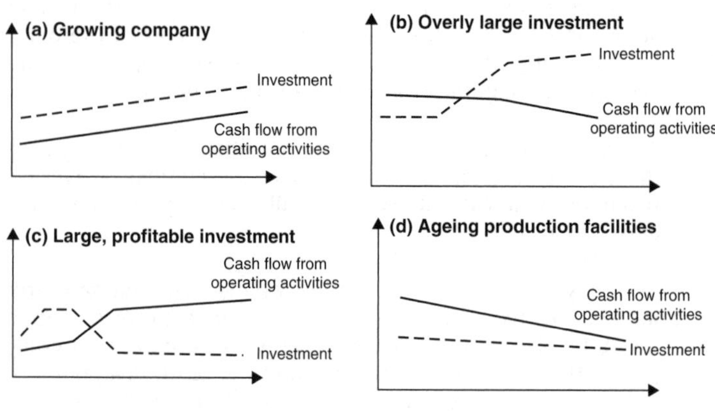

Figure 1.5: Virtuous circle of growth

You must compare investment with depreciation charges in order to answer the following questions:

- Is the company living off the assets it has already acquired (profit generated by existing fixed assets)?
- Is the company's production equipment ageing?
- Are the company's current capital expenditures appropriate, given the rate of technological innovation in the sector?

Naturally, the risk in this situation is that the company is 'resting on its laurels', and that its technology is falling behind that of its competitors. This will eat into the company's profitability and, as a result, into its cash flow from operating activities at the very moment it will mostly need cash in order to make the investments necessary to close the gap *vis-à-vis* its rivals.

> *The most important piece of information to be gleaned from a cash flow statement is the relationship between capital expenditure and cash flow from operating activities and their respective growth rates.*

Lastly, ask yourself the following questions about the company's divestments. Do they represent recurrent transactions, such as the gradual replacement of a rental car company's fleet of vehicles, or are they one-off disposals? In the latter case, is the company's insufficient cash flow forcing the company to divest? Or is the company selling old, outdated assets in order to turn itself into a dynamic, strategically-rejuvenated company?

References and Further Reading

Quiry, P., Dallocchio, M., Le Fur, Y. and Salvi, A., *Corporate Finance. Theory and Practice*, 3rd ed., John Wiley & Sons, 2011.

11. How can the credit risk of a company be assessed?

Short Answer

Analyzing the credit risk of a company means analyzing how the company is financed. This can be performed either by looking at several fiscal years, or on the basis of the latest available balance sheet.

Example

Looking at the cash flow statement of Indesit (see Question 2), we see that the cash flow from operating activity remains healthy from 2005 to 2007 (remaining over €200 million each year, even in 2005 when the activity slowed down slightly). Cash flows from operating activity are therefore sufficient to cover capital expenditure. In 2008 due to a sales decrease, the cash flow from operating activity is not enough to cover capital expenditure. However, in 2009, thanks to a deep reorganization, the cash flow from operating activity achieves an historical record at €333mn, while the operating profit is at its historical lowest.

In 2005 the free cash flows after financial expense are just enough to cover dividend payment; the net debt of the group therefore remains constant. In 2006 and 2007, Indesit generates large enough free cash flows to distribute dividends and to reduce its net debt level significantly. In 2008, the debt increases significantly before a considerable reduction in 2009 (€−257mn) thanks to the operating cash flow, a strong reduction of investments and the removal of dividends.

The combination of a reduction in net debt and an increasing EBITDA leads to a sharp decrease in net debt level measured by the ratio net debt/EBITDA (from 2.0x in 2005 to 1.1x in 2009).

Analyzing the balance sheet, the liquidity of the group in 2007 could be questioned as short-term debt (€276 million) is higher than the available cash and cash equivalent (€187 million). Digging a little further we find that c. 100 million euros of short term debt are against receivables. In addition, in 2006 the group secured for five years a syndicated loan of €350 million which is undrawn. We can therefore conclude that Indesit has no liquidity issue.

Long Answer

There are two approaches to assessing the credit risk of a company.

In the ***dynamic approach***, your main analytical tool will be the cash flow statement. **Cash flow from operating activities is the key metric**: it must cover capital expenditure, loan repayment and dividends. Otherwise, the company will have to borrow more to pay for its past use of funds.

In the ***static approach***, analysts try to answer two questions:

- Can the company repay its debts as scheduled? To answer this question, projected cash flow statements must be built, based on assumed rates of growth in sales, margins, working capital and capital expenditure. To perform a simplified analysis, the net debt/EBITDA (earnings before interest, taxes, depreciation, and amortization) ratio is calculated. If the company is to have an acceptable capacity to meet its repayment commitments as scheduled, the ratio should not be in excess of 4.
- Is the company running the risk of being illiquid? To answer this question, the dates at which the company's

liabilities will come due and the dates at which its assets will be liquidated must be compared. Assets should mature before liabilities. If they do, the company will remain liquid (Figure 1.6).

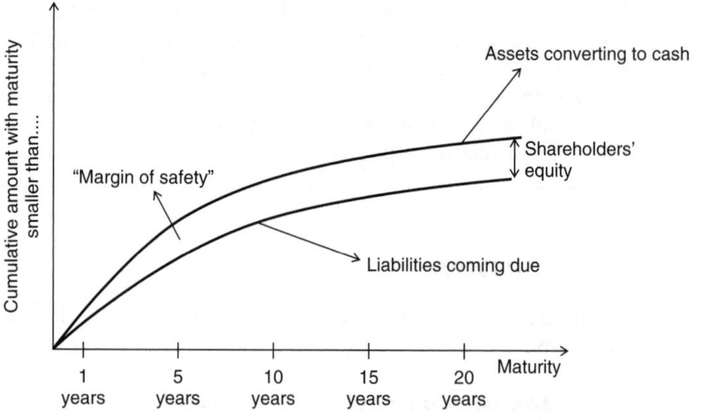

Figure 1.6: Liquidity

To measure liquidity, then, we must compare the maturity of the company's assets to that of its liabilities.

This rule gives rise to the following ratios, commonly used in loan covenants. They enable banks to monitor the risk of their borrowers.

1. **Current ratio**:

$$\frac{\textit{Current assets (less than one year)}}{\textit{Current liabilities (due in less than one year)}}$$

This ratio measures whether the assets to be converted into cash in less than one year exceed the debts to be paid in less than one year.

2. **Quick ratio**: is another measure of the company's liquidity. It is the same as the current ratio, except that inventories are excluded from the calculation. Using the quick ratio is a way of recognizing that a portion of inventories corresponds to the minimum the company requires for its ongoing activity. As such, they are tantamount to fixed assets. It also recognizes that the company may not be able to liquidate the inventories it has on hand quickly enough in the event of an urgent cash need. Certain inventory items have value only to the extent they are used in the production process. The quick ratio (also called the *acid test ratio*) is calculated as follows:

$$\frac{\textit{Current assets (less than one year) excluding inventories}}{\textit{Current liabilities (due in less than one year)}}$$

3. **Cash ratio**:

$$\frac{\textit{Cash and cash equivalents}}{\textit{Current liabilities (due in less than one year)}}$$

The cash ratio is generally very low. Its fluctuations often do not lend themselves to easy interpretation.

References and Further Reading

Almeida, H. and Campello, R., Financial Constraints, Asset Tangibility, and Corporate Investment, *Review of Financial Studies* **20**, 1429–1460, 2007.

Hackethal, A. and Schmidt, R., Financing Patterns: Measurement Concepts and Empirical Results, University of Frankfurt – Department of Finance, Working Paper n°125, 2004.

Morellec, A., Asset Liquidity, Capital Structure and Secured Debt, *Journal of Financial Economics* **61**, 173–206, 2001.

12. How do we measure the profitability of a company?

Short Answer

We can measure profitability only by studying returns in relation to the invested capital. If no capital is invested, there is no profitability to speak of.

Long Answer

Book profitability is the ratio of the wealth created (i.e. earnings) to the capital invested. Profitability should not be confused with margins. Margins represent the ratio of earnings to business volumes (i.e. sales or production), while profitability is the ratio of profits to the capital that had to be invested to generate the profits.

Above all, analysts should focus on the profitability of capital employed by studying the ratio of operating profit to capital employed, which is called the *Return On Capital Employed* (ROCE).

$$ROCE = \frac{Operating\ profit\ after\ tax}{Capital\ employed}$$

Return on capital employed can also be considered as the return on equity if the net debt is zero.

Much ink has been spilled over the issue of whether opening or closing capital employed or an average of the two figures should be used. We will leave it up to readers to decide for themselves. This said, care should be taken not to change the method decided upon as time goes on so that comparisons over longer periods are not skewed.

Return on capital employed can be calculated by combining a margin and turnover rate as follows:

$$ROCE = \frac{Operating\ profit\ after\ tax}{Capital\ employed}$$
$$= \frac{Operating\ profit\ after\ tax}{Sales} \times \frac{Sales}{Capital\ employed}$$

The first ratio – operating profit after tax/sales – corresponds to the operating margin generated by the company, while the second – sales/capital employed – reflects asset turnover or capital turn (the inverse of capital intensity), which indicates the amount of capital (capital employed) required to generate a given level of sales. Consequently, a 'normal' return on capital employed may result from weak margins, but high asset turnover (and thus weak capital intensity), e.g. in mass retailing. It may also stem from high margins, but low asset turnover (i.e. high capital intensity), e.g. whisky producers.

Analysts will have to decide for themselves whether, as we suggest here, they work on an after-tax basis. If so, they will have to calculate operating profit after theoretical tax (calculated based on the company's normalized tax rate), which is called NOPAT (net operating profit after tax).

Example

The following graph (Figure 1.7) shows the ROCE and its components achieved by some leading European groups during 2010.

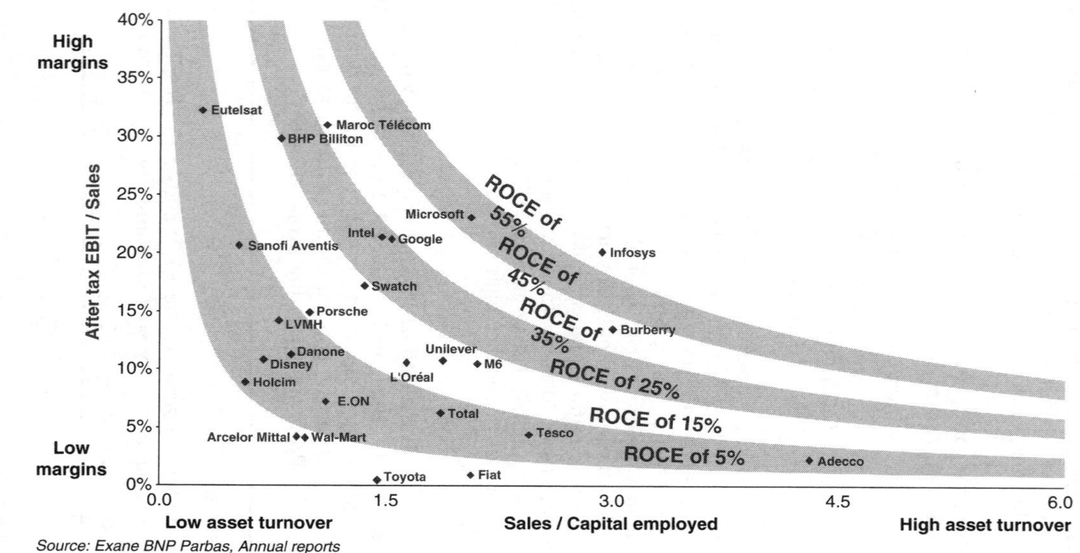

Source: Exane BNP Parbas, Annual reports

Figure 1.7: Return on capital employed (ROCE)

Table 1.10: ROE of European industries 1998–2007

ROE Sector	ICB code	1998	1999	2000	2001	2002	2003	2004	2005	2006	2007
Oil & Gas	5	5%	9%	12%	11%	8%	9%	12%	14%	12%	13%
Chemical	13	13%	12%	12%	9%	9%	6%	9%	12%	13%	16%
Basic Resources	17	9%	8%	12%	6%	6%	6%	10%	7%	13%	14%
Construction and Materials	23	12%	14%	14%	12%	12%	12%	14%	17%	20%	18%
Industrials Goods and Services	27	17%	15%	15%	9%	6%	8%	12%	15%	16%	17%
Automobiles & Parts	33	14%	9%	12%	8%	11%	10%	12%	13%	12%	14%
Food & Beverage	35	16%	14%	11%	11%	11%	12%	11%	13%	12%	14%
Personal & Household Goods	37	14%	14%	14%	9%	12%	12%	14%	15%	15%	17%
Health Care	45	9%	8%	7%	5%	3%	6%	5%	4%	3%	2%
Retail	53	17%	17%	15%	13%	13%	13%	14%	15%	15%	15%
Media	55	15%	14%	13%	1%	3%	8%	10%	15%	13%	13%
Travel & Leisure	57	12%	11%	9%	5%	8%	8%	9%	10%	12%	13%
Telecommunications	65	11%	11%	9%	1%	3%	7%	14%	13%	15%	17%
Utilities	75	10%	10%	9%	9%	10%	10%	9%	12%	14%	14%
Technology	95	19%	15%	5%	−4%	−6%	1%	7%	11%	11%	11%

Secondly, we can calculate the *return on equity* (ROE), which is the ratio of net income to shareholders' equity.

$$ROE = \frac{Net\ income}{Shareholders'\ equity}$$

In practice, most financial analysts take goodwill impairment losses and nonrecurring items out of net income before calculating return on equity.

Example

Table 1.10 reports the ROE of some European industries from 1998 to 2007.

References and Further Reading

Andersson, T., Haslam, C. and Lee, E., Financialized account: Restructuring and return on capital employed in the S&P 500, *Accounting Forum*, **30**, 21–41, June 2006.

13. What is the financial leverage effect and how does it work?

Short Answer

The leverage effect is the difference between return on equity and return on capital employed. Although it can lift a company's return on equity above return on capital employed, it can also depress it, turning the dream into a nightmare.

Example

Let's consider a company with capital employed of 100, generating a return of 10% after tax, which is financed entirely by equity. Its return on capital employed and return on equity both stand at 10%.

If the same company finances 30 of its capital employed with debt at an interest rate of 4% after tax and the remainder with equity, its return on equity is:

Operating profit after tax:	10% x 100 = 10
Interest expense after tax:	4% x 30 = 1.2
= Net income after tax:	= 8.8

When divided by shareholders' equity of 70 (100–30), this yields a return on equity after tax of 12.6% (8.8/70), while the after-tax return on capital employed stands at 10%.

The borrowing of 30 that is invested in capital employed generates operating profit after tax of 3 which, after post-tax interest expense (1.2), is fully attributable for an amount of 1.8 to shareholders. This surplus amount (1.8) is added to operating profit generated by the equity-financed investments

(70 × 10% = 7) to give net income of 7 + 1.8 = 8.8. The company's return on equity now stands at 8.8/70 = 12.6%.

The leverage effect of debt thus increases the company's return on equity by 2.6%, or the surplus generated (1.8) divided by shareholders' equity (1.8/70 = 2.6%).

Long Answer

The leverage effect explains a company's return on equity in terms of its return on capital employed and cost of debt.

All the capital provided by lenders and shareholders is used to finance all uses of funds, i.e. the company's capital employed. These uses of funds generate operating profit, which itself is apportioned between net financial expense (returns paid to debt holders) and net income attributable to shareholders.

If we compare a company's return on equity with its return on capital employed (after tax, to remain consistent), we note that the difference is due to its financial structure, apart from nonrecurring items and items specific to consolidated accounts.

The leverage effect works as follows. When a company raises debt and invests the funds it has borrowed in its industrial and commercial activities, it generates operating profit that normally exceeds the interest expense due on its borrowings. If this is not the case, it is not worth investing. So, the company generates a surplus consisting of the difference between the return on capital employed and the cost of debt related to the borrowing. This surplus is attributable to shareholders and is added to shareholders' equity. The leverage effect of debt thus increases the return on equity: hence its name.

Debt can therefore be used to boost a company's return on equity without any change in return on capital employed.

But readers will surely have noticed the prerequisite for the return on equity to increase when the company raises additional debt, i.e. its ROCE must be higher than its cost of debt. Otherwise, the company borrows at a higher rate than the returns it generates by investing the borrowed funds in its capital employed. This gives rise to a deficit, which reduces the rate of return generated by the company's equity. Its earnings decline and the return on equity dips below its return on capital employed.

When the return on capital employed falls below the cost of debt, the leverage effect of debt shifts into reverse and reduces the return on equity, which in turn falls below the return on capital employed.

Let's now formulate a **leverage effect equation**, with *i* representing the cost of debt, *D* the debt and *E* the equity:

$$ROE = \underbrace{ROCE + (ROCE - i) \times \frac{D}{E}}$$

Book return on capital employed, return on equity and cost of debt do not reflect the returns required by shareholders, providers of funds and creditors. These figures cannot be regarded as financial indicators because they do not take into account risk or valuation, two key parameters in finance. Instead, they reflect the historical book returns achieved and belong to the realms of financial analysis and control.

The leverage effect helps to identify the source of a good return on equity, which may come from either a healthy return on capital employed or merely from a company's capital structure, i.e. the leverage effect. This is its only real point. In the long run, only a healthy return on capital employed will ensure a decent return on equity. As we shall see, the leverage effect does not create any value. Although it may boost return on equity, it leads to an increase in risk that is proportional to the additional profit.

References and Further Reading

Campello, M. and Fluck, Z., Market Share, Financial Leverage and the Macroeconomy: Theory and Empirical Evidence, University of Illinois, Working Paper, 3 February 2004.

Dugan, M., Minyard, G. and Shriver, K., A Re-examination of the Operating Leverage – Financial Leverage Tradeoff, *Quarterly Review of Economics & Finance*, 327–334, Fall 1994.

Lang, L., Ofek, E. and Stulz, R., Leverage, Investment and Firm Growth, *Journal of Financial Economics*, 3–29, January 1996.

Nissim, D. and Penman, S., Financial Statement Analysis of Leverage and how it Informs about Profitability and Price-to-book Ratios, *Review of Accounting Studies*, **8**, 531–560, 2003.

Reilly, F., The Impact of Inflation on ROE, Growth and Stock Prices, *Financial Services Review*, **6**(1), 1997.

14. What are efficient markets?

Short Answer

An efficient market is one in which the prices of financial securities at any time *rapidly* reflect *all available relevant* information.

Example

On March 14, 2011 before market opening, Berkshire Hathaway, the investment vehicle of Warren Buffett announced it would launch an agreed takeover bid on Lubrizol, a specialty chemical company. Lubrizol's share price immediately reached the offer price of $135 with a very high level of shares exchanged (Figure 1.8).

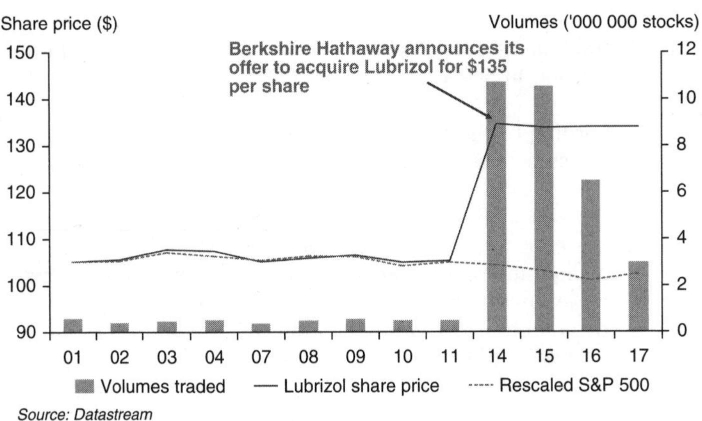

Figure 1.8: Lubrizol share price variations in March 2011

Example

A counterexample: speculative bubble and insider trading phenomena demonstrate that markets are inefficient at least under the strong hypothesis.

Long Answer

Eugene Fama (1970) has developed three tests to determine whether a market is efficient.

In a ***weak-form*** efficient market, it is impossible to predict future returns. Existing prices already reflect all the information that can be gleaned from studying past prices and trading volumes, interest rates and returns. This is what is meant by the 'weak form' of efficiency.

Extra returns can be obtained only if investors have future or privileged information.

According to the weak-form of efficiency, the price of an asset is the sum of three components:

1. the last available price (P_{-1});
2. the expected return from the security; and
3. a random component due to new information that might be learned during the period in question. This component of random error is independent from past events and unpredictable in the future.

$$P_0 = P_{-1} + \text{Expected return} + \text{Random error}$$

When prices follow this model, they follow a random walk.

The efficient market hypothesis says that technical analysis has no practical value, nor do martingales.

A ***semi-strong*** efficient market reflects all publicly available information, as found in annual reports, newspaper and magazine articles, prospectuses, announcements of new contracts, of a merger, of an increase in the dividend, etc.

Semi-strong efficiency is superior to weak-form efficiency because it requires that current prices include historical information (as assumed by the weak-form efficiency) *and* publicly available information. The latter, for example, is available in:

- financial statements;
- research on the company performed by external financial analysts; and
- company announcements.

This hypothesis can be empirically tested by studying the reaction of market prices to company events (event studies). In fact, the price of a stock reacts immediately to any announcement of relevant new information regarding a company. In an efficient market, no impact should be observable prior to the announcement, nor during the days following the announcement. In other words, prices should adjust rapidly only at the time any new information is announced.

In a ***strongly*** efficient financial market, investors with privileged or insider information or with a monopoly on certain information are unable to influence securities' prices. This is the 'strong form' of efficiency.

This holds true only when financial market regulators have the power to prohibit and punish the use of insider information.

In theory, professional investment managers have expert knowledge that is supposed to enable them to post better performances than the market average. However, without using any inside information, the efficient market hypothesis says that market experts have no edge over the layman. In fact, in an efficient market, the experts' performance is slightly below the market average, in a proportion directly related to the management fees they charge!

Actual markets approach the theory of an efficient market when:

- participants have low-cost access to all information;
- transaction costs are low;
- the market is liquid; and
- investors are rational.

In general, if we try to explain why financial markets have different degrees of efficiency, we could say that:

1. The lower transaction costs are, the more efficient a market is.
2. The more liquid a market is, the more efficient it is.
3. The more rational investors are, the more efficient a market is.

The last assumption in particular is the most feeble, because human beings and their feelings cannot be reduced to a series of mathematical equations. It has been demonstrated that the Dow Jones Industrial Average turns in below-average performance when it rains in Central Park, that stock market returns are lower on Monday than on Friday, and so on. These phenomena have given rise to ***behavioral finance***, which takes psychology into account when analyzing investor decisions. This field of research provides recent evidence that investors can make systematic errors in processing new information – information that is profitably exploited by other investors.

The vast majority of *evidence* regarding market efficiency has concerned the weak and semi-strong forms of efficiency.

The weak form of efficiency has been proven by the absence of serial correlation in daily returns.

The theory of semi-strong efficiency can be measured by looking at the event studies that examine the market's reaction to price-sensitive announcements from companies. More specifically, event-studies also estimate the cumulative abnormal returns (CAR), which are the sum of subsequent abnormal returns. Abnormal returns are measured by:

$$AR = \text{Return of the company} - \text{Return of the market}$$

If the market is efficient, the CAR before the announcement should be nil or very low. Thus, if abnormal returns grew during the previous period, there is good evidence that some investors might have received information before others. The analysis of *ex-post* CAR is also interesting because, in efficient markets, abnormal returns should be zero (Figure 1.9).

In short, the abnormal return should be confined to the announcement day and ideally no abnormal return should be registered before or after the announcement (graph a).

The higher the deviation from the fair market value and the more slowly it fades away, the less efficient is the financial market. In this instance we are faced with two alternative situations: the first is typical of a slow learning market (graph b) and the second is characteristic of excessive reaction (market overreaction – graph c).

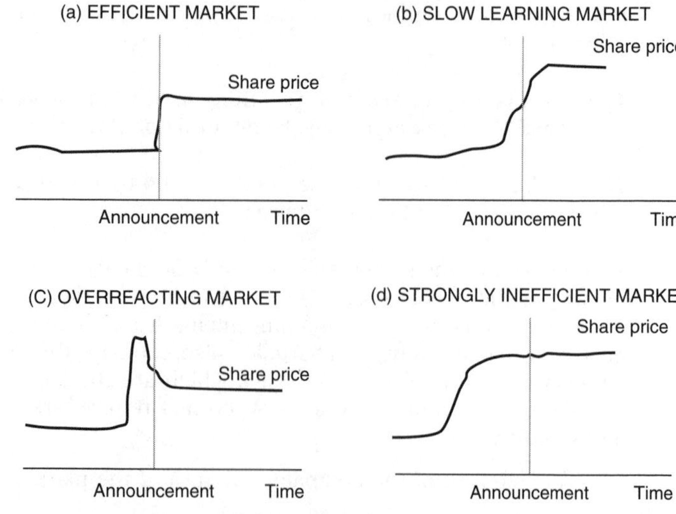

Figure 1.9: Analysis of *ex-post* CAR

If there is a clear (and otherwise inexplicable) trend in prices before the announcement, then it is reasonable to assume that a few privileged investors had access to the information before the formal announcement was made to the entire market (graph d).

References and Further Reading

Bhattacharya, U. and Daouk, H., The world price of insider trading, *Journal of Finance*, **57**(1), 75–108, February 2002.

Bressand, A. and Distler, C. (eds.), *Enhanced Transparency: Meeting European Investors' Needs*, Promethee publication for Standard & Poor's, 2003.

Dimson, E. and Mussavian, M., A brief history of market efficiency, *European Financial Management*, **4**(1), 91–103, March 1998.

Fama, E., Efficient capital markets: A review of theory and empirical work, *Journal of Finance*, 383–417, May 1970.

Fama, E., Efficient capital market II, *Journal of Finance*, 1575–1617, December 1991.

Fama, E., Market efficiency, long-term returns and behavioral finance, *Journal of Financial Economics*, **49**(3), 283–306, September 1998.

Fox, J., *The Myth of the Rational Market*, Harper Business, 2009.

Fuller, J. and Jensen, M., Just say no to Wall Street: Putting a stop to the earnings game, *Journal of Applied Corporate Finance*, **14**(4), 27–40, Winter 2002.

Gibbons, M. and Patrick, H., Day of the week effects and asset returns, *Journal of Business*, **54**, 579–596, October 1981.

Haugen, R. and Lakonishok, J., *The Incredible January Effect*, Irwin, 1989.

Hawawini, G. and Keim, D., The Cross Section of Common Stock Returns: A Review of the Evidence and some New Findings, Working Paper, Wharton School, University of Pennsylvania, May 1997.

Loughran, T., Book-to-market across firm size, exchange, and seasonality: Is there an effect? *Journal of Financial and Quantitative Analysis*, **32**, 249–268, September 1997.

Loughran, T. and Ritter, J., The new issue puzzle, *Journal of Finance*, **50**(1), 23–51, March 1995.

Malkiel, B., *A Random Walk down Wall Street*, 10th ed., New York, W.W. Norton & Company, 2011.

Marsh, P., Myths surrounding short-termism, in G. Bickerstaffe (ed.), *Mastering Finance*, London, FT/ Pitman Publishing, 1998.

Ritter, J., The long-run performance of IPOs, *Journal of Finance*, **46**(1), 3–27, March 1991.

Rubinstein, M., Rational markets: yes or no? The affirmative case, *Financial Analysts Journal*, May–June 2001.

15. What do we mean by discounting a sum?

Short Answer

To discount means to calculate the present value of a future cash flow.

Example

Consider an offer whereby someone will give you €1000 in five years' time. As you will not receive this sum for another five years, you can apply a discounting factor to it, for example, 0.6. The present, or today's, value of this future sum is then €600. Having discounted the future value to a present value, we can then compare it to other values. For example, it is preferable to receive €650 today rather than €1000 in five years, as the present value of €1000 five years ahead is €600, and that is below €650.

Long Answer

Discounting into today's euros helps to compare a sum that will not be produced until later. Technically speaking, what is discounting?

To discount is to 'depreciate' the future. It is to be more rigorous with future cash flows than present cash flows, because future cash flows cannot be spent or invested immediately. First, take tomorrow's cash flow and then apply to it a multiplier coefficient below one, which is called a discounting factor. The discounting factor is used to express a future value as a present value, thus reflecting the depreciation brought on by time.

Discounting makes it possible to compare sums received or paid out at different dates.

Discounting is based on the time value of money. After all, 'time is money'. Any sum received later is worth less than the same sum received today.

Remember that investors discount because they demand a certain rate of return. If a security pays you €110 in one year and you wish to see a return of 10% on your investment, the most you would pay today for the security (i.e. its present value) is €100.

At this price (€100) and for the amount you know you will receive in one year (€110), you will get a return of 10% on your investment of €100. However, if a return of 11% is required on the investment, then the price you are willing to pay changes. In this case, you would be willing to pay no more than €99.1 for the security because the gain would have been €10.9 (or 11% of €99.1), which will still give you a final payment of €110.

Discounting is calculated with the required return of the investor. If the investment does not meet or exceed the investor's expectations, he or she will forego it and seek a better opportunity elsewhere.

Discounting converts a future value into a present value. This is the opposite result of capitalization (Figure 1.10).

Discounting converts future values into present values, while capitalization converts present values into future ones.

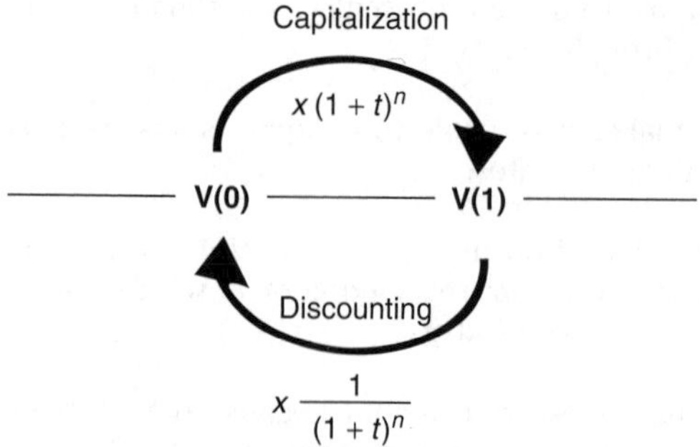

Figure 1.10: Capitalization and discounting

Hence, to return to the example above, €1,800,000 ten years in the future discounted at 33.5% is today worth €100,000. €100,000 today will be worth €1,800,000 when capitalized at 33.5% over ten years:

Capitalization:

$$100{,}000(1 + 33.5\%)^{10} \cong 1{,}800{,}000$$

Discounting:

$$1{,}800{,}000 \frac{1}{(1 - 33.5\%)^{10}} \cong 100{,}000$$

16. How do companies measure value creation?

Short Answer

The tools used for measuring creation of value (Figure 1.11) can be classified under three headings:

- **Economic indicators**: NPV, EVA and CFROI.
- **Market indicators**: MVA and TSR.
- **Accounting indicators**: EPS, ROE, ROCE and Equity per share.

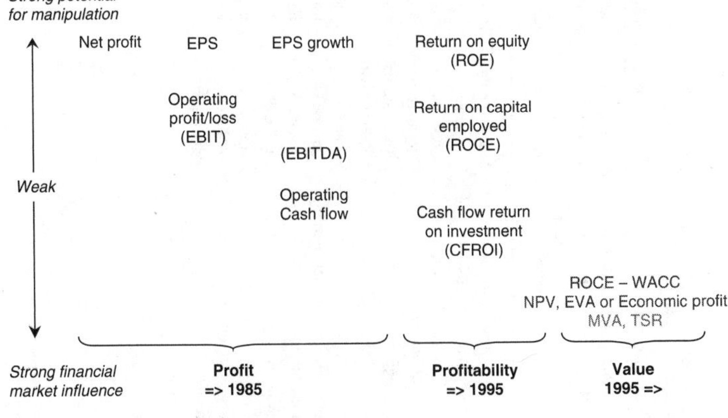

Figure 1.11: Evolution of financial indicators

Example

We show here in Table 1.11 a comparison between the different criteria.

Table 1.11: Comparison between the different criteria

	Economic criteria			Market criteria		Accounting criteria		
Ratio	**Net present value**	**Economic profit**	**Cash flow return on investment**	**Market value added**	**Total shareholder return**	**Earning per share**	**Accounting rates of return**	**Equity per share**
Acronym	**NPV**	**EVA**	**CFROI**	**MVA**	**TSR**	**EPS**	**ROE, ROCE**	
Strengths	The best criterion	Simple indicator leading to the concept of weighted average cost of capital	Not restricted to just one year	Astoundingly simple. Reflects the total rather than annual value created	Represents shareholder return in the medium to long term	Historical data. simple	Simple concepts.	
Weaknesses	Difficult to calculate for an external analyst	Restricted to one year. Difficult to evaluate changes over a period of time	Complex calculations	Subject to market volatility. Difficult to apply to unlisted companies	Calculated over too short a period. Subject to market volatility.	Does not factor in risks. Easily manipu-lated. Does not factor in the cost of equity	Accounting measures, thus do not factor in risks. Restricted to one year. To be significant, must be compared with the required rates of return.	Little con-nection with value creation.

Long Answer

Economic indicators

The factor in returns required by investors (the weighted average cost of capital) does not depend directly on the sometimes erratic price movements of markets.

NPV (net present value) is the most important of these (see Question 17 for further details).

Obviously, one should only allocate resources if the net present value is positive, in other words, if the market value is lower than the present value. Net present value reflects how allocation of the company's resources has led to the creation or destruction of value. On the one hand, there is a constant search for anticipated financial flows – while keeping in mind the uncertainty of these forecasts. On the other hand, it is necessary to consider the rate of return (*k*) required by the investors and shareholders providing the funds. The value created is thus equal to the difference between the capital employed and its book value. Book value is the amount of funds invested in the company's operations.

Creation of value = Enterprise value – Book value of capital employed

The creation of value reflects investors' expectations. Typically, this means that, over a certain period, the company will enjoy a rent with a present value allowing its capital employed to be worth more than its book value! The same principle applies to choosing a source of financing for allocating resources. To do so, one must disregard the book value and determine instead the value of the financial security issued and deduct the required rate of return. This approach represents a shift from the explicit or accounting cost to the financial cost, which is the return required on this category of security.

EVA (economic value added), the popular term for economic profit, measures how much the shareholder has increased his or her wealth over and above standard remuneration.

The key aspect of EVA is that it identifies the income level at which value is created. This is because EVA is calculated after deducting the capital charge, i.e. the remuneration of the funds contributed by creditors and shareholders. Economic profit or EVA first measures the excess of ROCE over the weighted average cost of capital. Then, to determine the value created during the period, the ratio is multiplied by the book value of the capital employed at the start of the reporting period.

$$\text{EVA} = \text{Capital employed} \times (\text{ROCE} - \text{WACC})$$

$$\text{EVA} = \text{NOPAT} - \text{WACC} \times \text{Capital Employed}$$

Economic profit is related to net present value, because NPV is the sum of the economic profits discounted at the weighted average cost of capital.

$$\text{NPV} = \sum_{i=0}^{\infty} \frac{\text{EVA}_i}{(1 + \text{WACC})^t}$$

However, since EVA has the drawback of being restricted to the financial period in question, it can thus be manipulated to yield maximum results in one period at the expense of subsequent periods.

The simplified version of cash flow return on investment (CFROI) compares EBITDA with gross capital employed, i.e. before amortization and depreciation of fixed assets.

$$\text{CFROI} = \frac{\text{EBITDA}}{\text{Capital employed}}$$

This ratio is used particularly in business sectors wherein charges to depreciation do not necessarily reflect the normal deterioration of fixed assets, e.g. in the hotel business.

Market indicators measure MVA (market value added), or the difference between the company's enterprise value and its book value:

$$\begin{aligned}\text{MVA} = {} & \text{Market capitalization} + \text{Net debt} \\ & - \text{Book value of capital employed}\end{aligned}$$

It is easy to demonstrate the relationship between MVA and intrinsic value creation in equilibrium markets, since:

$$\text{MVA} = \sum_{i=0}^{\infty} \frac{\text{EVA}_i}{(1 + \text{WACC})^i}$$

Total shareholder returns (TSR) is the rate of shareholder returns given the increase in the value of the share and the dividends paid out. These market tools are only useful over the medium term, because to be meaningful they should avoid the market fluctuations that can distort economic reality.

Accounting indicators have the main drawback of being designed for accounting purposes, i.e. they do not factor in risk or return on equity. They include:

1. **Earnings per share (EPS)** linked to the value of the share by the price earnings ratio (P/E). It can be a reliable indicator of value creation under three conditions only:
   - the risk on capital employed remains the same from one period to the next, or before and after operations such as mergers, capital increases or share buybacks, investments, etc.;
   - earnings growth remains the same before and after any given operation; and

  - the company's financial structure remains the same from one period to the next, or before and after a given operation.
2. **Accounting rates of return (ROE and ROCE).** In general, if the investment yields more than the required rate of return, the increase in the value of the company will exceed that of the sums invested. Financial managers should approach book rates of return with caution. These ratios are accounting measures, but not external measures. They assume that the company is operating in a closed system! The minimum criterion should be the return required by the financial system.
3. **Equity per share** is one way of measuring shareholder value. It therefore seems logical to assume that there is a coefficient linking the price of the share with equity per share. This is called the price-to-book ratio (PBR). However, the warnings against the P/E ratio apply to the PBR as well. Bear in mind that if equity has been correctly valued in the accounts, that is, if it includes unrealized capital gains on assets, the price-to-book ratio will be:
   - lower than 1 if the expected return on equity is lower than the return required by shareholders; and
   - higher than 1 if the expected return is higher than that required by the shareholders.

References and Further Reading

Andrade, G., Do Appearances Matter? The Impact of EPS Accretion and Dilution on Stock Prices. Harvard Business School Working Paper 00–07.

Boston Consulting Group, *Shareholder Value Metrics, Shareholder Value Management*, Boston Consulting Group, 1996.

Copeland, T., What do practitioners want? *Journal of Applied Finance*, **12**(1), 5–11, Spring/Summer 2002.

Deelder, B., Goedhart, M. and Agrawal, A., A better way to understand TSR, *The McKinsey Quartely*, **28**, 26–30, Summer 2008.

Dobbs, R. and Koller, T., Measuring long-term performance, *The McKinsey Quarterly*, special edition Value and Performance, 17–27, 2005.

Fama, E. and French, K., The corporate cost of capital and the return on corporate investment, *Journal of Finance*, **54**, 1939–1967, December 1999.

Monographic issue on 'EVA and incentive compensation' in the *Journal of Applied Corporate Finance*, **12**(2), Summer 1999.

17. What is the NPV of a project?

Short Answer

Net present value (*NPV*) is the difference between present value (*PV*) of future flows and the current market value of a security (V_0):

$$NPV = \sum_{n=1}^{N} \frac{F_n}{(1+r)^n} - V_0$$

Example

Consider the following example in Table 1.12 of an asset (e.g. a financial security or a capital investment) whose market value is 2 and whose cash flows are as follows:

Table 1.12: Cash flow

Year	1	2	3	4	5
Cash flow	0.08	0.08	0.08	0.08	0.08

A 20% discounting rate would produce the following discounting factors (Table 1.13):

Table 1.13: Discounting factors

Year	1	2	3	4	5
Discounting factor	0.833	0.694	0.579	0.482	0.402
Present value of cash flow	0.67	0.56	0.46	0.39	0.32

As a result, the present value of this investment is about 2.4. As its market value is 2, its NPV is approximately 0.4. If the discounting rate changes, the following values (Table 1.14) are obtained:

Table 1.14: Values discounting rate

	0%	10%	20%	25%	30%	35%
Present value of the investment	4	3.03	2.39	2.15	1.95	1.78
Market value	2	2	2	2	2	2
NPV	2	1.03	0.39	0.15	−0.05	−0.22

These values would then look like this graphically (Figure 1.12):

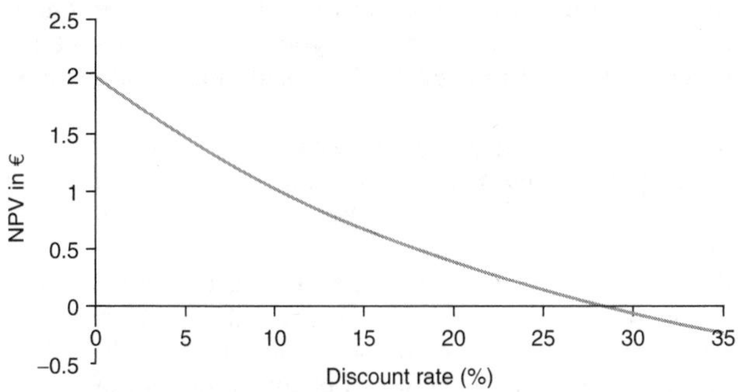

Figure 1.12: Net present value (NPV) and the discount rate

Long Answer

The present value (PV) of a security is the sum of its discounted cash flows; i.e.:

$$PV = \sum_{n=1}^{N} \frac{F_n}{(1+r)^n}$$

where F_n are the cash flows generated by the security, r is the applied discounting rate and n is the number of years for which the security is discounted.

All securities also have a *market value*, particularly on the secondary market. Market value is the price at which a security can be bought or sold.

Net present value (NPV) is the difference between present value and market value (V_0):

$$NPV = \sum_{n=1}^{N} \frac{F_n}{(1+r)^n} - V_0$$

If the NPV of a security is greater than its market value, then it will be worth more in the future than the market has presently valued it. Therefore, you will probably want to invest in it, i.e. to invest in the upside potential of its value.

If, however, the security's present value is below its market value, you should sell it at once, for *its market value is sure to diminish*.

If an imbalance occurs between a security's market value and its present value, efficient markets will seek to re-establish balance and reduce net present value to zero. Investors acting on efficient markets seek out investments offering positive NPV, in order to realize that value. When they do so, they push NPV towards zero, ultimately arriving at the fair value of the security.

In efficient, fairly valued markets, NPVs are zero, i.e. market values are equal to present values.

Up to this point, the discussion has been limited to financial securities. However, the concepts of present value and NPV can easily be applied to any investment, such as the construction of a new factory, the launch of a new product, the takeover of a competing company or any other asset that will generate positive and/or negative cash flows.

The concept of NPV can be interpreted in three different ways:

1. The value created by an investment – for example, if the investment requires an outlay of €100 and the present value of its future cash flow is €110 then the investor has become €10 wealthier.
2. The maximum additional amount that the investor is willing to pay to make the investment – if the investor pays up to €10 more, he or she has not necessarily made a bad deal, as he or she is paying up to €100 for an asset that is worth €110.
3. The difference between the present value of the investment (€100) and its market value (€110).

Calculating the NPV of a project is conceptually easy. There are basically two steps to be followed:

1. Write down the net cash flows that the investment will generate over its life.
2. Discount these cash flows at an interest rate that reflects the degree of risk inherent in the project.

The resulting sum of discounted cash flows equals the project's NPV. The *NPV decision rule* says to invest in projects when the present value is positive (greater than zero):

- NPV $>$ 0 invest
- NPV $<$ 0 do not invest

The NPV rule implies that firms should invest when the present value of future cash inflows exceeds the initial cost of the project. Why does the NPV rule lead to good investment decisions? The firm's primary goal is to maximize shareholder wealth. The discount rate r represents the highest rate of return (opportunity cost) that investors could obtain in the marketplace in an investment with equal risk. When the NPV of cash flow equals zero, the rate of return provided by the investment is exactly equal to investors' required return. Therefore, when a firm finds a project with a positive NPV, that project will offer a return exceeding investors' expectations.

Although this question highlights many of the advantageous qualities of the NPV approach, there are also a few weaknesses that are worth mentioning:

- it is less intuitive than other methodologies, such as the payback rule or the accounting return rule;
- it does not take into account the value of managerial flexibility, in other words the options that managers can exploit after an investment has been made in order to increase its value; and
- the NPV has a major competitor in the internal rate of return (IRR), whose use seems more widespread among corporations. In most cases, the two decision rules give the same information, but the IRR is more appealing to managers because it delivers a number that is more easily interpreted.

References and Further Reading

Hirshleifer, J., On the theory of optimal investment decision, *Journal of Political Economy*, **66**, 329–352, August 1958.

Tobin, J., Liquidity preference as behaviour towards risk, *Review of Economic Studies*, February 1958.

18. What is the IRR of a project?

Short Answer

The discounting rate that makes NPV equal to zero is called the internal rate of return (IRR) or yield to maturity.

Example

To calculate IRR, make r the unknown and simply use the NPV formula again. The rate r is determined as follows:

$$VAN = 0, or \sum_{n=1}^{N} \frac{F_n}{(1+r)^n} = V_0$$

Let's input some numbers:

$$\frac{0.8}{(1+r)} + \frac{0.8}{(1+r)^2} + \cdots + \frac{0.8}{(1+r)^5} + 2$$

In other words, an investment's IRR is the rate at which its market value is equal to the present value of the investment's future cash flows.

It is possible to use trial-and-error to determine IRR. This will result in an interest rate that gives a negative NPV and another that gives a positive NPV. These negative and positive values constitute a range of values, which can be narrowed until the yield to maturity is found, which in this case is about 28.6%.

Long Answer

The internal rate of return (IRR) is frequently used in financial markets because it immediately tells the investor the return to be expected for a given level of risk. The investor can then compare this expected return to his or her required return rate, thereby simplifying the investment decision.

The decision-making rule is very simple: if an investment's internal rate of return is higher than the investor's required return, he or she will make the investment or buy the security. Otherwise, the investment will be abandoned or the security sold.

Hence, at fair value, the IRR is identical to the market return. In other words, NPV is nil.

The limits of the internal rate of return

1. **The reinvestment rate.** Let's consider two investments in Table 1.15.

Table 1.15: Investment examples

	Year							NPV at 5%	IRR%
	1	**2**	**3**	**4**	**5**	**6**	**7**		
A	6	0.5						1.17	27.8
B	2	3	0	0	2.1	0	5.1	2.40	12.7

At first glance, investment *B* would appear to be the more attractive of the two. Its NPV is higher and it creates the most value: 2.40 vs. 1.17.

However, some might say that investment *A* is more attractive, as cash flows are received earlier than with investment *B* and therefore can be reinvested sooner in high return projects. While that is theoretically possible, it is the strong (and optimistic) form of the theory because competition among investors, and the mechanisms of arbitrage, tend to move NPVs towards zero. NPVs moving towards zero means that exceptional rates of return converge toward the required rate of return, thereby eliminating the possibility of long-lasting high-return projects.

Given the convergence of the exceptional rates toward required rates of return, it is more reasonable to suppose that cash flows from investment *A* will be reinvested at the required rate of return of 5%. The exceptional rate of 27.8% is unlikely to be recurrent.

And this is exactly what happens if we adopt the NPV decision rule. The NPV in fact assumes that the reinvestment of intermediate cash flows is made at the required rate of return (k):

$$\left[\sum_{n=1}^{N} F_n(1+k)^{N-n}\right](1+k)^{-N} - F_0 = \sum_{n=1}^{N} \frac{F_n}{(1+k)^n} - F_0$$

If we apply the same equation to the IRR, we observe that the reinvestment rate is simply the IRR again. However, in equilibrium, it is unreasonable to think that the company can continue to invest at the same rate of the (sometimes) exceptional IRR of a specific project. Instead it is much more reasonable to assume that, at best, the company can invest at the required rate of return.

2. **Multiple or no IRR.** Let's consider the following (Table 1.16) investment:

Table 1.16: Example investment

Year	0	1	2
Cash flow	−1	7.2	−7.2

The project has two IRRs, and we do not know which one is the right one (see Figure 1.13). There is no good reason to use one over the other. Investments with 'unconventional' cash flow sequences are rare, but they can happen. Consider a firm that is cutting timber in a forest. The timber is cut, sold and the firm gets an

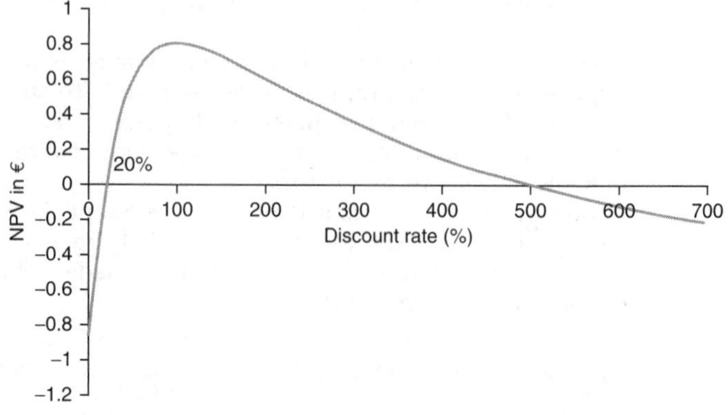

Figure 1.13: NPV and discount rate: multiple or no IRR

immediate profit. But, when harvesting is complete, the firm may be forced to replant the forest at considerable expense. Another example may be a strip-mining project, which normally requires a final investment to reclaim the land and satisfy the requirements of environmental legislation.

Consider now, in Table 1.17, the following investment:

Table 1.17: Example investment

Year	0	1	2
Cash flow	3.2	−7.1	4.0

A project like this has no IRR (see Figure 1.14). Thus, we have no benchmark for deciding if it is a good investment or not. Although the NPV remains positive for all the discount rates, it remains only *slightly* positive and the company may decide not to do it.

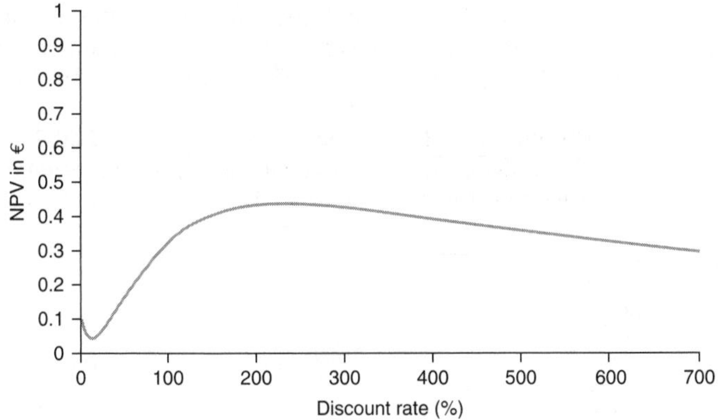

Figure 1.14: NPV and discount rate: no IRR

3. **Investing or financing?** Consider two projects (Table 1.18) with the following flows:

Table 1.18: Cash flow examples

Project	F_0	F_1	IRR	NPV (15%)
A	−100	120	20%	€4.35
B	100	−120	20%	−€4.35

Consider our trial-and-error method to calculate the IRR of project *B* (Table 1.19):

Table 1.19: Trial-and-error method

F_0	F_1	k	NPV
100	−120	15%	−€4.35
100	−120	20%	€0.00
100	−120	30%	€7.69

The reader will surely have noticed that the net present value of project *B* is *negative* when the discount rate is below 20%. Conversely, the NPV is positive when the discount rate is above 20%.

The curve of the NPV is upward sloping (similar to a loan): implying that the investment is *positively related* to the discount rate (see Figure 1.15).

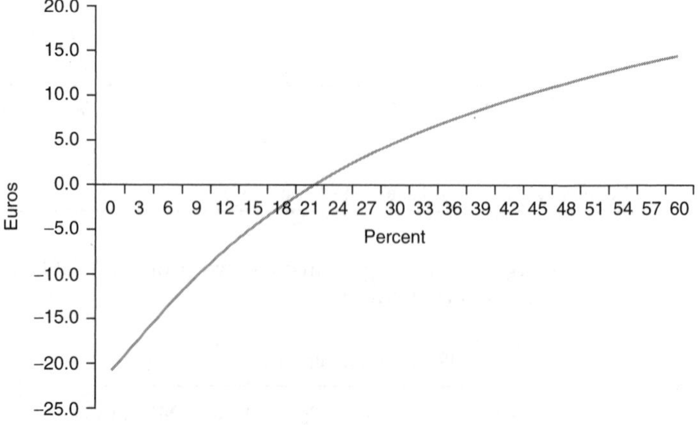

Figure 1.15: Curve of the NPV

Intuitively, the 'inverted IRR' rule makes sense. If the firm wants to obtain €100 immediately, it can either invest in project *B* or *borrow* €100 from a bank, which will have to be repaid in the following period with an interest rate of 20%. Thus, the project is actually a substitute for borrowing.

4. **Changing discount rates.** It is common to discount cash flows at a constant rate throughout a project's life. However, this may not be appropriate under certain

circumstances. In fact, the required rate of return is a function of interest rates and of the uncertainty of cash flows, both of which can change substantially over time. The necessity of using different discount rates can be easily overcome with the NPV criteria, whereby different discount rates can be set for each period. Conversely, the IRR method can only be compared with a single rate of return and cannot cope with changing discount rates.

19. How do companies deal with uncertainty in capital budgeting?

Short Answer

Companies and investors have developed a number of risk analysis techniques whose common objective is to *know more about a project* than just the information provided by the NPV. These techniques are:

- Sensitivity analysis;
- Scenario analysis and Monte Carlo simulation.

Long Answer

1. **Sensitivity analysis.** An important risk analysis consists in determining how sensitive the investment is to different economic assumptions (see Figure 1.16). This is done by *holding all other assumptions fixed* and then applying the present value to each different economic assumption. It is a technique that highlights the consequences of changes in *prices*, *volumes*, *rising costs* or *additional investments* on the value of projects. To perform a sensitivity analysis, the investor:

- fixes a base-case set of assumptions and calculates the NPV; and
- allows one variable to change while holding the others constant, and recalculates the NPV based on these assumptions. Usually analysts develop both pessimistic and optimistic forecasts for each assumption, and then analysts move to a more complete range of possible values of the key drivers (see the graph below for an example).

The sensitivity analysis requires a good understanding of the sector of activity and its specific constraints. The industrial analysis must be rounded off with a more financial analysis of the investment's sensitivity to the model's technical parameters, such as the discount rate or terminal value (exit multiple or growth rate to infinity).

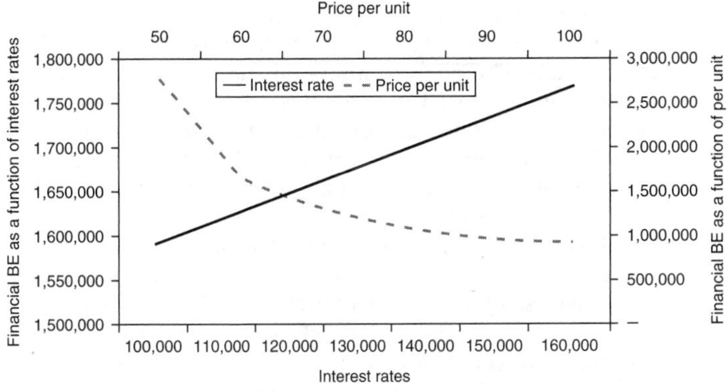

Figure 1.16: Sensitivity analysis of financial breakeven

2. **Scenario and Monte Carlo simulation**. With a *scenario analysis*, the analyst calculates the project NPV assuming simultaneously a whole set of new assumptions, rather than adjusting one assumption at a time. For example, the analyst may foresee that if production volume falls short of expectations, operating costs per unit may also be higher than anticipated. In this case, two variables change at the same time. But as the reader can easily understand, in reality the situation may be much more complex.

Although scenario analysis is appealing, it can be very difficult to understand how different variables are related to each other. The problem is two-sided:

- What are the assumptions that move together?
- What is the strength of their relationships?

As with sensitivity analysis, companies often build a base-case (or consensus) scenario and then move to optimistic and pessimistic scenarios.

An even more elaborate variation of scenario analysis is the Monte Carlo simulation, which is based on more sophisticated mathematical tools and software. It consists of isolating a number of the project's key variables or value drivers, such as turnover or margins, and allocating a probability distribution to each. The analyst enters all the assumptions about distributions of possible outcomes into a spreadsheet. The model then randomly samples from a table of pre-determined probability distributions in order to identify the probability of each result. Assigning probabilities to the investment's key variables is done in two stages:

1. Influential factors are identified for each key variable. For example, with turnover, the analyst would also want to evaluate sales prices, market size, market share, etc.
2. It is then important to look at available information (long-term trends, statistical analysis, etc.) to determine the uncertainty profile of each key variable using the values given by the influential factors.

Generally, there are several types of key variables, such as simple variables (e.g. fixed costs), compound variables (e.g. turnover = market × market share), or variables resulting from more complex, econometric relationships.

The investment's NPV is shown as an uncertainty profile resulting from the probability distribution of the key variables, the random sampling of groups of variables, and the calculation of net present value in this scenario.

Repeating the process many times gives us a clear representation of the NPV risk profile.

Once the uncertainty profile has been created, the question is whether to accept or reject the project. The results of the Monte Carlo method are not as clear cut as present value, and a lot depends upon the risk and reward trade-off that the investor is willing to accept. One important limitation of the method is the analysis of interdependence of the key variables, for example, how developments in costs are related to those in turnover, etc.

References and Further Reading

Benninga, S., *Financial Modelling*, 3rd ed., MIT Press, 2008.

20. How can real options be used in corporate finance?

Short Answer

Real options relate to industrial investments. Real options offer the right, but not the obligation, to *change* an investment project, particularly when new information on its prospective returns becomes available.

Example

In the example outlined in Figure 1.17 the project includes an option to defer its launch (wait and see), an option to expand if it proves successful and an option to abandon it completely.

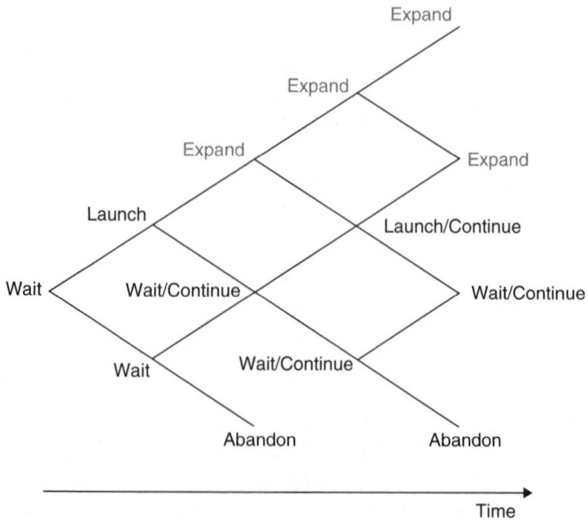

Figure 1.17: Real options

Long Answer

Given the potential value of hidden options, it is tempting to consider all investment uncertainties as a potential source of value. But the specific features of option contracts must not be overlooked. The following three factors are necessary to ensure that an investment project actually offers real options:

- The project must have a degree of *uncertainty*. The higher the underlying volatility, the greater the value of an option. If the standard deviation of the flows on a project is low, the value of the options will be negligible.
- Investors must be able to get *more information* during the course of the project, and this information must be sufficiently precise to be useful.
- Once the new information has been obtained, it must be possible to change the project *significantly and irrevocably*. If the industrial manager cannot use the additional information to modify the project, he or she does not really have an option but is simply taking a chance. In addition, the initial investment decision must also have a certain degree of irreversibility. If it can be changed at no cost, then the option has no value. And lastly, since the value of a real option stems from the investor's ability to take action, any increase in *investment flexibility generates value*, since it can give rise to new options or increase the value of existing options.

Real options apply primarily to decisions to invest or divest, but they can appear at any stage of a company's development. Some categories of real options:

- **The option to launch a new project** corresponds to a call option on a new business. Its exercise price is the startup investment, a component that is very important in the valuation for many companies. In these cases, they are not valued on their own merits, but according to their ability to generate new investment opportunities, even though the nature and returns are still uncertain.

- **The option to develop or extend the business.**
- **The option to reduce or contract business.** The implied sales price of the unrealized portion of the project consists of the savings on additional investments. This option can be described as a put option on a fraction of the project, even if the investment never actually materializes.
- **The option to postpone a project.** There is a certain time value in delaying the realization of a project, since in the meantime better information about the project's income and expenses may become available. This enables a better assessment of the potential for value creation.
- **The option to abandon.** The industrial manager can decide to abandon the project at any time.

The uncertainty inherent in the flexibility of an industrial project creates value, because the unknown represents risk that has a time value. As time passes, this uncertainty declines as the discounted cash flows are adjusted with new information. The uncertainty is replaced with an intrinsic value that progressively incorporates the ever changing expectations.

When a company has a real option, using NPV or any other traditional investment criterion implies that it will exercise its option immediately. It is important to keep in mind that this is not necessarily the best solution or the only reality that the company or investor faces.

In real options one of the most used models is the binomial model that uses the replicating portfolio approach: suppose that we know the value of the option at the end of the period, both in the up- and in the down-state.

We could simply obtain the value by discounting the expected value of the two returns at an appropriate discount rate. Although correct, this approach suffers two limitations:

- We do not know the probability of the up and down scenario. This problem can be overcome.
- The discount rate is not the cost of capital we use in estimating the NPV of the project without flexibility. A real option has different payouts and different risks than the underlying project. Thus, the cost of capital inappropriately reflects the riskiness of the cash flows of the project with flexibility.

It is sometimes possible to choose δ shares of a 'traded' or twin (of the project with flexibility!) security (an asset named S, which is perfectly correlated with the option) and B euros of risk-free debt. Suppose that if the price goes up the twin security price will be SU (supposedly known), while if the price goes down it will be SD (also known). In the up-state, the project with flexibility will return PU (a figure that we are able to estimate as we will see later on) while in the down-state it will return PD (also estimable). The result is two equations and two unknowns (B and δ):

$$\delta \times SU + B \times (1 + r_f) = PU$$
$$\delta \times SD + B \times (1 + r_f) = PD$$

The solution of this simple system is:

$$\delta = (PU - PD)/(SU - SD)$$
$$B = (PU - \delta \times SU)/(1 + r_f)$$

In each node, the present value of the project with flexibility is:

$$\delta \times \text{PV of the project at the node} + B/(1 + r_f)$$

We then work backward, node by node and in a similar way, to arrive at the present value of the project with real options, i.e. the expanded NPV.

The reader should be aware that the expanded NPV cannot be lower than the 'passive' NPV.

But what is this security that is perfectly correlated (the twin!) with a project with real options? The trick is to use the project itself, taking the present value without flexibility, as the twin security. In other words, we use the present value of the passive project as an estimate of the price it would have if it were traded on the market. This solution is extremely reasonable and useful because, after all, the project with flexibility has the highest asset correlation with the no-flexibility project.

It is now possible to take all of these tools and create some order out of this line of reasoning. The approach for option valuation is a five-step process.

STEP 1. Calculate the passive present value of the project, using the traditional discounted cash flow methods.

STEP 2. Build a so-called event tree, i.e. the lattice that models the values of the passive investment. This tree does not contain decision nodes and simply models the evolution of the present value of the project.

The up and down movements can be determined by the following formulae:

$$\textit{Up movement} = U = e^{\sigma\sqrt{\tau}}$$

$$\textit{Down movement} = D = e^{-\sigma\sqrt{\tau}}$$

The corresponding probabilities of up and down movements are:

$$\textit{Probability up} = (1 + r_f - D)/(U - D)$$

$$\textit{Probability down} = 1 - \textit{Probability up}$$

STEP 3. Turn the event tree into a decision tree, by identifying the managerial flexibility and building it into the appropriate nodes of the tree, i.e. when the flexibility is effectively possible.

STEP 4. Use the replication portfolio approach to value the present value of the project with flexibility. Then the entire decision tree can be solved by working from the final branches backward through time.

$$\delta \times \text{PV of the no-flexibility project at the node} + B/(1 + r_f)$$

STEP 5. Calculate the expanded net present value by subtracting the initial investment from the present value of the project with flexibility.

References and Further Reading

Cox, J., Rubinstein, M. and Ross, S., Option pricing: A simplified approach, *Journal of Financial Economics*, 229–263, September 1979.

Dixit, A. and Pindyck, R., The option approach to capital investment, *Harvard Business Review*, May–June 1995.

Myers, S. and Turnbull, S., Capital budgeting and the capital asset pricing model: Good news and bad news, *Journal of Finance*, **32** (2), 321–333, May 1997.

Trigeorgis, L., A conceptual options framework for capital budgeting, *Advances in Futures and Options Research*, **3**, 145–167, 1998.

Trigeorgis, L. and Schwartz, E., *Real Options and Investment under Uncertainty: Classical Readings and Recent Contributions*, MIT Press, September 2004.

www.real-options.com, website entirely dedicated to real options.

21. What is risk in finance?

Short Answer

Risk refers to the likelihood that we will receive a return on the investment that is different from the return we expect to make.

There is a difference between risk and uncertainty: risk has an unknown outcome, but we know what the underlying outcome distribution looks like. Uncertainty also implies an unknown outcome, but we don't know what the underlying distribution looks like. So games of chance like roulette or blackjack are risky, while the outcome of a war is uncertain. Frank Knight said that objective probability is the basis for risk, while subjective probability underlies uncertainty.

Example

Suppose you would like to give a party, to which you decide to invite a dozen of your friends. You think that ten of the invitees will come, but there is some uncertainty about the real number of people that will eventually show up, eight. However, this is not a risky situation only if a perfect forecast of the number of guests doesn't change your action.

For example, in providing for your guests, suppose you have to decide how much food to prepare. If you knew for sure that ten people would show up, then you would prepare exactly enough for ten – no more and no less. If twelve actually show up, there will not be enough food, and you will be displeased with that outcome because some guests will be hungry and dissatisfied. If eight actually show up, there will be too much food, and you will be displeased with that too because you will have wasted some of your limited resources on surplus food. Thus, the uncertainty matters and, therefore, there is risk in this situation.

On the other hand, suppose that you have told your guests that each person is to bring enough food for a single guest. Then it might not matter in planning the party whether more or fewer than ten people come. In that case, there is *uncertainty* but no risk.

Long Answer

There are various risks affecting the return of financial securities, including:

Industrial, commercial and labor risks, etc. There are so many types of risks in this category that we cannot list them all here. They include: lack of competitiveness, emergence of new competitors, technological breakthroughs, an inadequate sales network, strikes and others. These risks tend to lower cash flow expectations and thus have an immediate impact on the value of the stock.

Liquidity risk. This is the risk of not being able to sell a security at its fair value, as a result either of a liquidity discount or the complete absence of a market or buyers.

Solvency risk. This is the risk that a creditor will lose his entire investment if a debtor cannot repay him in full, even if the debtor's assets are liquidated. Traders call this counterparty risk.

Currency risk. Fluctuations in exchange rates can lead to a loss of value of assets denominated in foreign currencies. Similarly, higher exchange rates can increase the value of debt denominated in foreign currencies when translated into the company's reporting currency base.

Interest rate risk. The holder of financial securities is exposed to the risk of interest rate fluctuations. Even if the issuer fulfills his commitments entirely, there is still the risk of a capital loss, or at the very least, an opportunity loss.

Political risk. This includes risks created by a particular political situation or decisions by political authorities, such as nationalization without sufficient compensation, revolution, exclusion from certain markets, discriminatory tax policies, inability to repatriate capital, etc.

Regulatory risk. A change in the law or in regulations can directly affect the return expected in a particular sector. Pharmaceuticals, banks and insurance companies, among others, tend to be on the front lines here.

Inflation risk. This is the risk that the investor will recover his or her investment with a depreciated currency, i.e. that the investor will receive a return below the inflation rate. A flagrant historical example is the hyperinflation in Germany in the 1920s.

Fraud risk. This is the risk that some parties to an investment will lie or cheat, i.e. by exploiting asymmetries of information in order to gain unfair advantage over other investors. The most common example is insider trading.

Natural disaster risks. They include storms, earthquakes, volcanic eruptions, cyclones, tidal waves, etc., which destroy assets.

Economic risk. This type of risk is characterized by bull or bear markets, anticipation of an acceleration, a slowdown in business activity or changes in labor productivity.

Under the point of view of a company, we can split the risk into five categories:

1. **Market risk.** The exposure to unfavorable trends in product prices, interest rates, exchange rates, raw material

prices or stock prices. Market risk occurs at various levels:

- a position (e.g. a debt or an expected receipt of revenue in foreign currencies, etc.);
- a business activity (purchases paid in a currency other than that in which the products are sold, etc.); or
- a portfolio (short- and long-term financial holdings).

2. **Liquidity risk**. The impossibility at a given moment of meeting a debt payment, because:
   - the company no longer has assets that can rapidly be turned into cash;
   - a financial crisis (a market crash, for example) has made it very difficult to liquidate assets, except at a very great loss in value; or
   - it is impossible to find investors willing to offer new funding.
3. **Counterparty or credit risk.** The risk of loss on an outstanding receivable or, more generally, on a debt that is not paid on time. It naturally depends on three parameters: the amount of the debt, the likelihood of default and the portion of the debt that will be collected in the event of a default.
4. **Operating risks.** Risks of losses caused by errors on the part of employees, systems and processes, or by external events:
   - risk of deterioration of industrial facilities (accident, fire, explosion, etc.) that may also cover the risk of a temporary halt in business;
   - technological risk: am I in a position to identify or anticipate the arrival of new technology which will make my own technology redundant?
   - climate risks that may be of vital importance in some sectors, such as agriculture (how can cereal growers protect their harvests from the vagaries of the weather?) or the leisure sector (what sort of insurance should producers of outdoor concerts take out?);
   - environmental risks: how can I ensure that I'm in a position to protect the environment from the potentially

harmful impact of my activity? Am I in a position to certify that I comply with all environmental statutes and regulations in force?
   - etc.
5. **Political, regulatory and legal risks.** Risks that impact on the immediate environment of the company and that could substantially modify its competitive situation and even the business model itself.

Risk is always present. The so-called risk-free rate, to be discussed later, is simply a manner of speaking. Risk is always present, and to say that risk can be eliminated is to be excessively confident or to be unable to think about the future – both of which are very serious faults for an investor.

The knowledge gleaned from analysts with extensive experience in the business, mixed with common sense, allows us to classify risks into two categories:

- economic risks (political, natural, inflation, swindle and other risks), which threaten cash flows from investments and which come from the 'real economy'; and
- financial risks (liquidity, currency, interest rate and other risks), which do not directly affect cash flow, but nonetheless do come under the financial sphere. These risks are due to external financial events, and not to the nature of the issuer.

> *All risks, regardless of their nature, lead to fluctuations in the value of a financial security.*

Some securities are more volatile than others, i.e. their price fluctuates more widely. We say that these stocks are 'riskier'. The riskier a stock is, the more volatile its price is, and vice versa. Conversely, the less risky a security is, the less volatile its price is, and vice versa.

> *In a market economy, a security's risk is measured in terms of the volatility of its price (or of its rate of return). The greater the volatility, the greater the risk, and vice versa.*

Volatility can be measured mathematically by *variance* and *standard deviation* (see Question 23 for further details).

The degree of risk depends on the investment timeframe and tends to diminish over the long term. Yet rarely do investors have the means and stamina to think only of the long term and ignore short-to-medium-term needs. Investors are only human, and there is definitely risk in the short and medium terms!

22. Is there any relation between risk and return?

Short Answer

There is a trade-off between risk and return: low risks are associated with low potential returns, whereas high risks are associated with high potential returns.

Long Answer

Risk can penalize the financial performances of companies and their future cash flows. Obviously, if a risk materializes that seriously hurts company cash flows, investors will seek to sell their securities. Consequently the value of the security falls.

Moreover, if a company is exposed to significant risk, some investors will be reluctant to buy its securities. Even before risk materializes, investors' perceptions that a company's future cash flows are uncertain or volatile will serve to reduce the value of its securities.

Most modern finance is based on the premise that investors seek to reduce the uncertainty of their future cash flows. By its very nature, risk increases the uncertainty of an asset's future cash flows, and it therefore follows that such uncertainty will be priced into the market value of a security.

Investors consider risk only to the extent that it affects the value of the security. Risks can affect value by changing anticipations of cash flows or the rate at which these cash flows are discounted.

To begin with, it is important to realize that in corporate finance no fundamental distinction is made between the risk of asset revaluation and the risk of asset devaluation. That is to say, whether investors expect the value of an asset to rise or decrease is immaterial. It is the fact that risk exists in the first place that is of significance and affects how investors behave.

All risks, regardless of their nature, lead to fluctuations in the value of a financial security.

Example

Consider for example a security with the expected cash flows in Table 1.20.

Table 1.20: Cash flows expected for years from one to four

Year	1	2	3	4
Cash flow (in €)	100	120	150	190

Imagine the value of this security is estimated to be €2000 in five years. Assuming a 9% discounting rate, its value today would be:

$$\frac{100}{1.09}+\frac{120}{1.09^2}+\frac{150}{1.09^3}+\frac{190}{1.09^4}+\frac{2000}{1.09^5}=€1743$$

If a sudden sharp rise in interest rates raises the discounting rate to 13%, the value of the security becomes:

$$\frac{100}{1.13}+\frac{120}{1.13^2}+\frac{150}{1.13^3}+\frac{190}{1.13^4}+\frac{2000}{1.13^4}=€1488$$

The security's value has fallen by 15%. However, if the company comes out with a new product that raises projected cash flow by 20%, with no further change in the discounting rate, the security's value then becomes:

$$\frac{100 \times 1.20}{1.13} + \frac{120 \times 1.20}{1.13^2} + \frac{150 \times 1.20}{1.13^3} + \frac{190 \times 1.20}{1.13^4} + \frac{2000 \times 1.20}{1.13^5} = €1786$$

The security's value increases for reasons specific to the company, not because of a rise in interest rates in the market.

Now, suppose that there is an improvement in the overall economic outlook that lowers the discounting rate to 10%. If there is no change in expected cash flows, the stock's value would be:

$$\frac{120}{1.10} + \frac{144}{1.10^2} + \frac{180}{1.10^3} + \frac{228}{1.10^4} + \frac{2400}{1.10^5} = €2009$$

Again, there has been no change in the stock's intrinsic characteristics and yet its value has risen by 12.5%.

If there is stiff price competition, then previous cash flow projections will have to be adjusted downward by 10%. If all cash flows fall by the same percentage and the discounting rate remains constant, the value of the company becomes:

$$2009(1 - 10\%) = €1808$$

Once again, the security's value increases for reasons specific to the company, not because of a rise in the market.

In the previous example, a European investor would have lost 10% of his or her investment (from €2009 to €1808). If, in the interim, the euro had fallen from $1 to $0.86, a US investor would have lost 23% (from $2009 to $1555).

A closer analysis shows that some securities are more volatile than others, i.e. their price fluctuates more widely.

We say that these stocks are 'riskier'. The riskier a stock is, the more volatile its price is, and vice versa. Conversely, the less risky a security is, the less volatile its price is, and vice versa.

In general, for riskier assets, investors will require higher returns, as Figure 1.18 shows:

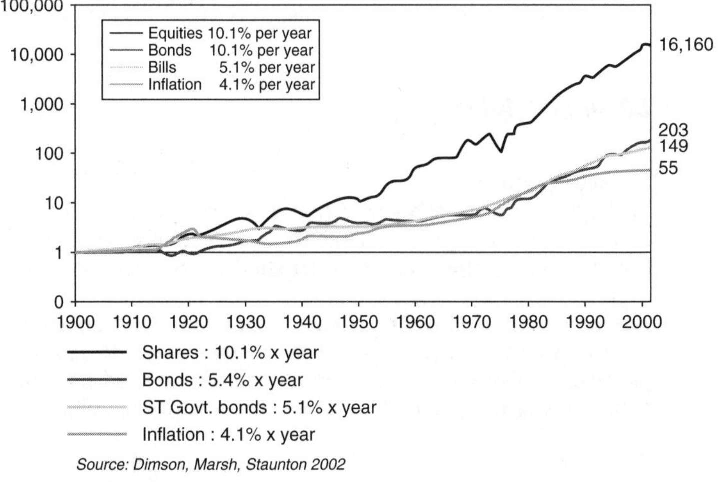

Figure 1.18: Nominal returns in the UK

As is easily shown by the graph in Figure 1.18, risk does dissipate, but only over the long term. In other words, an investor must be able to invest his or her funds and then do without them during this long-term timeframe.

23. How are risk and return measured?

Short Answer

Expected outcome $E(r)$, is a measure of expected return, and standard deviation $\sigma(r)$ measures the average dispersion of returns around expected outcome, in other words, risk.

Long Answer

Expected return

To begin, it must be realized that a security's rate of return and the value of a financial security are actually two sides of the same coin. The rate of return shall be considered first.

The holding-period return is calculated from the sum total of cash flows for a given investment, i.e. income, in the form of interest or dividends earned on the funds invested and the resulting capital gain or loss when the security is sold.

If just one period is examined, the return on a financial security can be expressed as follows:

$$F_1/V_0 + (V_1 - V_0)/V_0 = \text{income} + \text{capital gain or loss}$$

Here F_1 is the income received by the investor during the period, V_0 is the value of the security at the beginning of the period and V_1 is the value of the security at the end of the period.

In an uncertain world, investors cannot calculate their returns in advance, as the value of the security is unknown at the end of the period. In some cases, the same is true for the income to be received during the period.

Therefore, investors use the concept of expected return, which is the average of possible returns, weighted by their likelihood of occurring. Familiarity with the science of statistics should aid in understanding the notion of expected outcome.

Expected return or expected outcome is equal to:

$$E(r) = \sum_{t=1}^{n} r_t \times p_t = \bar{r}$$

where r_t is a possible return and p_t the probability of it occurring.

Variance

Intuitively, the greater the risk on an investment, the wider the variations in its return, and the more uncertain that return is. While the holder of a government bond is sure to receive his or her coupons (unless the government goes bankrupt!), this is far from true for the shareholder of an offshore oil drilling company. The shareholder could either lose everything, show a decent return or hit the jackpot.

Therefore, the risk carried by a security can be looked at in terms of the dispersion of its possible returns around an average return. Consequently, risk can be measured mathematically by the variance of its return, i.e. by the sum of the squares of the deviation of each return from expected outcome, weighted by the likelihood of each of the possible returns occurring, or:

$$V(r) = \sum_{t=1}^{n} p_t \times (r_t - \bar{r})^2$$

Standard deviation in returns is the most often used measure to evaluate the risk of an investment. Standard deviation is expressed as the square root of the variance:

$$\sigma(r) = \sqrt{V(r)}$$

Example

Given security A with 12 chances out of 100 of showing a return of –22%, 74 chances out of 100 of showing a return of 6% and 14 chances out of 100 of showing a return of 16%, its expected return would then be:

$$-22\%\frac{12}{100}+6\%\frac{74}{100}+16\%\frac{14}{100}\cong 4\%$$

The variance of investment A above is therefore:

$$\frac{12}{100}(-22\%-4\%)^2+\frac{74}{100}(6\%-4\%)^2+\frac{14}{100}(16\%-4\%)^2=1.04\%$$

---

24. What is diversification?

Short Answer

Diversification means that investors do not concentrate their entire wealth in only one financial asset, because they prefer to hold well-diversified portfolios. This behavior has the effect of reducing the risk of the investor's portfolio.

Example

Table 1.21 contains evidence of an interesting phenomenon, which gives the standard deviation for the daily return of ten Italian companies and the Italian S&P MIB index from 2003 to 2010:

Table 1.21: Standard deviation for the daily return of ten Italian companies and the Italian S&P MIB index 2003–2010

A2A	24.0%	Mediaset	24.0%
Brembo	33.2%	Pirelli	30.9%
ENEL	25.6%	Telecom Italia	26.5%
Finmeccanica	28.3%	Unicredit	34.7%
Generali	21.7%	**FTSE MIB index**	**23.3%**
Impregilo	27.9%		

The standard deviation of single assets is almost always higher than the standard deviation of the entire market (as given by the market index)! If investors buy portfolios of assets, instead of single assets, they can reduce the overall risk of their entire portfolio because asset prices move independently. They are influenced differently by macroeconomic conditions.

Long Answer

Adding securities to a portfolio makes it possible to reduce the idiosyncratic influence that single securities have on the total return of the portfolio. This 'diversification effect' is due to:

- the reduced weighting of single securities on the portfolio performance; and
- the higher balance that occurs between favorable and unfavorable securities.

When choosing securities, investors should evaluate the marginal contribution that each additional asset brings to the variance of the entire portfolio.

Fluctuations in the value of a security can be due to:

- fluctuations in the entire market. The market could rise as a whole after an unexpected cut in interest rates, stronger than expected economic growth figures, etc. All stocks will then rise, although some will move more than others. The same thing can occur when the entire market moves downward; or
- factors specific to the company that do not affect the market as a whole, such as a major order, the bankruptcy of a competitor, a new regulation affecting the company's products, etc.

These two sources of fluctuation produce two types of risk: market risk and specific risk.

- **Market, systematic or undiversifiable risk** is due to trends in the entire economy, tax policy, interest rates, inflation, etc., and affects all securities. Remember, this is the risk of the security *correlated* to market risk. To varying degrees, market risk affects all securities. For example, if a nation switches to a 35-hour work-week with no cut in wages, all companies will be affected. However, in such a case, it stands to reason that textile makers will be affected more than cement companies.

- **Specific, intrinsic or idiosyncratic risk** is independent of market-wide phenomena and is due to factors affecting just the one company, such as mismanagement, a factory fire, an invention that renders a company's main product line obsolete, etc.

Market volatility can be economic or financial in origin, but it can also result from anticipations of flows (dividends, capital gains, etc.) or a variation in the cost of equity. For example, an overheating of the economy could raise the cost of equity (i.e. after an increase in the central bank rate) and reduce anticipated cash flows due to weaker demand. Together, these two factors could exert a double downward pressure on financial securities.

Considering a portfolio composed of two stocks A and E the portfolio's variance is determined as follows:

$$\sigma^2(r_{A,E}) = X_A^2 \times \sigma^2(r_A) + X_E^2 \times \sigma^2(r_E) + 2X_A \times X_E \times \text{cov}(r_A, r_E)$$

$\text{Cov}(r_A, r_E)$ is the covariance between A and E. It measures the degree to which the two stocks fluctuate together. It is equal to:

$$\begin{aligned}\text{Cov}(r_A, r_E) &= E\left[(r_A - E(r_A)) \times (r_E - E(r_E))\right] \\ &= \sum_{i=1}^{n}\sum_{j=1}^{m} p_{i,j} \times (r_A - \overline{r_A}) \times (r_E - \overline{r_E}) \\ &= \rho_{A,E} \times \sigma(r_A) \times \sigma(r_E)\end{aligned}$$

$p_{i,j}$ is the probability of joint occurrence and $\rho_{A,E}$ is the correlation coefficient of returns offered by A and E. The correlation coefficient is a number between –1 (returns 100% inversely proportional to each other) and 1 (returns 100% proportional to each other). Correlation coefficients are usually positive, as most stocks rise together in a bullish market and most fall together in a bearish market.

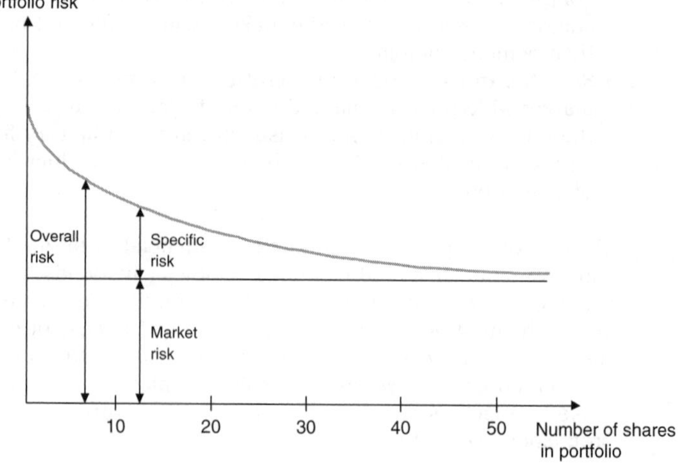

Figure 1.19: What diversification does

By plugging the variables back into our variance equation above, we obtain:

$$\sigma^2(r_{A,E}) = X_A^2 \times \sigma^2(r_A) + X_E^2 \times \sigma^2(r_E) + 2X_A \times X_E \times \rho_{A,E} \times \sigma(r_A) \times \sigma(r_E)$$

Given that:

$$-1 \leq \rho_{A,E} \leq 1$$

It is therefore possible to say:

$$\sigma^2(r_{A,E}) \leq X_A^2 \times \sigma^2(r_A) + X_E^2 \times \sigma^2(r_E) + 2X_A \times X_E \times \sigma(r_A) \times \sigma(r_E)$$

or:

$$\sigma^2(r_{A,E}) \leq (X_A \times \sigma(r_A) + X_E \times \sigma(r_E))^2$$

It is important to understand also the effect of the correlation coefficient on diversification (see Figures 1.19 and 1.20). Considering a portfolio of two stocks, Alcatel and ENI:

- if Alcatel and ENI were perfectly correlated (i.e. the correlation coefficient is 1) diversification would have no effect. All possible portfolios would lie on a line linking the risk and return point of Alcatel with that of ENI. Risk would increase in direct proportion to Alcatel's stock added;
- if the two stocks were perfectly inversely correlated (correlation coefficient –1) diversification would be total. However, there is little chance of this occurring, as both companies are exposed to the same economic conditions; and
- generally speaking, Alcatel and ENI are positively, but imperfectly, correlated and diversification is based on the desired amount of risk.

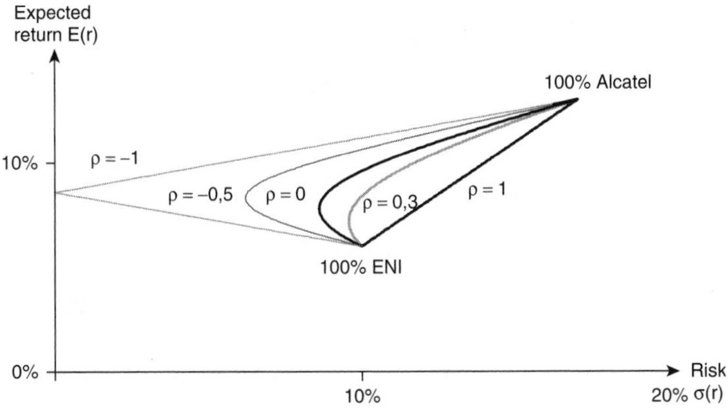

Figure 1.20: Impact of the correlation coefficient on risk and return

In sum, to formalize diversification can:

- either reduce risk for a given level of return; and/or
- improve return for a given level of risk.

References and Further Reading

Kritzman, M., What practitioners need to know... about time diversification, *Financial Analysts Journal*, 14–18, January–February 1994.

25. What are the efficient frontier and the capital market line?

Short Answer

The *efficient frontier* shows all the portfolios that offer investors the best risk–return ratio (i.e. minimal risk for a given return).

The *capital market line* links the market portfolio M to the risk-free asset. For a given level of risk, no portfolio is better than those located on this line.

Example

Efficient portfolios fall between Z and Alcatel. The portion of the curve between Z and Alcatel is called the efficient frontier (Figure 1.21).

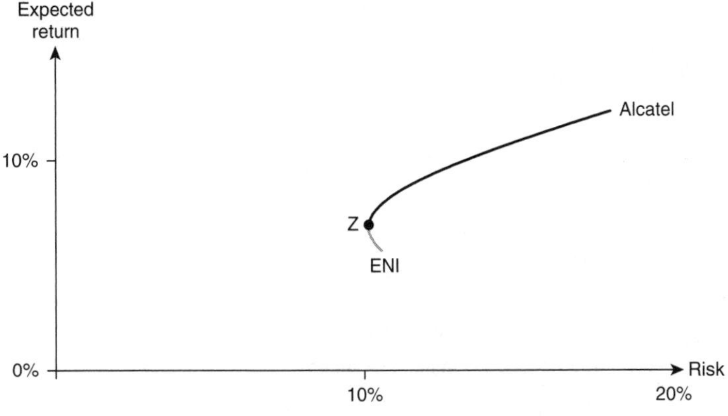

Figure 1.21: Efficient frontier

For any portfolio that does not lie on the efficient frontier, another can be found that, given the level of risk, offers a greater return, or that at the same return, entails less risk.

All subjective elements aside, it is impossible to choose between portfolios that have different levels of risk. There is no universally optimum portfolio and therefore it is up to the investor to decide, based upon his or her appetite for risk.

However, given the same level of risk, some portfolios are better than others. These are the efficient portfolios.

With a larger number of stocks, i.e. more than just two, the investor can improve his or her efficient frontier, as shown in Figure 1.22.

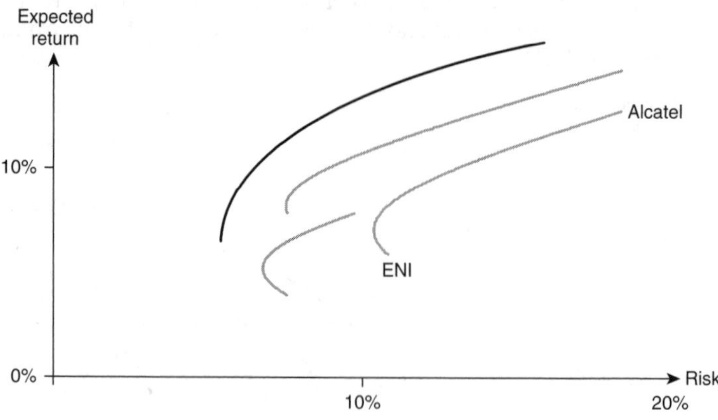

Figure 1.22: Improved efficient frontier

Long Answer

The risk and return profile can be chosen by combining risk-free assets and a stock portfolio (the Alpha portfolio in Figure 1.23). This new portfolio will be on a line that connects the risk-free rate to the efficient portfolio that has been chosen. In Figure 1.23, the portfolio located on the efficient frontier, M, maximizes utility. The line joining the risk-free rate to portfolio M is tangential to the efficient frontier.

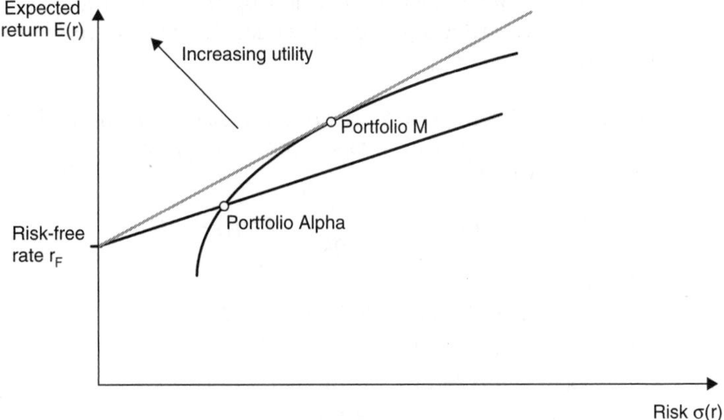

Figure 1.23: Combining risk-free assets and a stock portfolio

Investors' taste for risk can vary, yet Figure 1.23 demonstrates that the shrewd investor should be invested in portfolio M. It is then a matter of adjusting the risk exposure by adding or subtracting risk-free assets.

If all investors acquire the same portfolio, the latter must contain all existing shares. To understand why, suppose that stock *i* was not in portfolio M. In that case, nobody would want to buy it, since all investors hold portfolio M. Consequently, there would be no market for it and it would cease to exist.

The *market portfolio* includes all stocks at their market value. The market portfolio is thus weighted proportionally to the market capitalization of a particular stock market. The weighting of stock *i* in a market portfolio will necessarily be the value of the single security divided by the sum of all the assets. As we are assuming fair value, this will be the fair value of *i*.

The expected return of a portfolio consisting of the market portfolio and the risk-free asset can be expressed by the following equation:

$$E(r_P) = r_F + \frac{\sigma_P}{\sigma_M} \times [E(r_M) - r_F]$$

where:

$E(r_P)$ is the portfolio's expected return;
r_F, the risk-free rate;
$E(r_M)$, the return on the market portfolio;
σ_P, the portfolio's risk; and
σ_M, the risk of the market portfolio.

This is the equation of the capital market line, which is graphically tangent to the efficient frontier containing the portfolio M. The reason is that if there was a more efficient combination of risk-free and risky assets, the weighting of the risky assets would depart from that of the market portfolio, and supply and demand for these stocks would seek a new equilibrium.

The most efficient portfolios in terms of risk and return will always be on the capital market line. The tangent point at M constitutes the optimal combination for *all* investors. If we introduce the assumption that all investors have homogeneous expectations, i.e. that they have the same opinions on expected returns and risk of financial assets, then the efficient frontier of risky assets will be the same for all of them. The capital market line is the same for all investors and each of them would thus hold a combination of the portfolio M and the risk-free asset.

With the assumption of homogeneous expectations, it is reasonable to say that portfolio M includes all the assets weighted for their market capitalization. This is defined as the market portfolio.[1]

> *The market portfolio is the portfolio that all investors hold a fraction of, proportional to the market's capitalization.*

The *capital market line* links the market portfolio M to the risk-free asset. For a given level of risk, no portfolio is better than those located on this line.

These portfolios consist of two types of investments:

- an investment in the risk-free rate and in the market portfolio, between $\sigma = 0$ and $\sigma = \sigma_M$; and
- an investment in the market portfolio financed partly by debt at the risk-free rate, beyond σ_M.

A rational investor will not take a position on individual stocks in the hope of obtaining a big return, but rather on

---

[1]In practice, investors use wide-capitalization market indexes as a proxy for the market portfolio.

the market as a whole. That investor will then choose his or her risk level by adjusting the debt level or by investing in risk-free assets. This is the *separation theorem*. According to this theorem the financial decision of an investor requires 'two steps':

1. The investor collects data and information on financial assets, estimates the expected risk and return for each of them, simulates sets of combinations of assets, builds the efficient frontier of risky assets, links the risk-free asset with the efficient frontier, delineates the market portfolio (M); and then
2. chooses how to allocate wealth between M and the risk-free assets. This decision is a function of personal preferences and attitude toward risk.

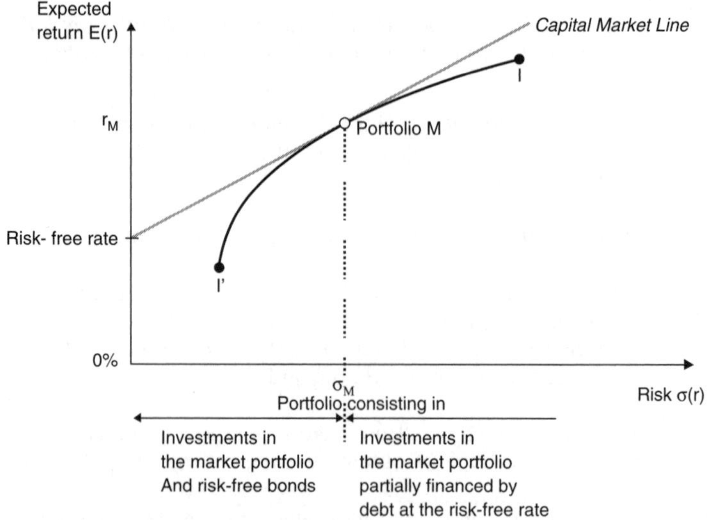

Figure 1.24: Separation theorem

26. What are the CAPM and the beta coefficients?

Short Answer

The CAPM (capital asset pricing model) is a financial model that says that if all investors hold the market portfolio, the risk premium they will demand is proportional to a coefficient normally named 'beta' (β).

The beta measures a security's sensitivity to market risk.

Example

$$r_f = 2.5\%$$
$$\beta = 1.5$$
$$r_m = 10\%$$

Then, the required rate of return is:

$$\textit{Required rate of return} = 2.5\% + 1.5(10\% - 2.5\%) = 13.75\%$$

Long Answer

The contribution of a single asset to the risk of a portfolio is measured by its covariance with the returns of the portfolio. This sensitivity measure is called the beta (β) of a financial asset.

For security J, it is mathematically obtained by performing a regression analysis of security returns vs. market returns. Hence:

$$\beta_J = \frac{\mathrm{Cov}(r_J, r_\mathrm{M})}{V(r_\mathrm{M})}$$

Here $\text{Cov}(r_J, r_\text{M})$ is the covariance of the return of security J with that of the market, and $V(r_\text{M})$ is the variance of the market return. This can be represented as:

$$\beta_J = \frac{\sum_{i=1}^{n}\sum_{k=1}^{n} p_{i,k} \times (r_{J_i} - \overline{r_J}) \times (r_{\text{M}_k} - \overline{r_\text{M}})}{\sum_{i=1}^{n} p_i \times (r_{\text{M}_i} - \overline{r_\text{M}})^2}$$

More intuitively, β corresponds to the slope of the linear regression of the security's return vs. that of the market.

The line we obtain is defined as the *characteristic line of a security.*

We can fruitfully consider three cases:

- $\beta = 1$, the asset is expected to perform as the market;
- $\beta > 1$, the asset is expected to amplify the movements of the market;
- $\beta < 1$, the asset is less volatile than the market.

Figure 1.25 shows this graphically.

The CAPM was developed in the late 1950s and 1960s, based on the pioneering work of Harry Markowitz, then followed by William Sharpe, John Lintner and Jack Treynor.

This model is based on the assumption that investors act rationally and have at their disposal all relevant information on financial securities. They seek to maximize their return, at a given level of risk.

From *portfolio selection*, we know that the investors:

1. consider the efficient portfolios, that is the portfolios that offer the highest return for a given level of risk (measured by the standard deviation);

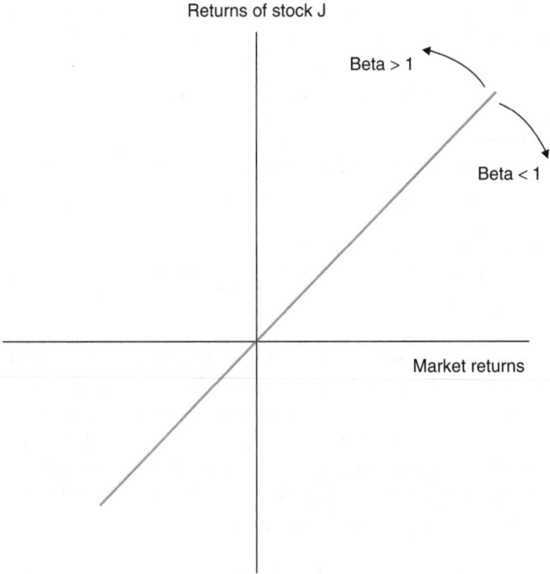

Figure 1.25: The characteristic line of a security

2. introduce the risk-free asset. The tangent point between the risk-free asset and the efficient frontier is the portfolio with the highest ratio of risk premium to standard deviation; and
3. hold the same portfolio as everybody else as long as there are homogeneous expectations among investors. This portfolio is the market portfolio.

From the analysis of risk of individual securities, it has been shown that:

- the contribution of a stock to a portfolio depends on the stock's sensitivity to the returns of the portfolio; and

- the sensitivity to the returns of the market portfolio is known as beta (β).

The expected return of an asset will then be a linear function of beta:

$$\text{Expected return on a financial asset} = \text{Risk-free rate} + \beta \times (\text{Expected return of market portfolio} - \text{Risk-free rate})$$

Remember that in order to minimize total risk, investors seek to reduce that component which can be reduced, i.e. the specific risk. They do so by diversifying their portfolios.

As a result, when stocks are efficiently priced, investors will expect a return only on the *portion of risk that they cannot eliminate: the market risk (also named systematic or non-diversifiable risk)*. Indeed, in a market in which arbitrage is theoretically possible, they will not be remunerated for a risk that they could otherwise eliminate themselves by simply diversifying their portfolios.

Portfolio theory's essential contribution is to show that an investor's required rate of return is not linked to total risk, but solely to market risk.

> *Conversely, in an efficient market, diversifiable (or intrinsic or firm-specific) risks are not remunerated.*

This means that the required rate of return (k) is equal to the risk-free rate r_f, plus the risk premium for the non-diversifiable risk, i.e. the market risk.

This can be expressed as follows:

$$\text{Required rate of return} = \text{Risk-free rate} + \beta \times \text{Market risk premium}$$

$$k = r_f + \beta(r_m - r_f)$$

Where r_m is the required rate of return for the market and β the sensitivity coefficient described previously.

Note that the coefficient β measures the non-diversifiable risk of an asset, not its total risk. So it is possible to have a stock that is, on the whole, highly risky, but with a low β if it is only loosely correlated with the market.

The difference between the return expected on the market as a whole and the risk-free rate is called the equity risk premium. This averages 3–5% in developed economies, but is higher in emerging markets (Figure 1.26).

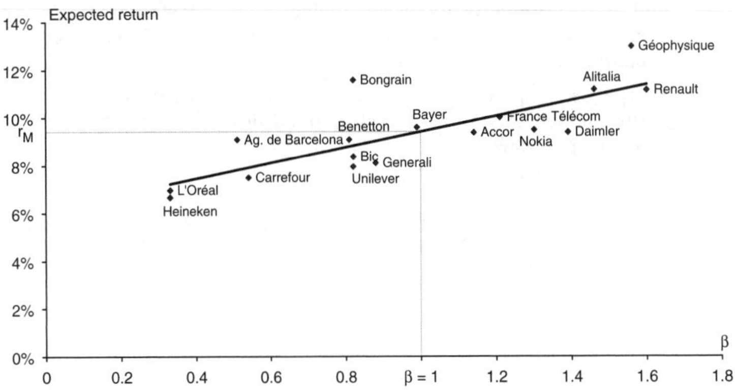

Figure 1.26: Security market line for the euro zone

References and Further Reading

Blume, M., Betas and their regression tendencies, *Journal of Finance*, **30**, 785–795, June 1975.

Campbell, J., Lettau, M., Malkiel, B. and Xu, Y., Have individual stocks become more volatile? An empirical exploration of idiosyncratic risk, *Journal of Finance*, **56**, 1–43, February 2001.

Fama, E. and French, K., Size and book-to-market factors in earnings and returns, *Journal of Finance*, **50**, 131–155, 1995.

Ferguson, M. and Shockley, R., Equilibrium 'anomalies', *Journal of Finance*, **58**, 2549–2580, December 2003.

Groenewold, N. and Fraser, P., Forecasting beta: how does the 'five-year rule of thumb' do?, *Journal of Business & Accounting*, **27**, 953–982, Sept/Oct 2000.

Lintner, J., The valuation of risk assets and the selection of risky investments in stock portfolios and capital budgets, *Review of Economics and Statistics*, **47**, 13–37, February 1965.

Roll, R., A critique of the asset pricing theory's tests Part I: on past and potential testability of the theory, *Journal of Financial Economics*, **4**, 129–179, March 1997.

Sharpe, W., Capital Asset Prices: a theory of market equilibrium under conditions of risk, *Journal of Finance*, **19**, 425–442, September 1964.

27. What is the cost of capital and how can it be estimated?

Short Answer

The cost of capital is the minimum rate of return on the company's investments that can satisfy both shareholders (the cost of equity) and debt-holders (the cost of debt). The cost of capital is thus the company's total cost of financing.

Example

Different ratings imply different risks and different costs of capital, as shown in Figure 1.27.

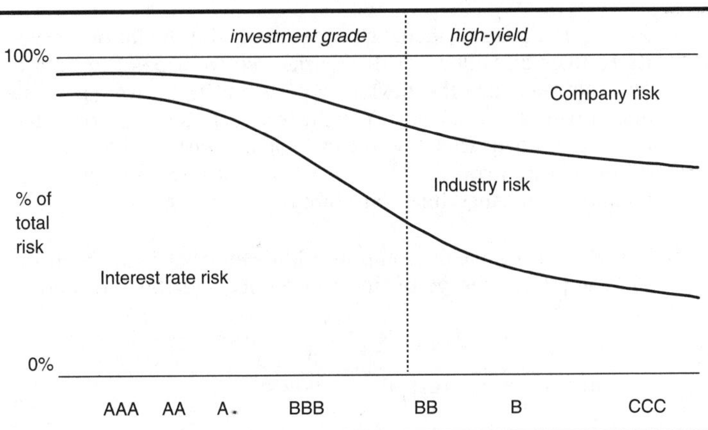

Figure 1.27: Ratings, risks and costs of capital

Long Answer

The cost of capital can be calculated in three ways: directly, indirectly or via enterprise value.

Direct calculation via the β of assets

Since a company's liabilities merely provide a 'screen' between the asset side of the company and the financial market, the rate of return required to satisfy investors is equal to the risk-free rate plus a risk premium related to the company's activity.

Applying the CAPM gives us:

$$k = r_F + \beta_A \times (r_M - r_F)$$

Where k is the weighted average cost of capital, r_F the risk-free rate, r_M the market rate of return and β_A the beta of assets or unlevered beta, that is the β of a debt-free company.

Just as the beta of a security measures the deviation between its returns and those of the market, so too does the beta of an asset measure the deviation between its future cash flows and those of the market. Yet these two betas are not independent. A firm that invests in projects with a high β_A, in other words, projects that are risky, will have a high β_E on its shares because its profitability will fluctuate widely.

The β_A can be easily computed knowing that it is equal to the weighted average of the β of equity and the β of debt:

$$\beta_{Asset} = \beta_{Equity} \times \frac{V_E}{V_E + V_D} + \beta_{Debt} \times \frac{V_D}{V_E + V_D}$$

β_A can also be expressed as follows:

$$\beta_{Asset} = \frac{\beta_{Equity} + \beta_{Debt} \times \dfrac{V_D}{V_E}}{1 + \dfrac{V_D}{V_E}}$$

β_D corresponds to the beta of the net debt and it should be computed exactly the same way as the beta of equity, i.e. by regressing the returns on listed debt against market returns of the debt of the same credit quality. However, it is reasonable to assume that β_D is equal to zero for weakly leveraged companies. Thus, the previous equation can be simplified as follows:

$$\beta_{\text{Asset}} = \frac{\beta_{\text{Equity}}}{1 + \dfrac{V_D}{V_E}}$$

We believe that it is not reasonable to simplify the analysis by assuming that $\beta_D = 0$ only when the leverage of a company is not negligible. In fact, the higher the leverage the less the financial debt depends on the level of interest rates and the more it will be linked to the specific characteristics of the company (fixed costs/variable costs) and its industry (cyclicality). In these cases, debt then begins to behave more like equity.

More frequently, financial analysts prefer using the following formula (called the 'Hamada formula'):

$$\beta_A = \frac{\beta_E}{\left[1 + (1 - T_C) \times \dfrac{V_D}{V_E}\right]}$$

This way of computing β_D makes two strong assumptions, following propositions from Modigliani and Miller (1963) that:

- the company can borrow at the risk-free rate, whatever its capital structure is; and
- the value of the firm is equal to the unlevered value plus the value of the tax shield of debt, computed as the product of the net debt multiplied by the corporate tax rate.

Although these two assumptions are useful for simplifying the analysis, they are frequently unrealistic. The first, because even the borrowing rate of companies with AAA rating (e.g. Exxon) includes a credit spread. The second, because the financial distress cost is not considered in the analysis, even if its magnitude is close to the value of tax shield for highly levered companies.

Indirect calculation

In practice, to determine the rate of return required by all of the company's providers of funds, it is necessary to calculate the cost of capital by valuing the various securities issued by the company.

The cost of capital is related to the value of the securities and represents the amount the company would have to pay to refund all its liabilities, regardless of the cost of its current resources. As such, it symbolizes the application of financial market logic to the corporation.

To calculate a company's cost of capital, we determine the rate of return required of each type of security and weight each rate according to its relative share in financing. This is none other than the WACC formula:

$$k = \text{WACC} = k_{\text{E}} \times \frac{V_{\text{E}}}{V_{\text{E}} + V_{\text{D}}} + k_{\text{D}} \times (1 - T_{\text{C}}) \times \frac{V_{\text{D}}}{V_{\text{E}} + V_{\text{D}}}$$

Thus, a company with equity financing of 100 at a rate of 15.7%, and debt financing of 50 at a pre-tax cost of 7%, has a cost of capital of 12% (with a 35% tax rate, T_{C}).

This is the most frequently used method to calculate the cost of capital. Nevertheless, beware of relying too much on spreadsheets to calculate the cost of capital, instead of getting your hands dirty by working on some examples yourself.

When performing simulations, it is all too tempting to change the company's capital structure while forgetting that the cost of equity and the cost of debt are not constant: they are a function of the company's structure. It is all too easy to reduce the cost of capital on paper by increasing the relative share of net debt, because debt is always cheaper than equity!

In the preceding example, if the share of debt is increased to 80% without changing either the cost of debt or equity, then the cost of capital works out to 5.1%. While the arithmetic may be correct, this is totally wrong financially.

Do not forget that higher debt translates into a higher cost of both equity and net debt, as shown in Figure 1.27.

Implicit calculation based on enterprise value

The cost of capital can be estimated based on enterprise value and a projection of anticipated future free cash flows, since:

$$V = V_E + V_D = \sum_{t=0}^{\infty} \frac{FCF_t}{(1+k)^t}$$

It is then necessary to solve the equation with k as the unknown factor. However, this calculation is rarely used because it is difficult to determine the market consensus for free cash flows.

References and Further Reading

Amihud, Y. and Mendelson, H., Asset pricing and the bid ask spread, *Journal of Financial Economics*, **17**, 223–249, 1986.

Botosan, C., Evidence that greater liquidity lowers the cost of capital, *Journal of Applied Corporate Finance*, **12**(4), 8–25, Winter 2000.

Bruner, R., Eades, K., Harris, R. and Higgins, R., Best practices in estimating the cost of capital: survey and synthesis, *Financial Practice and Education*, 13–29, Spring/Summer 1998.

Fama, E. and French, K., The corporate cost of capital and the return on corporate investment, *Journal of Finance*, **54**(6), 1939–1967, December 1999.

Gitman, L. and Vandenberg, P., Cost of capital techniques used by major US firms: 1997 vs. 1980, *Financial Practice and Education*, 54–68, Fall/Winter 2000.

Graham, J. and Harvey, C., The theory and practice of corporate finance: evidence from the field, *Journal of Financial Economics*, 187–243, May 2001.

Modigliani, F. and Miller, M., Corporate income taxes and the cost of capital: a correction, *American Economic Review*, **53**, 433–443, June 1963.

Myers, S., Interactions of corporate financing and investment decisions – implication for capital budgeting, *Journal of Finance*, **29**(1), 1–25, March 1974.

Pratt, S., *Cost of Capital. Estimation and applications*, 3rd ed., John Wiley & Sons, 2010.

Schramm, R. and Wang, H., Measuring the cost of capital in an international CAPM framework, *Journal of Applied Corporate Finance*, **12**(3), 63–72, Autumn 1999.

Stulz, R., Globalisation, corporate finance and the cost of capital, *Journal of Applied Corporate Finance*, **12**(3), 8–25, Autumn 1999.

28. What are the most important debt products for companies' financing?

Short Answer

Debt securities are *bonds*, *commercial papers*, *notes*, *certificates of deposit* and *mortgage-backed bonds* or *mortgage bonds*. Furthermore, the current trend is to securitize loans to make them negotiable.

Example of a corporate bond

Table 1.22: Lafarge – 6.125% May 2008–May 2015 Bond Issue

Amount:	€750,000,000
Denomination:	€50,000
Issue price:	99.529% or €49,764.5 per bond, payable in one installment on the settlement date
Date of issue:	28 May 2008
Settlement date:	28 May 2008
Maturity:	7 years
Annual coupon:	6.125%, i.e. €3062.50 per bond payable in one installment on 28 May of each year, with the first payment on 28 May 2009
Yield to maturity for the subscriber:	On the settlement date
Average life:	7 years
Normal redemption date:	The bonds will be redeemed in full on 28 May 2015 at par value.
Guarantee:	no guarantee

(*continued overleaf*)

Table 1.22: *(continued)*

Further issues (fungibility):	The issuer may, without prior permission from the bondholders, create and issue new bonds with the same features as the present bonds with the exception of the issue price and the first coupon payment date. The present bonds could thus be exchanged with the new bonds.
Rating:	Baa2 (Moody's), BBB (Standard & Poor's)
Listing:	Luxembourg Stock Market.

Long Answer

Marketable debt securities

Medium- to long-term debt securities Bonds are an important medium-term market financing vehicle used by corporations, particularly in the five-to-ten year segment. Bonds can be subordinated, convertible or redeemable in shares.

Bonds can be issued in a currency other than that of the issuer. The most liquid currencies are the euro, the dollar, sterling and the Swiss franc.

High-yield bonds are generally subordinated debt, typically taking the form of five-, six- or ten-year bonds. These bonds are issued by companies in the process of being turned around or with a weak financial base, in particular LBOs. Their high yields match the level of risk involved, making them a speculative investment. Their holders enter into a debt subordination agreement whereby, in the event of bankruptcy proceedings (whether court-ordered or amicable) their claims are not settled until all claims held by traditional bank lenders have been fully repaid.

Medium-term notes are negotiable notes with a maturity of more than one year. The market for medium-term notes is still in its infancy and, as in the case of the bond market, investors in continental Europe would rather entrust their medium-term funds to institutional investors such as insurance companies and financial institutions than to medium-sized industrial companies. In any event, the issuing of both negotiable medium-term notes and high-yield bonds is virtually impossible without a credit rating.

Commercial paper A commercial paper is a negotiable debt security issued on the money market for periods ranging from one day to one year. The average maturity of commercial paper is generally very short, between one to three months. They are issued in minimum denominations of €150 thousands at fixed or variable rates. Issuers can also launch variable rate commercial paper linked with a variable rate/fixed rate swap or paper denominated in US dollars with a euro swap, allowing them to separate the company's financing from interest or exchange-rate risk management.

Commercial paper enables companies to borrow directly from other companies without going through the banking system at rates very close to those of the money market.

Obtaining at least a short-term credit rating for a commercial paper issue is optional, but implicitly recommended since companies are required to indicate whether they have called on a specialized rating agency and, if so, must disclose the rating given. Moreover, any issuer can ask a bank for a commitment to provide financing should the market situation make it impossible to renew the note. Companies have to have such lines if they want their commercial paper issues to get an investment grade rating.

In addition to lower issue costs, commercial paper gives companies some autonomy vis-à-vis its bankers. It is very flexible in terms of maturity and rates, but less so in terms of issue amounts.

In addition to straight commercial paper, companies can use the commercial paper market for securitization transactions. A vehicle is then created to receive trade receivables from one or several corporates (usually the vehicle is kept alive and 'refilled' by the corporates). The vehicle is financed on the commercial paper market. This specific market segment called asset backed commercial paper (ABCP) had outstanding issues of €85 bn in 2003 (€59 for the European market and €26 for domestic markets).

Bank debt products

Banks have developed a number of credit products that, contrary to market financing, are tailored to meet the specific needs of their clients.

Business loans Business loans have two key characteristics: they are based on interest rates and take into account the overall risk to the company.

They are business loans because they are not granted for a specific purpose (investments, trade payables, inventories, etc.). There is no connection between the funds advanced and the company's disbursements. They can even be used to finance an investment already made.

Business loans are based on interest rates and the cheapest usually wins. They rarely come with ancillary services, such as debt recovery, and are determined according to the maturity schedule and margin on the market rate.

Financial loans are a type of credit that, in theory, is repaid by the cash flow generated by the company and is guaranteed by its assets-in-place.

Syndicated loans are typically set up for facilities exceeding €100 million that a single bank does not want to take on alone. The lead bank (or banks depending on the amounts involved) is in charge of arranging the facility and organizing a syndicate of five to twenty banks that will each lend part of the amount.

A syndicated loan (or credit facility) is a relatively large loan to a single borrower structured by a lead manager(s) and the borrower. Funds are provided by a group of banks (rather than a single lender).

There are 4 types of credit or lending facilities:

1. **Committed facilities.** A legally enforceable agreement that binds banks to lend up to stated amounts.
2. **Revolving credits**. In this case, the borrower has the right to borrow or 'draw down' on demand, re-pay and then draw-down again. The borrower is charged a commitment fee on unused amounts. Options include:
   - Multi-currency option: right to borrow in several currencies.
   - Competitive bid option: solicit best bid from syndicate members.
   - Swing line: Overnight lending option from lead manager.
3. **Term loans.**
4. **Letters of credit, equipment lines, etc.**

Overdrafts on current accounts are the corporate treasurers' means of adjusting to temporary cash shortages, but given their high interest charges they should not be used too frequently or for too long. Small enterprises can only obtain overdrafts against collateral, making the overdraft more of a secured loan.

Commercial loans are short-term loans that are easy to set up, which is why they are very popular.

The bank provides the funds for the period specified by the two parties. The interest rate is the bank's refinancing rate plus a margin negotiated between the two parties. It generally ranges from 0.10% to 1.50% per year depending on the borrower's credit-worthiness since there are no other guarantees.

Commercial loans can be made in foreign currencies either because the company needs foreign currencies or because the lending rates are more attractive.

The repeated use of commercial loans may result in a short or medium-term confirmed credit line. When the credit facility is confirmed, an engagement or confirmation commission amounting to anywhere from 1/16% to 1/18% is paid. The commission is based on the borrower's credit-worthiness and the duration of the credit and allows the company to discount the commercial paper as and when needed.

Extending this concept leads us to the *master credit agreement*, which is a confirmed credit line between several banks offering a group (and by extension its subsidiaries) a raft of credit facilities ranging from overdrafts, commercial credit lines, backup lines, foreign currency advances or guarantees for commercial paper issues. These master agreements take the form of a contract and give rise to an engagement commission on all credits authorized, in addition to the contractual remuneration of each line drawn down. Large groups use such master agreements as multi-currency and multi-company backup lines, umbrella lines and secure financing from their usual banks according to market conditions. Smaller companies sometimes obtain similar financing from their banks. Engagement commissions are usually paid on these credit lines.

Master agreements take into account the borrower's organization chart by organizing and regulating its subsidiaries' access to the credit lines. At the local level, the business relationship between the company's representatives and the bank's branches may be based on the credit conditions set up at group level.

Master agreements are based on a network of underlying guarantees between the subsidiaries party to the agreement and the parent company. In particular, the parent company must provide a letter of comfort for each subsidiary.

Banks include a certain number of *covenants* in the loan agreements, mainly regarding accounting ratios, financial decisions and share ownership. These covenants fall into four main categories:

- **Positive or affirmative covenants** are agreements to comply with certain capital structure or earnings ratios, to adopt a given legal structure or even to restructure.
- **Negative covenants** can limit the dividend payout, prevent the company from pledging certain assets to third parties (negative pledges), or from taking out new loans or engaging in certain equity transactions, such as share buybacks.
- **Pari passu clauses** are covenants whereby the borrower agrees that the lender will benefit from any additional guarantees it may give on future credits.
- **Cross default clauses** specify that if the company defaults on another loan, the loan which has a cross default clause will become payable even if there is no breach of covenant or default of payment on this loan.

Securitization

Securitization was initially used by credit institutions looking to refinance part of their assets, in other words, to convert customer loans into negotiable securities.

Securitization (Figure 1.28) works as follows: a bank first selects mortgages or consumer loans, or unsecured loans such as credit card receivables, based on the quality of the collateral they offer or their level of risk. To reduce risk, the loans are then grouped into an SPV (special purpose vehicle) so as to pool risks and take advantage of the law of large numbers. The SPV buys the loans and finances itself by issuing securities to outside investors: equity, mezzanine debt, subordinated debt, senior debt, commercial paper, etc., so as to offer different risk–return profiles to investors. Usually the vehicle is kept alive and 'refilled' progressively by banks with new loans when old loans mature. The new entity, such as a debt securitization fund receives the flow of interest and principal payments emanating from the loans it bought from the banks (or nonbank companies). The fund uses the proceeds to cover its obligations on the securities it has issued.

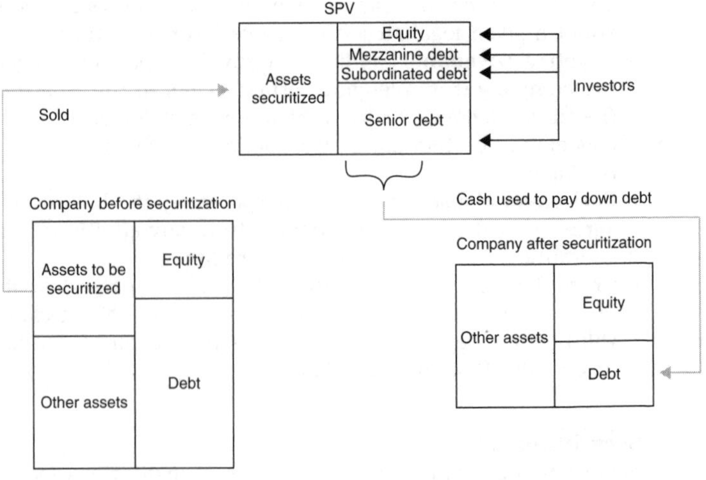

Figure 1.28: How securitization works

To boost the rating of the securities, the SPV buys more loans than the volume of securities to be issued, the excess serving as enhancement. Alternatively, the SPV can take out an insurance policy with an insurance company. The SPV might also obtain a short-term line of credit to ensure the payment of interest in the event of a temporary interruption in the flow of interest and principal payments.

Most of the time, the securitization vehicle subcontracts administration of the fund and recovery to one service provider and cash management to another.

With the help of securitization specialists, some industrial companies regularly securitize accounts receivable, inventories, buildings or other assets. In short, the whole balance sheet can be made liquid. Once isolated certain assets are of higher quality than the balance sheet as a whole, thus allowing the company to finance them at preferential rates. This said, the cost of these arrangements is higher than that of straight debt, especially for a high-quality borrower with an attractive cost of debt.

The subprime crisis has badly hurt securitization of banks' assets due to a fear of finding subprime loans or debts of highly leveraged LBOs (leveraged buyouts) among the securitized assets. For industrial groups, the securitization market is still open provided the SPV structure is crystal clear and its assets of undisputed quality.

Leasing

Types of leases In a lease contract the firm (lessee) commits itself to making fixed payments (usually monthly or semiannually) to the owner of the asset (lessor) for the right to use the asset.

These payments are either fully or partially tax-deductible, depending on how the lease is categorized for accounting purposes. The lessor is either the asset's manufacturer or an independent leasing company.

If the firm fails to make fixed payments it normally results in the loss of the asset and even bankruptcy, although the claim of the lessor is normally subordinated to other lenders.

The lease contract may take a number of different forms, but normally is categorized as either an operating or a financial lease.

For *operating leases*, the term of the lease contract is shorter than the economic life of the asset. Consequently, the present value of lease payments is normally lower than the market value of the asset. At the end of the contract the asset reverts back to the lessor, who can either offer to sell it to the lessee or lease it again to somebody else. In an operating lease, the lessee generally has the right to cancel the lease and return the asset to the lessor. Thus, the lessee bears little or no risk if the asset becomes obsolete.

A *financial (or capital) lease* normally lasts for the entire economic life of the asset. The present value of fixed payments tends to cover the market value of the asset. At the end of the contract, the lease can be renewed at a reduced rate or the lessee can buy the asset at a favorable price. This contract cannot be cancelled by the lessee.

From an accounting point of view, leasing an asset rather than buying it substitutes lease payments as a tax deduction for the payments that the firm would have claimed if it had owned the asset – depreciation and interest expenses on debt.

SIC-15 clarifies the recognition of incentives related to operating leases by both the lessee and lessor. SIC-17, 'Leases', has been effective for annual financial statements since 1999. According to these principles:

- Finance leases are those that transfer substantially all risks and rewards to the lessee.

- Lessees should capitalize a finance lease at the lower of the fair value and the present value of the minimum lease payments.
- Rental payments should be split into (i) a reduction of liability, and (ii) a finance charge designed to reduce in line with the liability.
- Lessees should calculate depreciation on leased assets using useful life, unless there is no reasonable certainty of eventual ownership. In the latter case, the shorter of useful life and lease term should be used.
- Lessees should expense operating lease payments.

Reasons for leasing There are different reasons a firm can prefer leasing.

- The firm may not have the borrowing capacity to purchase an asset.
- Operating leases provide a source of off-balance sheet financing for heavily leveraged firms. However, this opportunity does not reduce the firm's financial risk. Lenders are in fact careful in considering the cash flow effects of lease payments.
- The firm may want to avoid bond covenants.

To lease or buy? The analysis regarding whether a firm should buy or lease follows the same principles illustrated so far of investment analysis. Thus, we have basically three alternatives in valuing the relative convenience of leases:

- The decisions can be made according to the present value of incremental after-tax cash flows of the two alternatives. In computing the present value of a lease's cash flows, we should use the after-tax cost of borrowing since we are comparing two borrowing alternatives. A lease payment is like the debt service on a secured bond issued by the lessee, and the discount rate should be approximately the same as the interest rate on such debt.

- Alternatively, we can compare the IRR of the two alternatives and choose the one with the lower rate.
- Finally, we could compute the difference between the two cash flows (buying and leasing) and compute the internal rate of return on these differential cash flows. This rate should then be compared with the after-tax cost of debt to determine which alternative is more attractive.

References and Further Reading

Choudry, M., *The Bond & Money Markets*, Butterworth-Heinemann, 2002.

Fabozzi, F., *The Handbook of Fixed Income Securities*, 7th ed., McGraw-Hill, 2008.

Freixas, J., Hartmann, P. and Mayer, C., *Handbook of European Financial Markets and Institutions*, Oxford University Press, 2008.

Santos, I., Is the secondary loan market valuable for borrowers?, *The Quarterly Review of Economics and Finance*, 1410–1428, November 2009.

29. What do we mean by stock market analysis of a company?

Short Answer

Share analysis is centered on changes in stock market prices, multiples (especially price-to-earnings ratio), dividends and returns, compared with required returns.

Example

Table 1.23: Key market data on Indesit

In euros	Past		Current	Future	
	2009	2010	2011	2012	2013
Adjusted share price					
High	8.70	10.4			
Low	1.62	7.9			
Average or last	7.80	8.56			
Absolute data					
Number of fully diluted shares (m)	103	103			
Market capitalization (bn)	803	882			
Equity, group share (bn)	506				
Value of net debt (bn)	368				
Enterprise value (bn)	1171				
Multiples					
Fully diluted EPS	0.32	0.78	0.82	0.88	
EPS growth	–41%	+144%	+5%	+7%	
P/E	24.4	11.0	10.4	9.7	
After-tax operating profit (m)	118	177	183	193	

(continued overleaf)

Table 1.23: (*continued*)

In euros	Past		Current	Future	
	2009	2010	2011	2012	2013
EBIT multiple	1.6				
Price/Book Ratio (PBV)					
Dividend	0.13	0.35	0.41	0.44	
Dividend per share (DPS)	nm	+169%	+17%	+7.0%	
DPS growth	1.7%	4.0%	4.8%	5.1%	
Net yield	41%	45%	50%	50%	
Payout					
Return	1.10	0.99			
Beta(β)	6.8%	6.5%			
Risk premium: $r_M - r_F$	4.0%	4.0%			
Risk-free rate: r_F	11.5%	10.4%			
Required rate of return: k_E	15%				
Return on equity: r_E	82.0%	14.3%			
Free float	20%	20%	20%		

Long Answer

Basic concepts to analyze the value of a share

1) Voting rights Shares are normally issued with one voting right each. For our purposes, this is more of a compensation for the risk assumed by the shareholder than a basic characteristic of stock.

A company can issue shares with limited or without voting rights. These are known under different names, including preference shares, savings shares or, simply, non-voting shares.

2) Earnings per share (EPS) EPS is equal to net attributable profit divided by the total number of shares in issue. EPS reflects the theoretical value creation during a given year, as net profit belongs to shareholders.

There is no absolute rule for presenting EPS. However, financial analysts generally base it on restated earnings, as shown below.

Net attributable profit:

- Exceptional (after-tax) profit.
- Other nonrecurring items not included in exceptional profit + depreciation and goodwill amortization.

Some companies have outstanding equity-linked securities, such as convertible bonds, warrants and stock options. In this case, analysts calculate, in addition to standard EPS, fully diluted EPS.

3) Dividend per share (DPS) Dividends are generally paid out from the net earnings for a given year but can be paid out of earnings that have been retained from previous years. Companies sometimes pay out a quarterly or half-year dividend.

4) Dividend yield Dividend yield per share is the ratio of the last dividend paid out to the current share price:

$$\text{Dividend yield} = \frac{\text{Dividend per share}}{\text{Share price}} = \frac{DPS_0}{P_0}$$

Yield is either gross (including the tax credit) or net (without the tax credit).

Yield is based on market value and never on book value.

5) Payout ratio The payout ratio is the percentage of earnings from a given year that is distributed to shareholders in the form of dividends. It is calculated by dividing dividend by earnings for the given year:

$$\text{Payout ratio} = d = \frac{\text{Cash dividend}}{\text{Net income}}$$

It will be clear that the higher the payout ratio, the weaker future earnings growth will be. The reason for this is that the company will then have less funds to invest. Mature companies are said to have moved from the status of a growth stock to that of an income stock.

6) Cash flow per share Cash flow per share has no theoretical basis, in that it does not constitute true creation of value. Cash flow per share is nonetheless used for two reasons:

- when EPS is very low, it can be used for comparisons where EPS cannot;
- one of its components, depreciation, in some cases has little connection to real wear and tear and instead results from a tax strategy. Consolidated accounts fortunately offset this drawback. Such calculations assume that cash flow provides a better picture of real earnings than reported earnings do. However, cash flow is not equal to real earnings, only proportional to them.

When the expression price to cash flow is mentioned, it is best to check what exactly is included in the vague term 'cash flow'.

7) Equity value (book value or net asset value) per share Equity value (book value or net asset value) per share is the accounting estimate of the value of a share. While book value may appear to be directly comparable to equity value, it is determined on an entirely different basis – it is the result of strategies undertaken up to the date of the analysis and corresponds to the amount invested by the shareholders in the company (i.e. new shares issued and retained earnings).

8) Cost of equity (expected rate of return) According to the CAPM, the cost of equity is equal to the risk-free rate plus a risk premium that reflects the stock's market (or systematic) risk.

$$K_E = r_f + \beta \times (r_M - r_f)$$

9) Shareholder return (historical rate of return) In a given year, shareholders receive a return in the form of dividends (dividend yield) and the increase in price or market value (capital gain):

$$\frac{P_1 - P_0}{P_0} + \frac{\text{Div}_1}{P_0}$$

Total shareholder return (TSR) is calculated in the same way, but over a longer period.

10) Liquidity A security is said to be liquid when it is possible to buy or sell a large number of shares on the market without too great an influence on the price. Liquidity is a typical measure of the relevance of a share price. It would not make much sense to analyze the price of a stock that is traded only once a week, for example.

A share price is relevant only if the stock is sufficiently liquid. A share's liquidity is measured mainly in terms of (i) free float and (ii) trade volumes.

The free float is the proportion of shares available to purely financial investors, to buy when the price looks low and sell when it looks high. Free float can be measured either in millions of euros or in percentage of total shares. It is becoming more common to use free-float based indices, i.e. indices composed with the relative free float value of each company. The free float factor is normally given by the percentage of shares remaining after the block ownership and restricted shares adjustments are applied to the total number of shares:

Free Float Factor (%)
= 100% – [Larger of Block Ownership
and Restricted Shares Adjustments (%)]

The free float market capitalization is the portion of a stock's total market capitalization that is available for trading:

Free Float Market Capitalization
= Capitalization Free Float Factor × Total Market

Thus, it may happen that a company with a high total market value has a lower percentage in the free float index because the percentage of shares 'free to float' is low. At the same time, mid-caps could increase their relevance in the indices if relevant shareholders hold a low portion of the entire equity.

Liquidity is also measured in terms of volumes traded daily. Here, again absolute value is the measure of liquidity, as a major institutional investor will first try to determine how long it will take to buy (or sell) the amount it has targeted. But volumes must also be expressed in terms of percentage of the total number of shares and even as a percentage of free float.

11) Market capitalization Market capitalization is the market value of company equity. It is obtained by multiplying the total number of shares outstanding by the share price. However, rarely can the majority of the shares be bought at this price at the same time, for example, in an attempt to take control and appoint new management: a premium most often must be paid.

All too often, only the shares in free float are counted in determining market capitalization. All shares must be included, as market cap is the market value of company equity and not of the free float.

12) Price to book ratio (PBR) PBR measures the ratio between market value and book value:

$$\text{PBR} = \frac{\text{Price per share}}{\text{Book value per share}} = \frac{\text{Market capitalization}}{\text{Book value of equity (Net worth)}}$$

PBR can be calculated either on a per share basis or for an entire company. Either way, the result is the same.

It is not hard to show that a stock's PBR will be above one if its market value is above book value, when return on equity (r_E) is above the required rate of return (k_E). The reason for this is that if a company consistently achieves 15% ROE, whereas shareholders require only 10%, a book value of 100 would mean an equity value of 150, and the shareholders will have achieved their required rate of return:

$$\frac{15\% \times 100}{150} = 10\%, \text{and PBR is } 1.5$$

In order to understand the level of stock prices, investors must make some comparisons with comparable investments; to achieve this objective investors normally relate the stock price to a financial item.

There are two basic categories of *multiples*:

- those which allow a direct estimate of the market capitalization; and
- those which don't consider the capital structure of the company.

EBIT multiple investors interested in estimating the market value of the capital employed of a company can frequently find that the stock market believes that a fair value for similar companies could be, for example, eight times their EBIT (or operating profit).

Investors name this ratio the EBIT multiple:

$$\text{EBIT multiple} = \frac{\text{Enterprise value}}{\text{Operating profit}}$$

Enterprise value is normally estimated summing the market value of equity and the book value of net debt, assuming that rarely is the difference between the book value of debt and the corresponding market value enormous.

Price to earnings (P/E) A lot of market operators now value shares based on EPS multiplied by the P/E ratio:

$$\text{P/E} = \frac{\text{Price per share}}{\text{EPS}}$$

Another way to put this is to consider the aggregate values:

$$\text{P/E} = \frac{\text{Market capitalization}}{\text{Net income}}$$

EPS reflects theoretical value creation over a period of one year. Unlike a dividend, EPS is not a revenue stream.

The widespread use of P/E to determine equity value has given rise to the myth of EPS as a financial criterion to assess a company's financial strategy. Such or such decision might or might not be taken on the basis of its positive or negative impact on EPS. This is why P/E is so important.

One way to understand P/E is to note that it expresses market value on the basis of the number of years of earnings that are being bought. Thus an equity value of 100, with earnings of 12.5 is valued at eight times these earnings. The P/E is thus eight. This means that if EPS remains constant, the investor will have to wait eight years to recover his or her investment, while ignoring the residual value of the investment after eight years, omitting the discount, and assuming that the investor receives all of the EPS. If the EPS rises (falls), the investor will have to wait less (more) than eight years.

In an efficient market, the greater EPS growth is, the higher the P/E, and vice versa.

P/E is inversely proportional to interest rates: all other factors being equal, the higher the interest rates the lower the P/Es and vice versa, again assuming efficient markets.

The greater the perceived risk, the lower the P/E, and vice versa.

P/E can only be used for valuation purposes if the comparable companies have the same EPS growth and the same risks on both the operating and financial levels.

References and Further Reading

Quiry, P., Dallocchio, M., Le Fur, Y. and Salvi A., *Corporate Finance*, 3rd ed. John Wiley & Sons, 2011.

30. What are financial options?

Short Answer

An option gives you the right to buy or sell an asset at a pre-determined price during a pre-determined period.

Example

Let's say Peter sells Helmut a call option (Figure 1.29) on the insurance company Allianz having an €85 strike price and maturing in nine months. For nine months (US-style option) or after nine months (European-style option), Helmut will have the right to buy one Allianz share at a price of €85, regardless of Allianz's share price at that moment. Helmut is not required to buy a share of Allianz from Peter, but if Helmut wants to, Peter must sell him one for €85.

Obviously, Helmut will exercise his option only if Allianz's share price is above €85. Otherwise, if Helmut wants to buy an Allianz share, he will simply buy it on the market for less than €85.

Now let's say that Paul buys from Clara put options (Figure 1.30) on $1 million in currency at an exchange rate of €1.1/$, exercisable six months from now. Paul may, in six months' time (if it's a European-style option) sell $1 million to Clara at €1.1/$, regardless of the dollar's exchange rate at that moment. Paul is not required to sell dollars to Clara, but if he wants to, Clara must buy them from him at the agreed upon price.

Obviously, Paul will only exercise his option if the dollar is trading below €1.1.

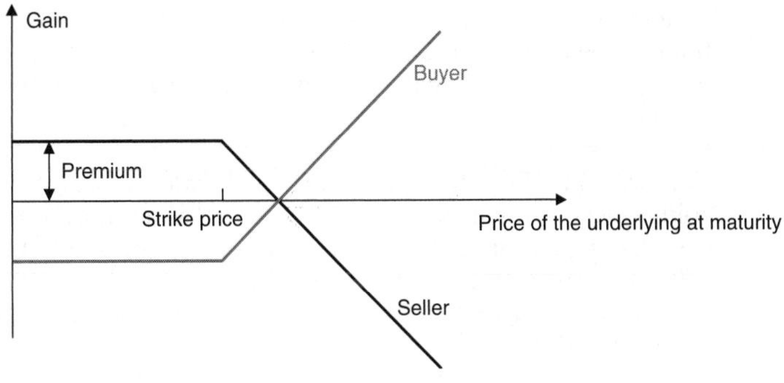

Figure 1.29: Call option

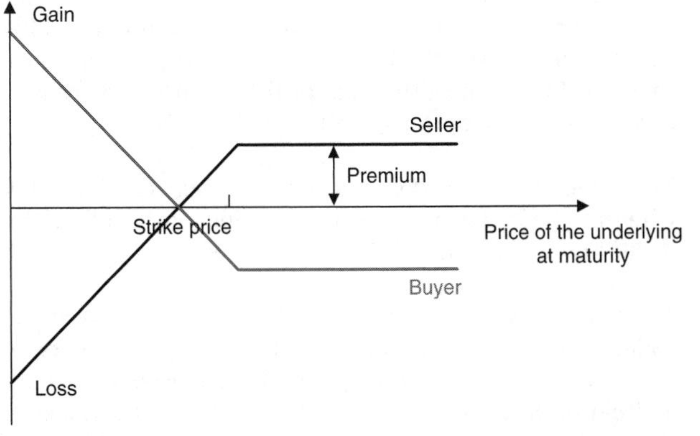

Figure 1.30: Put option

Long Answer

There are *call (buy) options* and *put (sell) options*. The asset that can thereby be bought or sold is called the underlying asset. This can be either a financial asset (stock, bond, Treasury bond, forward contract, currency, stock index, etc.) or a physical one (e.g. a raw material or mining asset).

The price at which the underlying asset can be bought or sold is called the strike price. The holder of an option may exercise it (i.e. buy the underlying asset if he or she holds a call option or sell it if he or she holds a put option) either at a given date (exercise date) or during a period called the exercise period.

A distinction is made between 'US-style options' (the holder can exercise his or her right at any moment during the exercise period) and 'European-style options' (the holder can only exercise his or her right on a given date, called the exercise date). Most listed options are US-style options, and they are found on both sides of the Atlantic, whereas most over-the-counter options are European-style.

The buyer of any option has the right but not the obligation, whereas the seller of any option is obliged to follow through if the buyer requests.

The value at which an option is bought or sold is sometimes called the premium. It is obviously paid by the buyer to the seller, who thereby obtains some financial compensation for a situation in which he or she has all the obligations and no rights.

Hence, a more precise definition of an option:

An option is a contract between two sides, under which one side gives the other side the right (but not the obligation) to buy from them (a call option, see Figure 1.31) or to sell to them (a put option, see Figure 1.32) an asset, in exchange for the payment of a premium.

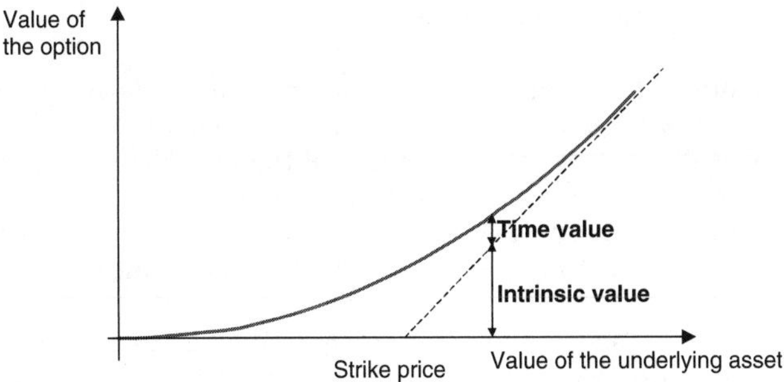

Figure 1.31: Value of a call option

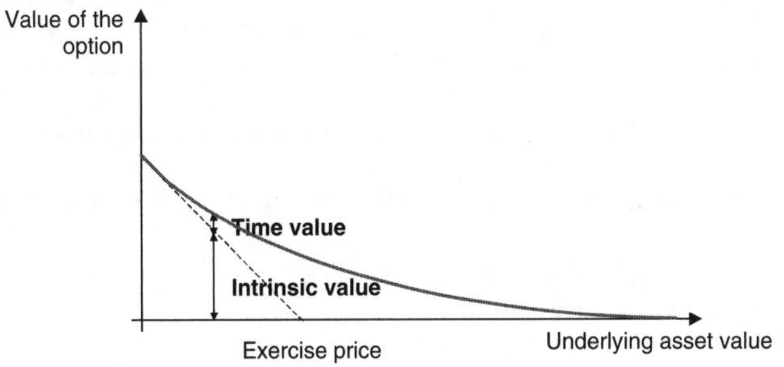

Figure 1.32: Value of a put option

This asset will be bought (or sold) at a pre-determined price called the strike price, during a period of time (the exercise period for US-style options), or at a precise date (the exercise date for European-style options).

Intrinsic value is the difference (if it is positive) between the price of the underlying asset and the option's strike price. For a put option, it's the opposite.

A call option is said to be:

- **out of the money** when the price of the underlying asset is below the strike price (zero intrinsic value);
- **at the money** when the price of the underlying asset is equal to the strike price (zero intrinsic value);
- **in the money** when the price of the underlying asset is above the strike price (positive intrinsic value).

Now let's imagine that sterling is trading at €1.4 in October. The option would be out of the money (€1.4 is less than the €1.5 strike price) and the holder would not exercise it. Does this mean that the option is worthless? No, because there is still a chance, however slight, that sterling will move over €1.5 by the end of December. This would make the option worth exercising. So the option has some value, even though it is not worth exercising right now. This is called *time value.*

$$\text{Option's value} = \text{intrinsic value} + \text{time value}$$

There are six criteria for determining the value of an option:

- the price of the underlying asset;
- the strike price;
- the volatility of the underlying asset;
- the option's maturity;
- the risk-free rate; and
- if applicable, the dividend or the coupon if the underlying asset is a share or a bond that pays one during the life of the option.

Models have been developed for valuing options, the main ones being the Black & Scholes and binomial models.

Black and Scholes (B&S) model: the B&S model is the continuous-time version of the discrete-time binomial model.

The model calculates the possible prices for the underlying asset at maturity, as well as their respective probabilities of occurrence, based on the fundamental assumption that this is a random variable with a log-normal distribution.

For a call option, the B&S formula is as follows:

$$\text{Value of the call option} = \mathrm{N}(d_1) \times V - \mathrm{N}(d_2) \times K \times \mathrm{e}^{-Tr_\mathrm{F}}$$

with:

$$d_1 = \frac{\ln\left(\frac{V}{K}\right) + \left(r_\mathrm{F} + \frac{\sigma^2}{2}\right) \times T}{\sigma \times \sqrt{T}} \quad \text{and } d_2 = d_1 - \sigma \times \sqrt{T}$$

where:

$V =$ current price of the underlying asset,
$\mathrm{N}(d)$ is a cumulative standard normal distribution (average = 0 standard deviation = 1),
$K =$ the option's strike price,
$\mathrm{e} =$ exponential function,
$r_\mathrm{F} =$ the continual annual risk-free rate,
$\sigma =$ instantaneous standard deviation of the return on the underlying asset,
$T =$ the time remaining until maturity (in years), and ln the natural logarithm.

In practice, the instantaneous return is equal to the difference between the logarithm of the share price today and yesterday's share price.

$$r = \ln V_1 - \ln V_0$$

Binomial model. The binomial method is an alternative to B&S. Let's take the example of a call option with a €105 strike price on a given stock (currently trading at €100) and for a given maturity.

Let's also assume that there are only two possibilities at the end of this period: either the stock is at €90, or it is at €110.

At maturity, our option will be worth its intrinsic value, i.e. either €0 or €5, or €0 or €20 for four options.

We can try to obtain the same result (€0 or €20) in the same conditions using another combination of securities (a so-called *replicating portfolio*). If we achieve this result, the four call options and this other combination of securities should have the same value. If we can determine the value of this other combination of securities, we will have succeeded in valuing the call option.

To do so, let's say a sum is borrowed (at 5%, for example) whose value (principal and interest) will be €90 at the end of the period concerned, and then a share is bought for €100 today. At the end of the period:

- either the share is worth €110, in which case the combination of buying the share and borrowing money is worth €110 – €90 = €20;
- or the share is worth €90, in which case the replicating portfolio is worth 90 – 90 = 0.

Since the two combinations – the purchase of four call options, on the one hand, and borrowing funds and buying the share directly – produce the same cash flows, regardless of what happens to the share price, their values are identical. Otherwise, arbitrage traders would quickly intervene to re-establish the balance. So what is the original value of this combination? Let's look at it this way:

$$\text{Purchase of a share : €100}$$
$$-\text{ borrowing of a sum that at maturity would be worth}$$
$$\text{€90, hence, at 5\%, } 90/1.05$$
$$= \text{€85.7} = \text{value : €14.3}$$

€14.3 corresponds also to the value of the four call options. We thus deduce that the call option at a €105 strike is worth €3.58. We have valued the option using arbitrage theory.

'Delta' is the number of shares that must be bought to duplicate an option. In our example, four calls produce a profit equivalent to the purchase of one share. The option's delta is therefore 1/4, or 0.25.

More generally, delta is defined as the ratio between the variation in the option's value, and the variation in the price of the underlying asset.

Hence:

$$\delta = \frac{5-0}{110-90} = 0.25$$

We can therefore conclude (Figure 1.33) that:

Value of a call option $= \delta$

$\times$ (Price of the underlying asset – PV of capital borrowed)

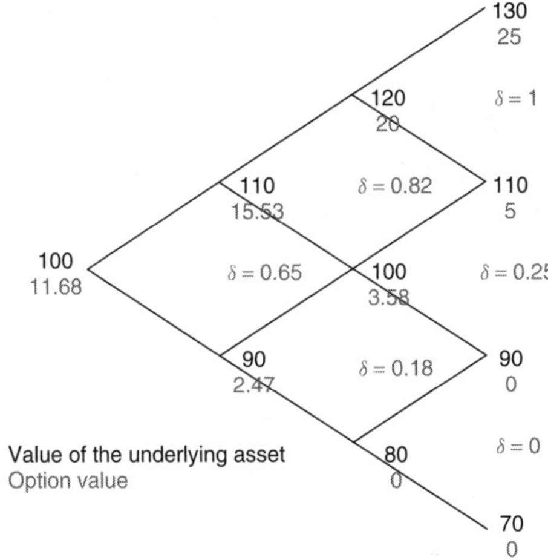

Figure 1.33: Binomial tree

References and Further Reading

Black, F. and Scholes, M., The valuation of option contracts and a test of market efficiency, *Journal of Finance*, **27**, 399–417, May 1972.

Black, F. and Scholes, M., The pricing of options and corporate liabilities, *Journal of Political Economy*, **18**, 637–654, May–June 1973.

Cox, J., Ross, S. and Rubinstein, M., Option pricing: a simplified approach, *Journal of Financial Economics*, **7**, 229–263, September 1979.

Gerlach, S., Ramaswamy, S. and Scatigna, M., 150 years of financial markets volatility, *BIS Quarterly Review*, 77–91, September 2006.

Hull, J., *Fundamentals of future and options markets*, 7th ed., Prentice Hall, 2010,

McMillan, L., *McMillan on Options*, 2nd edition, John Wiley & Sons, 2004.

Merton, R., Theory of rational option pricing, *Bell Journal of Economics and Management Services*, **4**, 637–654, Summer 1976.

Merton, R., Options pricing when underlying stock returns are discontinuous, *Journal of Financial Economics*, **3**, 125–144, January–March 1973.

Roll, R., An analytic valuation formula for unprotected American call options on stocks with known dividends, *Journal of Financial Economics*, 251–258, November 1977.

31. What are hybrid securities?

Short Answer

Hybrid securities are essentially bonds with an equity component.

Long Answer

Hybrid instruments are found in a multitude of guises. The range of possibilities can seem bewildering, but it is this very flexibility that proves a huge attraction for investors, issuers and financial institutions. We will look here at the main categories.

Warrants

A warrant is a security that allows the holder to subscribe another newly issued security (normally shares) during a given period, in a proportion and at a price fixed in advance.

Subscription warrants may be attached to an issue of shares or bonds, in which case the issue is said to be one of 'shares cum warrants' or 'bonds cum warrants'. Attached warrants to buy shares may be called an 'equity sweetener' or 'equity kicker'. Warrants can also be issued and distributed to existing shareholders at no charge. Once securities with attached warrants have been issued, the whole is split into its two component parts: the shares or bonds become traditional securities, and the warrants take on a life of their own. The warrants can be traded separately after issue.[2]

---

[2]As liquidity in the stock and bond markets has increased, financial institutions have taken the opportunity to issue warrants on existing securities independently of the company that issued the underlying shares. These securities are also called *covered warrants* because the issuing institution covers itself by buying the underlying securities on the market.

Conceptually, *a warrant is similar to a call option* sold by a company on shares in issue or to be issued. The exercise price of this option is the price at which the holder of the warrant can acquire the underlying security; the expiry date of the option is the same as the expiry date of the warrant.

A warrant, however, has a few particular characteristics that must be taken into account in its valuation:

- It will normally have a long life (typically two–three years), which increases its time value and makes it more difficult to accept the assumption of constant interest rates used in the Black & Scholes model.
- The underlying asset is more likely to pay a periodic return during the time the warrant is held. For an equity warrant, the payment of dividends on the underlying share lowers the value of that share and thereby reduces the value of the warrant. More generally, any transaction that changes the value of the share affects the value of the warrant.
- Lastly, in the case of subscription warrants, the dilution associated with the exercise of the warrants entails a gradual change in the value of the underlying security. When investors exercise warrants, the number of outstanding shares increases, and the issuing firm receives the strike price as a cash inflow. When investors exercise call options, no change in outstanding shares occurs, and the firm receives no cash.

To get round these difficulties, traders use models derived from the binomial and Black–Scholes models, taking into account the fact that the exercise of warrants can create more shares and thus affect the stock price. This is the case with warrants, management options and convertible bonds. As a general rule, using an unadjusted option pricing model to value these options will overstate their value.

Fortunately, there is a simple and reasonable solution if we want to continue to use the Black–Scholes formula. We must:

1. value a 'traditional' call option similar to those of a warrant, then
2. multiply the call value by an adjustment factor for dilution.

If N_1 represents the number of 'old shares' outstanding and N_2 represents the number of new shares issued as a result of the warrant being exercised, then the price of the warrant equals the price of an identical call option, C, multiplied by the following dilution factor: $\frac{N_1}{N_1+N_2}$.

$$\text{Value of a warrant} = C \times \frac{N_1}{N_1 + N_2}$$

Convertible bonds

A convertible bond is like a traditional bond except that it also gives the holder the right to exchange it for one or more shares of the issuing company during a conversion period set in advance.

A convertible bond is similar to a bond cum warrant. The most important difference is that warrants can be separated into distinct securities and a convertible cannot (directly, but investors can hedge part of the product, in practice: the two products are therefore very similar).

This is a financial product of considerable flexibility in use. The interest rate can be fixed, variable, indexed, floating, adjustable or determined in some other way (also under the form of a zero coupon), and any amortization schedule can be specified for return of principal.

The *conversion period* is specified in the bond indenture or issue contract. It may begin on the issue date or at a later date. It may run to the maturity date, or a decision may be forced if the company calls the bonds before maturity, in which case investors must choose between converting or redeeming them.

The bond may be convertible into one or more shares. This ratio, called the *conversion ratio*, is set at the time of issue. The conversion ratio is adjusted for any capital increases or decreases, mergers, asset distributions or distributions of bonus shares in order to preserve the rights of holders of the convertibles as if they were shareholders at the time of issue.

The *conversion premium* is the amount by which the conversion price exceeds the current market price of the share. The conversion premium is typically used. In our ABB example, the conversion premium is 30%. Since ABB offered no redemption premium, ABB shares must rise 30% by the maturity date of the bonds for investors to be willing to convert their bonds into shares rather than redeem them for cash. The calculation is slightly different when a redemption premium is involved.

Some convertible bonds are issued with a *call provision* that allows the issuer to buy them back at a pre-determined price. Holders must then choose between redeeming for cash and converting into shares. The indenture may provide for a minimum period of time during which the call provision may not be exercised ('hard non-call' period) and/or set a condition for exercising the call provision, such as that the share price has exceeded the conversion price for more than 20 or 30 days ('soft call' provision).

In some cases, the issuer may at conversion provide either newly issued shares or existing shares held in portfolio, for example, following a share buyback.

The value of a convertible bond during its life is the sum of three components:

1. The value of the straight bond alone is called the *investment value* (or just the *bond value*) of the convertible

bond. It is calculated by discounting the future cash flows on the bond at the market interest rate, assuming no conversion.
2. The *conversion value*, which is what the bonds would be worth if they were immediately converted in the stock at current market price.
3. The *option value*. The value of convertible generally exceeds both the straight bond and the conversion value because holders of convertibles have the option to wait and convert later on (time value of the option). The option to take advantage of whichever is greater in the future – the straight bond value or the conversion value – raises the value of the convertible over both the straight bond and the conversion value.

$$\text{Value of a convertible bond} = \text{The greater of (Straight bond or Conversion value)} + \text{Option value}$$

The attractiveness of convertible bonds to some investors is given by their 'defensive' quality, since the bond value provides a *floor* to the price of the security while giving the opportunity for price appreciation if the underlying stock rises. The bond value thus represents a minimum value: the convertible will never be worth less than this floor value, even if the share price falls significantly. It also cushions the impact of a falling share price on the price of the convertible. Bear in mind, though, that investment value is not a fixed number but one that varies as a function of changes in interest rates.

Example

As an example, in June 2008 Vilmorin issued a convertible bond with the characteristics shown in Table 1.24

Table 1.24: Vilmorin June 2008 Convertible Bond Issue ($150 M)

Issue price:	$155.96
Face value:	$155.96
Issue date:	6 June 2008
Maturity:	1 July 2015
Interest rate:	4.50% ($7.0182 coupon)
Redemption price:	$155.96
Conversion ratio:	1 share for 1 bond
Conversion period:	From 6 June 2008 to 22 June 2015
Vilmorin share price at the time of issue:	€129.97

Contingent convertible capital

The largest problem for issuers with a convertible bond is that it is very likely to remain debt (i.e. to be redeemed in cash) if the company is in a difficult financial situation and be converted into equity only if the financial performance is good. Therefore, for lenders (and rating agencies) and us in a financial analysis, convertible bonds remain considered as debt up until they are converted into equity (or are deeply in the money).

Investment bankers have recently created a new product that solves this drawback of convertible bonds. This product, named 'contingent capital', *is a convertible bond that mechanically turns into equity if certain events happen or certain ratios are breached by the issuer.*

This has been initially developed for financial institutions to help them enhance their solvency ratios. Typically, a bank would issue a bond that would convert automatically to equity if the core tier one ratio of the bank fell below, for example, 5%. This bond clearly helps the solvency of the institution when times are tough. Lloyds issued such a product.

Based on that idea of a *triggering event*, other products can be imagined to increase the solvency of an issuer: senior debt that stops paying coupon in difficult times, senior bonds that turn into preferred shares, or even debt that is repaid with a specific asset (and not in cash). The idea is always the same: provide the issuer with additional margins for maneuver if its financial situation is deteriorating.

Preference shares

Preference shares are created on the occasion of a capital increase by decision of the shareholders at a (extraordinary where applicable) general meeting.

The advantages conferred on preference shares may include:

- a claim to a higher proportion of earnings than is paid out on other shares;
- priority in dividend distributions, meaning the dividend on preference shares must be paid before any ordinary dividend is paid on other shares;
- a cumulative dividend, so that if earnings are insufficient to pay the preference dividend in full, the amount not distributed becomes payable from future earnings;
- a firm cannot go into default if it misses paying some dividends;
- rating agencies and financial analysts consider preference shares as a part of equity (thus improving the rating of the company).

At the same time, there are two important disadvantages in issuing preference shares:

- for the issuer, because the dividends are generally non tax-deductible; and
- for investors, because they have limited voting rights.

Special features can be added to preference shares to make them more attractive to investors or less risky to issuers:

- *adjustable rate preference share*: the dividend rate is pegged to an index rate, such as a Treasury bill or Treasury bond;
- *participating preference share*: the dividend is divided into a fixed and a variable component. The latter is generally set as a function of earnings;
- *trust preference share*: the dividend on these stocks is tax deductible like interest expenses. Firms issuing this security get the tax shield of debt and keep leverage low (because preference shares are treated like equity by analysts and rating agencies).

Valuation of preference shares follows the same principles as valuation of ordinary shares, but the flow of dividends is greater and more certain. Let's suppose we want to calculate the value of a *perpetual preferred stock*. The formula is similar to that of a perpetuity:

$$V_{\text{preferred}} = \frac{\text{Annual dividend}}{\text{Expected dividend yield}}$$

An approach of this kind will normally give a higher market value for the preference share than for the ordinary share. What is frequently observed, however, is a discount in the value of the preference share compared with the ordinary share. The origins of this discount are the lesser liquidity of the secondary market in preference shares and the limited voting rights belonging to this category of shareholders.

Convertible preferred stocks

Recent financial innovation has introduced a new distinct class of securities – convertible preferred securities – which are designed to provide issuers with the dual benefits of maintaining the dilution-limiting benefits of convertible debt while providing significant rating agency, balance sheet and (in limited cases) regulatory equity content. In addition, all classes of convertible securities can be structured such that issuer interest payments are tax-deductible.

Their main characteristics are: (i) deep subordination; (ii) long-dated maturity; (iii) multiyear dividend/interest deferral; (iv) various common stock conversion features.

Within the convertible preferred stock category, there are two primary security types:

- Conventional convertible preferred. Typically structured as either perpetual or 30-year preferred stock.
- Mandatory convertible preferred stock. Short-maturity preferred securities that automatically convert into common stock at maturity.

An important attribute of these securities is the amount of 'equity' that rating agencies assign to the product. S&P tends to view this equity in percentage terms while Moody's assigns content in distinct groupings. The factors that influence the 'amount' of equity are the following:

- the type of equity-linked product being used;
- the amount of other hybrid equity products on the issuer's balance sheet;
- the industry or sector of the issuer; and
- management credibility.

Mandatory convertibles

Unlike convertible bonds, for which there is always some risk of non-conversion, mandatory convertibles are necessarily transformed into equity capital (unless the issuing company goes bankrupt in the meantime), since the issuer redeems them by delivering shares; no cash changes hands at redemption.

Mandatory convertibles are hybrid securities, which automatically convert into a pre-determined number of shares dependent on the stock price at the time of conversion. They are closer to equity than debt because they redeem in shares instead of cash, and provide little downside protection (just the coupon payments).

The value of a bond redeemable in shares is the present value of the interest payments on it plus the present value of the shares received upon redemption. In pure theory, this is equal to the value of the share increased by the present value of the interest and decreased by the present value of the dividends that will be paid before redemption. The discount rate for the interest is the required rate of return on a risky debt security, while the discount rate for the dividends is the company's cost of equity.

Deeply subordinated debt

These financial instruments present the four following features, which are also presented by ordinary share capital and provide the undertaking with financial flexibility.

1. *Permanency*: the instrument must be perpetual, and early redemption features must be under the sole control of the issuer.
2. *Ranking*: in case of liquidation, the securities must rank senior only to share capital.
3. *Conditional payment of interest*: under certain conditions, such as non-payment of dividends to shareholders, payment of coupon/dividend to investors must be left at the issuers' entire discretion. Such non-payment must not be considered as a default event, but as a cancellation of the remuneration, with no deferred remuneration (non-cumulative coupon). Moreover, should the payment endanger the solvency soundness of the undertaking, the non-payment must be compulsory. Step-up remuneration clauses are forbidden.
4. *Loss absorption mechanism*: the securities must give the issuer the ability, in addition to the non-payment of interest, to absorb potential losses by a reduction of the

nominal value of the securities, in order to pursue its activity.

Tracking stocks

A tracking stock is an issue of shares for which performance is indexed to the earnings of a subsidiary or division. Tracking stock is technically a class of the parent company's shares. It confers no right to vote on the decisions of the subsidiary that it supposedly represents. If the business is sold, however, the holder of shares of tracking stock has the right to receive a portion of the capital gain.

The value of a share of tracking stock is theoretically equal to what a share of the subsidiary would be worth if it were publicly traded. However, in the absence of effective control over the subsidiary, the legal complexity and the often low liquidity generally result in a sharp discount to the theoretical value.

Exchangeable bonds

An exchangeable bond is a bond issued by one company that is redeemable in the shares of a second company in which the first company holds an equity interest. Thus while a convertible bond can be exchanged for specified amounts of common stock in the issuing firm, an exchangeable bond is an issue that can be exchanged for the common stock of a company other than the issuer of the bond.

At maturity, two cases are possible. If the price of the underlying shares has risen sufficiently, holders will exchange their bonds for the shares; the liability associated with the bonds will disappear from the first company's balance sheet, as will the asset associated with the shares. If the price has not raised enough, holders will redeem their bonds for cash, and the first company will still have the underlying shares. In neither case will there be any contribution of equity capital.

Exchangeable bonds, like convertibles, can have a behavior divided in 'time zones' (bond, hybrid and equity) according to the price evolution of the underlying asset.

References and Further Reading

Billett, M. and Vijh, A., The market performance of tracking stocks, Working paper, NBER, 2000.

Brennan, M. and Schwartz, E., The case for convertibles, *Journal of Applied Corporate Finance*, **1**, 55–64, 1988.

Burlacu, R., The probability of conversion as a measure of the equity and bond component of convertible bonds, research document, Affi Congress, 1999.

Chemmanur, T., Nandy, D. and Yan, A., Why issue mandatory convertibles? Theory and empirical evidence, working paper, NBER, July 2003.

Clayton, M. and Qian, Y., *Wealth gains from tracking stocks: long-run performance and ex-date returns*, working paper, NBER, 2003.

Fridson, M., Do high-yield bonds have an equity component?, *Financial Management*, Summer 1994, 82–84.

Ganshaw, T. and Dillon, D., Convertible securities: a toolbox of flexible financial instruments for corporate issuers, *Journal of Applied Corporate Finance*, **13**(1), 22–30, Spring 2000.

Jen, F., Choi, D. and Lee, S., Some new evidence on why companies use convertible bonds, *Journal of Applied Corporate Finance*, **10**(1), 44–53, Summer 1997.

Jensen, M. and Meckling, W., The theory of the firm: managerial behavior, agency costs, and capital structure, *Journal of Financial Economics*, **3**, 305–360, 1976.

Langner, S., *Tracking stocks*, working paper, NBER, 2002.

Lewis, C., Rogalski, R. and Seward, J., Understanding the design of convertible debt, *Journal of Applied Corporate Finance*, **11**(1), 45–53, Summer 1998.

Mayers, D., Why firms issue convertible bonds: the matching of financial and real investment options, *Journal of Financial Economics*, **47**, 83–102, 1998.

Myers, S. and Majluf, N., Corporate financing and investment decisions when firms have information that investors do not have, *Journal of Financial Economics*, **13**, 187–221, 1984.

Nyborg, K., Rationale for convertible bonds, in G. Bickerstaffe (Editor) *Mastering Finance*, London, Financial Times: Pitman Publishing, 1998, 241–247.

Smithson, C. and Chew, D., The use of hybrid debt in managing corporate risk, in J. Stern and D. Chew (Editors), *The Revolution in Corporate Finance*, 4th ed., McGraw Hill, 2003.

Stein, J., Convertible bonds as backdoor equity financing, *Journal of Financial Economics,* **32**, 1992.

32. How are securities sold on capital markets?

Short Answer

The company's main goal in selling its securities to investors is to obtain the highest possible price.

For the sale to be successful, the company must offer investors a return or a potential capital gain. Otherwise, it will be harder to gain access to the market in the future.

Example

The types of offering can be seen in Figure 1.34.

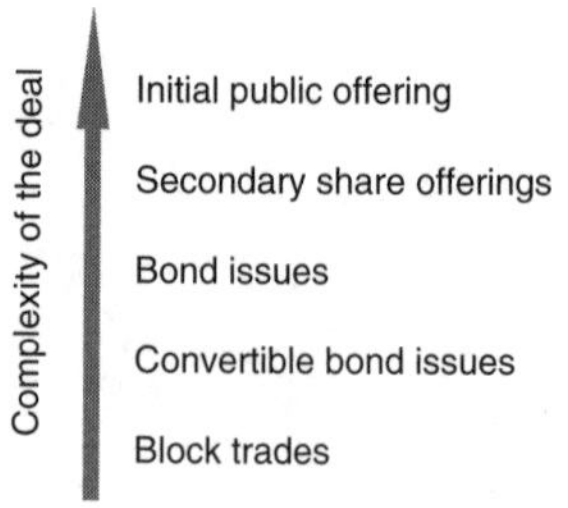

Complexity of the deal ↑

- Initial public offering
- Secondary share offerings
- Bond issues
- Convertible bond issues
- Block trades

Figure 1.34: Types of offering

Long Answer

IPO

A number of techniques exist for selling the shares of a company on a stock market for the first time (initial public offerings or IPOs). However, IPOs on regulated markets have almost all been in the same form, that of an *underwritten deal with institutional investors* and a *retail public offering with retail investors*.

Offerings of securities to institutional investors are often underwritten. This is the main tranche in almost all IPOs. Under this system, one or more banks organize the marketing and sale of securities to investors via a preliminary *book building*. The price set after book building will serve as a basis for setting the price of the retail public offering.

IPOs that make use of book building take place in several phases.

The initial *review phase* is handled by the banks. It consists in assessing and preparing the legal and regulatory framework of the deal (choice of market for listing, whether to offer shares in the US, etc.); structuring the deal; supervising documentation (due diligence, prospectus), as well as underwriting and execution agreements; preparing financial analysis reports; designing a marketing campaign (i.e. the type and content of management presentations, program of meetings between management and investors).

Then comes the *execution phase*; with the publishing of financial analysis notes by syndicate banks. This is a pre-marketing period lasting one to two weeks prior to the effective launch of the operation. The notes are presented to investors during 'warm-up' meetings, which help test investor sentiment. Analysts' research notes cannot be published during the black-out period that precedes the launch. The terms of the transaction and in particular the price range are set on the basis of conclusions from this pre-marketing exercise.

The *marketing campaign phase* then begins, and the offering is under way. During this period, full information is distributed via draft prospectuses (certified by market authorities), which may be national or international in scope. The prospectus includes all information on the company and the transaction. The offering is marketed within a price range of about 15%. Company managers are mobilized during this period for numerous meetings with investors (road shows) or for one-on-one meetings.

In the meantime, investor intentions to subscribe in terms of volumes and prices are recorded in an order book, on the basis of the preliminary price range.

After this period, which can last five to 15 days, the sale price of the existing shares and/or newly issued shares is set. The price reflects market conditions, overall demand as reflected in the order book and the price sensitivity that investors may have expressed.

Not until after this phase might banks enter into a firm underwriting agreement. The shares are then immediately allocated, thus limiting the bank's risk. After allocation, investors are theoretically committed. However, up to the actual settlement and delivery of the shares (three days after the transaction), banks still face counterparty risk. There is also business risk in that an institutional investor may decide he does not wish to take delivery of the shares after all. In sum, the only risks the syndicate take are that of a market crash between the moment the price is set and the moment when the shares are allocated, and that of stabilizing the price for around a month after the transaction by buying shares on the market.

The guarantee given by the bank to the company is also implicitly a guarantee for the market. The bank determines a value after review of internal information. This partly resolves the problem of asymmetry of information. The signal is no longer negative, because a bank with access to internal information is taking the risk of buying the shares at a set price if the market does not.

The final prospectus (with the issue price) is sent out after the price is set and the subscription period is closed. The lead bank knows the quantity and quality of demand. The book runner allocates the new shares to investors in concert with the issuer and/or seller, who can thus 'choose' his shareholders to a certain extent.

The shares are allocated on the basis of certain criteria determined in advance. Allocation is discretionary but not arbitrary. Generally, the main goal in allocation is to favor 'quality' investors, i.e. those who are unlikely to sell their shares in the immediate after-market. The banks may steer the issuer to what it believes are quality investors, thus limiting excessive *flow back*, namely the sale of securities immediately after the offering.

Book building offers several advantages, including greater flexibility (Figure 1.35). For one thing, the price can be

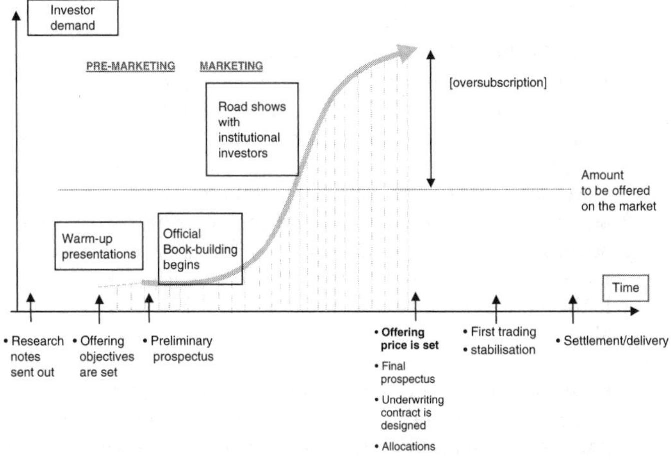

Figure 1.35: Book building

adjusted as necessary during the marketing phase, which can sometimes last several weeks. Moreover, shareholders can still be chosen via discretionary allocation of shares.

Generally, a retail public offering is made to retail investors at the same time. In a retail public offering, a price range is set before the offering, but the exact price is set after the offering. The final price reflects market demand. When the offer to retail investors is a fixed price offer, the issue price is preset. Generally identical to the price offered to institutional investors, it is totally independent of the market. Minimum price offerings and full listings using standard market procedures are rarely used these days.

Capital increases and secondary offerings
The method chosen for a capital increase depends:

1. on whether the company is listed or not,
2. on how eager current shareholders are to subscribe.

(See Table 1.25) Listed companies
When the large majority of current shareholders are expected to subscribe to the capital increase and it is not necessary or desirable to bring in new shareholders, the transaction comes with *pre-emptive subscription rights* (the transaction is then called a *rights issue*). The issue price of the new shares is set and announced in advance and the offering then unfolds over several days. The price is set at a significant discount to the market price, so that the transaction will go through even if the share price drops in the run-up to the listing of new shares.

However, when current shareholders are not expected to subscribe or when the company wants to widen its shareholder base, no pre-emptive subscription rights are issued. The issue price is then not set until a marketing and pre-placement period has been completed, with a very slight discount to

Table 1.25: Which method should be used for a capital increase?

Rights issue subscribed mainly by:	Listed company	Unlisted company
Current shareholders.	Pre-emptive subscription rights.	Pre-emptive subscription rights with a steep discount if current shareholders wish to raise cash.
	Steep discount to the market price.	Pre-emptive subscription rights with no discount or no pre-emptive rights if current shareholders do not want to raise cash.
New shareholders.	Offer without pre-emptive subscription rights (at a slight discount to the current share price).	Pre-emptive subscription rights with a steep discount if shareholders want to raise cash.
	In some cases, a reserve rights issue.	Reserved rights issue if shareholders do not want cash.

the share price at the end of this period. There are no pre-emptive subscription rights, but there may be a period during which current shareholders are given priority in subscribing.

Unlisted companies

In this case, the issue price discount will not be dictated by the fear that the share price will fluctuate during the operation (as the company is not listed), but rather by the wish of current shareholders to raise cash by selling the subscription rights they may have received.

If current shareholders do not wish to raise cash, the company will issue pre-emptive subscription rights at a price about equal to the share price, or may issue shares to identified investors that have been found via a private placement.

Block trades of shares

A block is a large number of shares that a shareholder wishes to sell on the market. Normally, only a small fraction of a company's shares are traded during the course of a normal day. Hence, a shareholder who wants to sell, for example 5% of a company's shares, cannot do so directly on the market. If she did, she could only do so over a long period and with the risk of driving down the share price. They are sold via book building and/or *bought deals*.

Bonds

Bond offering techniques have evolved towards those used for shares, and market regulations have followed suit. For example, competitive bidding has gradually given way to book building.

Competitive bidding consists in a tender from banks. The issuer chooses the establishment that will head up the offering on the basis of the terms offered (mainly price). It thus takes the risk of giving the lead mandate to a bank that is overly aggressive on price. The reason this is risky is that prices of bonds on the secondary market may fall after the operation begins as the bonds were issued at too high a price (hence at an excessively low rate). Buyers will not like this and will demand a higher interest rate the next time the issuer comes to the primary market. Competitive bidding is similar to a bought deal and is often used by State-owned companies, as well as companies that have already tapped the bond markets.

Book-building helps avoid price weakness after launch, as the issue price (or spread) is not pre-set. The lead bank suggests a price range and sounds out investors to see what price they are willing to pay. The lead then builds a book of volumes and prices (either rate or spread) offered by each investor interested in the issue. There is little risk of miscalculation, as the issue price is set by the market. The period between when the price is set and the effective delivery of the shares is called the *gray market* (as well as for IPOs and rights issues). Shares are traded on the gray market without, technically, even existing. Transactions on the gray market are unwound after settlement and delivery and the first official quotations. The lead intervenes on the gray market to maintain the spread at which the issue has been priced. This is especially useful when an issue requires intense marketing or would benefit from it. Companies wishing to market investors aggressively (notably to return to the market when they wish), will use book building (Figure 1.36).

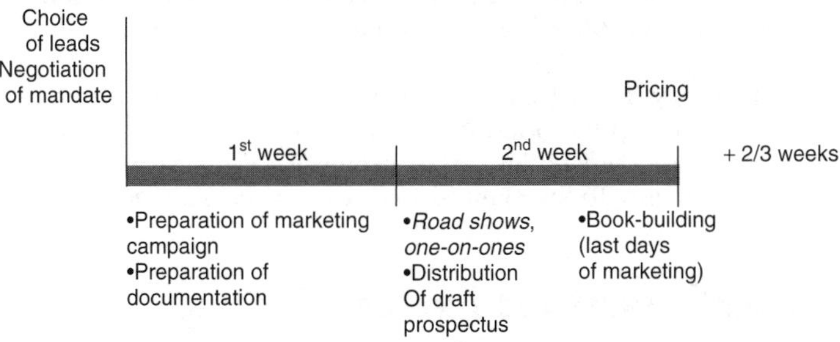

Figure 1.36: Timing of a book-building

The role of the lead is not just to market the paper, but to advise the client, where applicable, for the obtaining of a rating. It determines the spread possible through comparisons with issuers having a similar profile and chooses the members of the syndicate to help sell the bonds to the largest number possible of investors.

High-yield issues take longer and require more aggressive marketing than a standard issue, as there are fewer potential buyers (Figure 1.37):

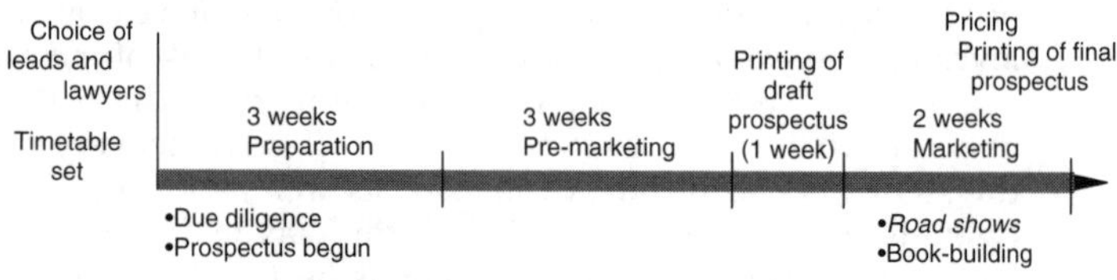

Figure 1.37: Timing of a high-yield issue

Convertible and exchangeable bonds are issued via accelerated book building or bought deals.

There is little problem of asymmetry of information between the investor and issuer in the case of a convertible bond, as the convertible's bond component protects the investor.

The only factor that could make an investor hesitate to invest in a convertible bond is the product's complexity. However, CBs are now well known to professional investors, and are sold mainly to specialized investors or *hedge funds*.

References and Further Reading

Altinkilic, O. and Hansen, R. Are there economies of scale in underwriting fees? Evidence of rising external financing costs, *Review of Financial Studies*, **13**, 191–218, 2000.

Benveniste, L. and Busaba, W., Bookbuilding versus fixed price: An analysis of competing strategies for marketing IPOs, *Journal of Financial and Quantitative Analysis*, **32**, 383–403, December 1997.

Chollet, P. and Ginglinger, E., The pricing of French unit seasoned equity offerings, *European Financial Management*, **7**(1), 23–38, March 2001.

Cornelli, F. and Goldreich, D., Bookbuilding and Strategic Allocation, *Journal of Finance*, **56**, 2337–2370, December 2001.

Cornelli, F. and Goldreich, D., Bookbuilding: How informative is the order book?, working paper, London Business School, 2001.

Datta, S., Datta, M. and Patel, A., The market pricing of debt IPOs, *Journal of Applied Corporate Finance*, **12**(1), Spring 1999.

Dechow, P., Hutton, A. and Sloan, R., Solving the new equity puzzle, in G. Bickerstaffe (Editor), *Mastering Finance*, Financial Times, Pitman publishing, 175–183, 1998.

Derrien, F. and Womack, K., Auction vs. book-building and the control of underpricing in hot IPO markets, *Review of Financial Studies*, forthcoming.

Eckbo, B., Masulis, R. and Norli, O., Seasoned public offerings: resolution of the new issues puzzle, *Journal of Financial Economics*, **56**(2), 251–291, May 2000.

Ely, D. and Salehizadeh, M., American depositary receipts. An analysis of international stock price movements, *International Review of Financial Analysis*, **10**, 243–363, 2001.

Helwege, J. and Kleiman, P., The pricing of high-yield debt IPOs, *Journal of Fixed Income*, **8**(2), 61–68, September 1998.

Karolyi, A., Sourcing equity internationally with Depositary Receipt Offerings: two exceptions that prove the rule, *Journal of Applied Corporate Finance*, **10**(4), 90–101, Winter 1998.

Karolyi, A., DaimlerChrysler AG, the truly global share, *Journal of Corporate Finance*, **9**, 409–430, 2003.

Lee, I., Lochhead, S., Ritter, J. and Zhao, Q., The cost of raising capital, *Journal of Financial Research*, **19**, 59–74, 1996.

Ljungqvist, A., Jenkinson, T. and Wilhelm, W., Has the introduction of bookbuilding increased the efficiency of international IPOs?, working paper, April 2000.

Loughran, T. and Ritter, J., Why don't issuers get upset about leaving money on the table in IPOs?, *Review of Financial Studies*, **15**, 413–444, July 2002.

Miller, D., The market reaction to international cross-listings: evidence from Depositary Receipts, *Journal of Financial Economics*, **52**, 103–123, 1999.

Reese, W. and Weisbach, M., Protection of minority shareholder interests, cross-listings in the United States, and subsequent equity offerings, *Journal of Financial Economics*, **66**, 65–104, 2002.

Ritter, J. and Loughran, T., The new issues puzzle, *Journal of Finance*, **50**(1), March 1995.

Ritter, J. and Welch, I., A review of IPO activity, pricing, and allocations, *Journal of Finance*, August 2002.

Rock, K., Why new issues are underpriced, *Journal of Financial Economics*, **15**, 187–212, January 1986.

33. What are the most important corporate valuation methodologies?

Short Answer

There are two major approaches used to value the equity of a company: the *direct method* and the *indirect method*. In the direct method, we value equity directly. In the indirect method, we first value the firm as a whole (what we call 'enterprise' or 'firm' value), then subtract the value of net debt to get the equity value (Figure 1.38 and Table 1.26).

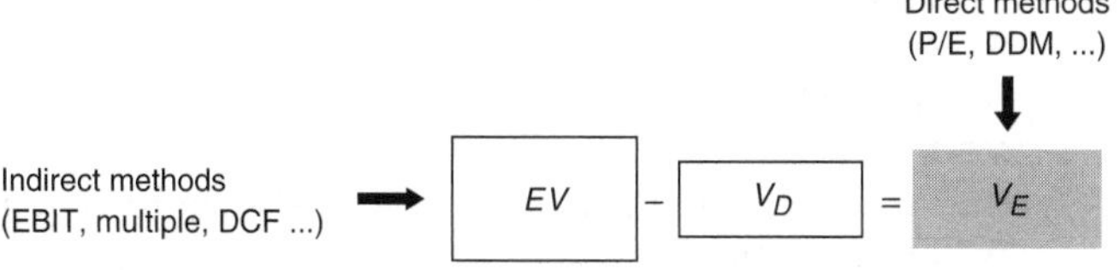

Figure 1.38: Direct and indirect methods

Long Answer

Discounted cash flow (DCF) is a methodology based on the notion that the value of the company is equal to the amount of free cash flows expected to be generated by the company in the future and discounted at a rate commensurate with its risk profile. The discount rate applied is the weighted average cost of capital (WACC). DCF calculation is performed as follows:

- future free cash flows are discounted over the explicit forecast period, i.e. the period over which there is visibility on the company's operations;
- a discounted terminal value is calculated on the basis of an estimated growth rate carried to perpetuity;

Table 1.26: Which method and approach?

	Indirect approach	**Direct approach**
Intrinsic value method (discounted present value of financial flows)	Present value of free cash flows discounted at the weighted average cost of capital (k)–value of net debt	Present value of dividends or free cash flows to equity at the cost of equity capital: k_E
Peer comparison method (multiples of comparable companies)	EBIT multiple × EBIT − value of net debt	Multiple (P/E) × net income

- the value of equity is the difference between the enterprise value obtained above and the value of the company's net debt.

The *comparables* or *multiples* method is a comparative approach that sets off the company to be valued against other companies in the same sector. With this approach, the enterprise value of the company is estimated via a multiple of its profit-generating capacity before interest expense. EBIT and EBITDA multiples are among those commonly used. The multiple used in the comparison can be either a market multiple or a transaction multiple.

The value of net debt is deducted from this enterprise value to get the value of equity. Equity can also be directly valued through a multiple of net income, cash flow or book equity.

The *sum-of-the-parts* (SOTP) method consists in valuing and summing up the company's different assets, divisions or subsidiaries and deducting liabilities. It is a method well suited for diversified groups or conglomerates for which consolidated accounts projections give too global a view.

The SOTP method is relatively simple. It consists in systematically studying the value of each asset and each liability on the company's balance sheet. For a variety of reasons – accounting, tax, historical – book values are often far from reality. They must therefore be restated and revalued before they can be assumed to reflect a true net asset value. The sum-of-the-parts method is an *additive method*. Revalued assets are summed, and the total of revalued liabilities is subtracted.

For diversified groups, the SOTP (or net asset value, NAV) method implies valuing subsidiaries or activities pro-rata the ownership level using either the DCF or the multiples of comparable companies method. Then the debt of the mother company is deducted as well as the present value of central costs.

Several basic types of value are used in the SOTP method:

- **market value**: this is the value we could obtain by selling the asset. This value might seem indisputable from a theoretical point of view, but it virtually assumes that the buyer's goal is liquidation. This is rarely the case. Acquisitions are usually motivated by the promise of industrial or commercial synergies;
- **value in use**: this is the value of an asset that is used in the company's operations. It is a kind of market value at replacement cost;
- **liquidation value**: this is the value of an asset during a fire sale to get cash as soon as possible to avoid bankruptcy. It is market value minus a discount.

The SOTP method is the easiest to use and the values it generates are the least questionable when the assets have a value on a market that is independent of the company's operations, such as the property market, the market for airplanes, etc. The value of the inventories and vineyards of a wine company is easy to determine and relatively undisputed. A wide variety of values is available when we apply the SOTP method. Possible approaches are numerous. We can assume discontinuation of the business – either sudden or gradual – or that it will continue as a going concern, for example. The important thing is to be consistent, sticking to the same approach throughout the valuation process.

To the financial manager, the market for corporate control is nothing but a segment of the broader capital market. From this principle it follows that there is no such thing as control value other than the strategic value deriving from synergies.

Industrial synergies generally make a company's strategic value higher than its financial or standalone value. The essence of negotiation lies in determining how the strategic value pie will be divided between the buyer and the seller, with both parties trying, unsurprisingly, to obtain the largest possible share.

References and Further Reading

Cheng, Y. and McNamara, R., The valuation accuracy of the price-earnings and price-book benchmark valuation methods, *Review of Quantitative Finance and Accounting*, **15**(4), 349–370, December 2000.

Damodaran, A., *Investment valuation*, 2nd ed., John Wiley & Sons, 2006.

Fernandez, P., Company valuation methods. The most common errors in valuation, *Investment Management and Financial Innovations Journal*, **2**(2), 128–141, July 2005.

Koller, T., Goedhart, M. and Wessels, D., *Valuation: Measuring and Managing the Value of Companies*, 5th ed., John Wiley & Sons, 2010.

Kruschwitz, L. and Löffler, A., *Discounted Cash Flow: A Theory of the Valuation of Firms*, John Wiley & Sons, 2005.

Ofek, E. and Richardson, M., Dotcom mania: The rise and fall of internet stock prices, *Journal of Finance*, **58**(3), 1113–1137, June 2003.

Quiry, P., Dallocchio, M., Le Fur, Y. and Salvi, A., *Corporate Finance*, 3rd ed., John Wiley & Sons, 2011.

34. What is the DCF method?

Short Answer

The discounted cash flow (DCF) method consists of applying the investment decision techniques to the firm value calculation, discounting a series of future cash flows.

Example

Let's look at Indesit's financial projections in Table 1.27 produced by the broker Exane BNP Paribas, as of 2007.

Table 1.27: Indesit's financial projections as of 2007

in €m	2007	2008E	2009E	2010E	2011E	2012E	2013E	2014E
Profit and loss statement								
Turnover	3438	3502	3623	3739	3795	3852	3910	3968
EBITDA	317	317	358	388	427	431	408	402
−Depreciation and amortization	−127	132	133	−138	−156	−159	−162	−167
= EBIT	190	185	225	250	271	272	246	235
Balance sheet								
Fixed assets	1169	1171	1179	1183	1190	1196	1201	1203
+ Working capital	−48	−10	4	16	24	32	40	48
= Capital employed	1121	1161	1183	1199	1214	1228	1241	1251
Operating margin after 37% tax	3.50%	3.30%	3.90%	4.20%	4.50%	4.50%	4.00%	3.70%
ROCE after 37% tax	10.70%	10.00%	12.00%	13.10%	14.00%	14.00%	12.50%	11.80%

These projections are moderately ambitious, with operating margin expected to rise from 3.5% in 2007 to a peak in 2011 (4.5%) before sliding back to around 3.5% in 2014. Over the period, the ROCE is projected to rise from 10.7% to a peak of 14% in 2011 before losing most of its gains at 11.8% in

2014. Projected after-tax free cash flows are as follows in Table 1.28:

Table 1.28: Indesit's projected after-tax cash flows

in €m	2008E	2009E	2010E	2011E	2012E	2013E	2014E
EBIT	185	225	250	271	272	246	235
- Corporate income tax at 37%	−68	−83	−93	−100	−101	−91	−87
+ Depreciation and amortization	132	133	138	156	159	162	167
- Capital expenditure	−150	−158	−161	−163	−165	−167	−169
- Change in working capital	−34	−10	−7	−8	−8	−8	−8
= Free cash flow	65	107	127	159	157	142	138

Using a weighted average cost of capital of 10%, the beginning-2008 present value of the free cash flows generated during the explicit forecast period is €600m.

Long Answer

The aim of the DCF is to value the company as a whole (i.e. to determine the value of the capital employed, what we call enterprise value). After deducting the value of net debt, the remainder is the value of the company's shareholders' equity.

As we have seen, the cash flows to be valued are the after-tax amounts produced by the firm. They should be discounted out to perpetuity at the company's weighted average cost of capital.

$$\mathrm{EV} = \sum_{t=0}^{\infty} \frac{\mathrm{FCFF}_t}{(1+k)^t}$$

In practice, we project specific cash flows over a certain number of years. This period is called the *explicit forecast period*. The length of this period varies depending on the sector. It can be as short as two to three years for a high-tech company, five to seven years for a consumer goods company and as long as 20–30 years for a utility. For the years beyond the explicit forecast period, we establish a *terminal value*.

> *The forecast period should therefore correspond to the time during which the company will live off its current configuration, or will lose its current competitive advantage.*

If it is too short, the terminal value will be too large and the valuation problem will only be shifted in time. Unfortunately, this happens all too often. If it is too long (more than ten years), the explicit forecast is reduced to an uninteresting theoretical extrapolation.

It is very difficult to estimate a terminal value, because it represents the value at the date when existing business development projections will no longer have any meaning. Often analysts assume that the company enters a phase of maturity after the end of the explicit forecast period. In this case, the terminal value can be based either on the capital employed or on the free cash flow in the last year of the explicit forecast period.

The most commonly used terminal value formula is the *Gordon formula*. It consists of a *normalized cash flow*, or annuity, that grows at a rate (g) out to perpetuity:

$$\text{Value of the company at the end of the explicit forecast period} = \frac{\text{Normalized free cash flow}}{k - g}$$

However, the key challenge is in choosing the normalized free cash flow value and the perpetual growth rate. The normalized free cash flow must be consistent with the assumptions of the business plan. It depends on long-term growth, the company's investment strategy and the growth in the company's working capital. Lastly, normalized free cash flows may be different from the free cash flow in the final year of the explicit forecast period, because normalized cash flow is what the company will generate after the end of the explicit forecast period and will continue to generate to perpetuity.

Concerning the growth rate to perpetuity (*g*), do not get carried away.

- Apart from the normalized cash flow's growth rate to perpetuity, you must take a hard cold look at your projected long-term growth in return on capital employed. For how long can the economic profit it represents be sustained? How long will market growth last?
- Most importantly, the company's rate of growth to perpetuity cannot be significantly greater than the long-term growth rate of the economy as a whole.

In the case of Indesit, the normalized cash flow must be calculated for the year 2015, because we are looking for the present value at the end of 2014 of the cash flows expected in 2015 and every subsequent year to perpetuity. Given the necessity to invest if growth is to be maintained, the assumptions in Table 1.29 could be used to determine the normalized cash flow.

Remember that if you compute a terminal value greater than book value (or, which is equivalent, if you assume that the ROCE will be higher than the cost of capital), you are implying that the company will be able to maintain

Table 1.29: Normalized cash flow

Normalized 2015 EBIT	240
– Corporate income tax at 37%	(89)
+ Depreciation and amortization	170
– Capital expenditure	(171)
– Change in working capital	(9)
= Normalized 2015 free cash flow	141

forever a return on capital employed in excess of its weighted average cost of capital.

If you choose a lower value, you are implying that the company will enter a phase of decline after the explicit forecast period and that you think it will not be able to earn its cost of capital in the future. Lastly, if you assume that terminal value is equal to book value, you are implying that the company's economic profit falls immediately to zero.

As we value cash flow to the firm, the discount rate is the WACC or simply, the cost of capital. Calculating an accurate cost of capital is one of the key drivers of any valuation exercise, based on the discounted cash flow approach.

Once you obtain the enterprise value using the above methodology, you must remove the value of net debt to derive equity value. *Net debt is composed of financial debt net of cash*, i.e. of all bank borrowings, bonds, debentures and other financial instruments, (short, medium or long term), net of cash, cash equivalents and marketable securities. Theoretically, the value of net debt is equal to the value of the future cash outflows (interest and principal payments) it represents, discounted at the market cost of similar borrowings. When all or part of the debt is listed or traded over the counter (listed bonds, syndicated loans), you can use the market value of the debt. You then subtract the market value of cash, cash equivalents and marketable securities.[3]

This approach makes sense especially when the debt has been contracted not long ago, or when it carries a variable rate and the company's risk profile has not fundamentally changed. If the interest rate or the risk of the company has changed significantly from when the debt was issued, then the market value of net debt is different from its book value. When the company's business is seasonal, year-end working capital may not reflect average requirements, and debt on the balance sheet at the end of the year may not represent real funding needs over the course of the year. Some companies also perform year-end 'window-dressing' in order to show a very low level of net debt. In these cases, if you notice that interest expense does not correspond to debt balances, you should restate the amount of debt by using a monthly average of outstanding net debt, for example.

Provisions for risks and contingencies must only be included if cash flows exclude them. If the business plan's EBIT does not reflect future charges for which provisions have been set aside – such as for restructuring, site closures, etc. – then the present value of the corresponding provisions on the balance sheet must be deducted from the value of the company.

Normally, *pension liabilities should be treated as debt*. The present value of future outflows for pension, net of pension assets, should be subtracted from the enterprise value.

With rare exceptions, *deferred tax liabilities* generally remain relatively stable. In practice, they are rarely paid out. Consequently, they are usually not considered as debt equivalents.

[3]The book value of net debt is often used as a first approximation of its present value.

If tax-loss carry forwards are not yet included in the business plan, you will have to value any tax-loss carry forward separately, discounting tax savings until deficits are exhausted. We advise discounting savings at the cost of equity capital as they are directly linked to the earnings of the company and are as volatile (if not more so).

If *unconsolidated or equity-accounted financial investments* are not reflected in the projected cash flows (via dividends received), you should add their value to the value of discounted cash flows. In this case, use the market value of these assets including, if relevant, tax on capital gains and losses. For listed securities, use listed market value. Conversely, for minor, unlisted holdings, the book value is often used as a shortcut. However, if the company holds a significant stake in the associated company – this is sometimes the case for holdings booked using the equity method – you will have to value the affiliate separately. This may be a simple exercise, applying, for example, a sector-average P/E to the company's pro-rata share of the net income of the affiliate. It can also be more detailed, by valuing the affiliate with a multi-criteria approach if the information is available.

Future free cash flows calculated on the basis of consolidated financial information will belong partly to the shareholders of the parent company and partly to minority shareholders in subsidiary companies, if any. If minority interests are significant, you will have to take them into account by either:

- performing a separate DCF valuation of the subsidiaries in which some minority shareholders hold a stake and subtract from the enterprise value the minority share of the subsidiary; or
- including only the group share in consolidated cash flows (which requires detailed information about the group subsidiaries).

Naturally, this assumes you have access to detailed information about the subsidiaries. You can also use a multiple approach. Simplifying to the extreme, you could apply the group's implied P/E multiple to the minority shareholders' portion of net profit to get a first-blush estimate of the value of minority interests. Alternatively, you could apply the group's price-to-book ratio to the minority interests appearing on the balance sheet. In either case, we would not recommend using book value to value minority interests unless amounts are low.

You might be wondering what to do with instruments that give future access to company equity, such as convertible bonds, warrants and stock options. If these instruments have a market value, your best bet will be to subtract that value from the enterprise value of the company to derive the value of equity capital, just as you would for net debt. The number of shares to use in determining the value per share will then be the number of shares currently in circulation.

35. What are valuation multiples?

Short Answer

The peer comparison or multiples approach is based on three fundamental principles:

- the company is to be valued in its entirety;
- the company is valued at a multiple of its profit-generating capacity. The most commonly used are the P/E ratio, EBITDA and EBIT multiples;
- markets are efficient and comparisons are therefore justified.

Example

Consider the following two similarly-sized companies, Ann and Valeria, operating in the same sector and enjoying the same outlook for the future, with the characteristics shown in Table 1.30.

Table 1.30: Characteristics of Ann and Valeria

Company	Ann	Valeria
Operating income	150	177
– Interest expense	30	120
– Corporate income tax (40%)	48	23
= Net profit	72	34
Market capitalization	1800	?
Value of debt (at 10% p. a.)	300	1200

As Ann's NOPAT is 150 × (1 – 40%) = 90, the multiple of Ann's NOPAT is 2100/90 = 23.3. Valeria's enterprise value is therefore equal to 23.3 times its NOPAT, or 23.3 × 106 = 2470.

We now subtract the value of the debt (1200) to obtain the value of equity capital, or 1270.

Long Answer

Multiples can derive from a sample of comparable, listed companies or a sample of companies that have recently been sold.

The latter sample has the virtue of representing actual transaction prices for the equity value of a company. These multiples are respectively called market multiples and transaction multiples, and we will look at them in turn. As these multiples result from comparing a market value with accounting figures, keep in mind that the two must be consistent. The enterprise value must be compared with operating data, such as turnover, EBITDA or EBIT. The value of equity capital must be compared with a figure after interest expense, such as net profit or cash flow.

For *market multiples*, a peer group comparison consists of setting up a sample of comparable listed companies that have not only similar sector characteristics, but also similar operating characteristics, such as ROCE and expected growth rates. Given that the multiple is usually calculated on short-term projections, you should choose companies whose shares are liquid and are covered by a sufficient number of financial analysts.

For *transaction multiples* you should use transactions in the same sector as the company you are trying to value. The transactions should not be too old otherwise they will reflect different market conditions. In addition, the size and geographical characteristics of the deals should be similar to the one contemplated. There is often a trade-off between retaining a sufficient number of transactions and having deals that can be qualified as similar.

There are two major groups of multiples: those based on the enterprise value (i.e. the value of capital employed) and those based on the value of equity.

Multiples based on the value of capital employed are multiples of operating balances before subtracting interest expense. We believe NOPAT is the best denominator, i.e. EBIT less corporate income taxes on EBIT. But many practitioners use EBIT, which is not a major problem provided corporate income tax rates are roughly the same for all the companies in the sample. The EBITDA multiple is also widely used.

Multiples based on the value of equity are multiples of operating balances after interest expense, principally net income (P/E multiple), as well as multiples of cash flow and multiples of underlying income – i.e. before nonrecurring items.

Multiples based on enterprise values

The *EBIT multiple* is the ratio of the value of capital employed to EBIT (operating income). It enables us to compare the genuine profit-generating capacity of the sample companies.

A company's genuine profit-generating capacity is the normalized operating profitability it can generate year after year, excluding exceptional gains and losses and other nonrecurring items.

The *EBITDA multiple* follows the same logic as the EBIT multiple. It has the merit of eliminating the sometimes significant differences in depreciation methods and periods. *It is very frequently used by stock market analysts for companies in capital-intensive industries.*

Be careful when using the EBITDA multiple, however, especially when the sample and the company to be valued have widely disparate levels of margins. In these cases, the EBITDA multiple tends to overvalue companies with low margins and undervalue companies with high margins, independently of depreciation policy. EBITDA does not capture certain (other) elements of profitability. Applying the sample's multiple therefore introduces a distortion.

Another multiple used is the EV/FCF (the ratio of enterprise value to free cash flow), a similar concept to P/E. P/E represents the number of times net recurrent income is capitalized by the value of equity, and EV/FCF represents the number of times free cash flow is capitalized by enterprise value. For example, in Table 1.31 are the levels of capitalization of free cash flow for a few European groups (as of 2010).

Table 1.31: Levels of capitalization of free cash flow for European groups as of 2010

Group	Multiple
Tesco	146.0
Endesa	61.3
H&M	24.0
L'Oreal	21.2
easyJet	18.7
Novartis	16.1
Unilever	14.9
Deutsche Telekom	14.1
Maroc Telecom	13.7
Eni	13.7
Siemens	11.1

Theoretically, since free cash flow is the cash that the company could pay out to its providers of funds, shareholders and lenders, after having financed its investments, this ratio should be a better indicator than P/E, which is more easily manipulated due to the accounting nature of the denominator.

However, such a conclusion would be overlooking the fact that EV/FCF is of little significance for companies in a high growth phase (whether external or internal growth), that accordingly have low or negative cash flow. An example of such a company is the mass retailer Tesco.

At 146 times, the figure doesn't mean much, except perhaps that investors are expecting current investments to bear fruit in the future, and that the return ratio will fall within the average.

In other words, this ratio is more relevant for groups that have reached maturity and make large investments of generally similar amounts, resulting in high free cash flow.

Accordingly, we should not be surprised at the popularity of this ratio, nor of that of its opposite – free cash flow yield – evidence of an era in which there is little expectation of growth, and so not much chance of finding any!

Operating multiples can also be calculated on the basis of other measures, such as turnover.

Some industries have even more specific multiples, such as multiples of the number of subscribers, number of visitors or page views for Internet companies, tons of cement produced, etc. These multiples are particularly interesting when the return on capital employed of the companies in the sample is standard. Otherwise, results will be too widely dispersed. They are only meaningful for small businesses such as shops where there are a lot of transactions and where in many countries turnover gives a better view of the profitability than the official profit figure.

These multiples are generally used to value companies that are not yet profitable: they were widely used during the Internet bubble, for instance. They tend to ascribe far too much value to the company to be valued and we recommend that you avoid them.

Multiples based on equity value

You may also decide to choose multiples based on operating balances after interest expense. These multiples include the P/E ratio, the cash flow multiple and the price-to-book ratio. All these multiples use market capitalization at the valuation date (or price paid for the equity for transaction multiples) as their numerator. The denominators are net profit, cash flow and book equity, respectively. The net profit used by analysts is the company's bottom line restated to exclude nonrecurring items and the depreciation of goodwill, so as to put the emphasis on recurrent profit-generating capacity.

Transaction multiples

The approach is slightly different, but the method of calculation is the same. The sample is composed of information available on recent transactions in the same sector, such as the sale of a controlling block of shares, a merger, etc.

If we use the price paid by the acquirer, our multiple will contain the control premium the acquirer paid to obtain control of the target company. As such, the price includes the value of anticipated synergies. Using the listed share prices leads to a so-called 'minority value', which we now know is nothing other than the standalone value. In contrast, transaction multiples reflect majority value – i.e. the value including any control premium for synergies. For listed companies it has been empirically observed that control premiums are around

25% of pre-bid market prices (i.e. prices before the announcement of the tender offer).

You will find that it is often difficult to apply this method, because good information on truly comparable transactions is often lacking.

References and Further Reading

Lie, E. and Lie, H., Multiples used to estimate corporate value, *Financial Analysts Journal*, **58**, 44–54, March 2002.

Quiry, P., Dallocchio, M., Le Fur, Y. and Salvi, A., *Corporate Finance*, 3rd ed. John Wiley & Sons, 2011.

36. What does the Modigliani and Miller theorem say?

Short Answer

Modigliani and Miller demonstrated that, barring any distortions, the enterprise value of a company must be independent of its financing mix.

Long Answer

In a seminal article published in 1958, Franco Modigliani and Merton Miller showed that, in a perfect market and without taxes, there is no optimal capital structure and the overall cost of equity (*k* or WACC) remains the same regardless of the firm's debt policy.

The main assumptions behind their theorem are:

- companies can issue only two types of securities: risk-free debt and equity;
- financial markets are frictionless;
- there is no corporate and personal taxation;
- there are no transaction costs;
- firms cannot go bankrupt;
- insiders and outsiders have the same set of information.

The key insight is that, in a world where their assumptions hold, investors can take on debt just like companies. So in a perfect market, they have no reason to pay companies to do something they can handle themselves at no cost.

Example

Imagine two companies that are completely identical, except for their capital structure. The value of their respective debt and equity differs, but the sum of both, i.e. the enterprise value of each company, is the same. If the reverse were true, equilibrium would be restored by arbitrage.

We shall demonstrate this using the examples of companies X and Y in Table 1.32, which are identical except that X is unlevered and Y carries debt of 80,000 at 5%. If the traditional approach were correct, Y's weighted average cost of capital would be lower than that of X and its enterprise value higher.

Table 1.32: Example of companies X and Y

	X	Y
Operating profit: EBIT	20,000	20,000
Interest expense (at 5%): IE	0	4000
Net profit: NP	20,000	16,000
Dividend : DIV = NP*	20,000	16,000
Cost of equity: k_E	10%	12%
Equity: $V_E = \text{DIV}/k_E$†	200,000	133,333
Debt: $V_D = \text{IE}/k_D^2$	0	80,000
Enterprise value: $V = V_E + V_D$	200,000	213,333
Weighted average cost of capital: $k = \text{EBIT}/V$	10%	9.4%
Gearing : V_D/V_E	0%	60%

*To simplify calculations, the payout ratio is 100%.
†To simplify calculations, we adopt an infinite horizon.

Y's cost of equity is higher than that of X since Y's shareholders bear both the operating risk and that of the capital structure (debt), whereas X's shareholders incur only the same operating risk. As a matter of fact, the operating risk of X is the same as that of Y as X and Y are identical but for their capital structures.

Modigliani and Miller demonstrated that Y's shareholders can achieve a higher return on their investment by buying shares of X, at no greater risk.

Thus, if a shareholder holding 1% of Y shares (equal to 1333) wants to obtain a better return on investment, they must:

- sell his or her Y shares;
- *replicate* Y's debt/equity structure in proportion to his or her 1% stake, that is, borrow 1333 × 60% = 800 at 5%;
- invest all this (800 + 1333 = 2133) in X shares.

The shareholder's risk exposure is the same as before the operation: the shareholder is still exposed to operating risk, which is the same on X and Y, as well as to financial risk, since his or her exposure to Y's debt has been transferred to the shareholder's personal borrowing. However, the personal wealth invested by our shareholder is still the same (1333).

Formerly, the investor received annual dividends of 160 from company Y (12% × 1333 or 1% of 16,000). Now, his or her net income on the same investment will be:

Dividends (company X)	2133 × 10%, = 213
– Interest expense	800 × 5%
= Net income	= 173

The investor is now earning 173 every year instead of the former 160, *on the same personal amount invested and with the same level of risk.*

Y's shareholders will thus sell their Y shares to invest in X shares, reducing the value of Y's equity and increasing that of X. This arbitrage will cease as soon as the enterprise values of the two companies come into line again.

Thus, barring any distortions, the enterprise value of a company must be independent of its financing policy, or the value of a levered firm (V_L) is equal to the value of an unlevered firm (V_U):

$$V_L = V_U$$

Investing in a leveraged company is neither more expensive nor cheaper than investing in a company without debt; in other words, the investor should not pay twice, once when buying shares at enterprise value and again to reimburse the debt. The value of the debt is deducted from the price paid for the equity.

While obvious, this crucial principle is frequently forgotten. And yet it should be easy to remember: the value of an asset, be it a factory, painting, subsidiary or house, is the same regardless of whether it was financed by debt, equity or a combination of the two. As Merton Miller explained when receiving the Nobel Prize for Economics, 'it is the size of the pizza that matters, not how many slices it is cut up into.' Or, to restate this: the weighted average cost of capital does not depend on the sources of financing. True, it is the weighted average of the rates of return required by the various providers of funds, but this average is independent of its different components, which adjust to any changes in the financial structure.

References and Further Reading

Modigliani, F. and Miller, M., The cost of capital, corporation finance and the theory of investment, *American Economic Review*, **47**, 261–297, June 1958.

37. What happens to the Modigliani and Miller theorem if we consider taxes and financial distress costs?

Short Answer

If we include taxes and financial distress costs in the analysis, the 1958 conclusions (see previous question) no longer hold: the value of the firm could be affected by the way the company is financed.

Long Answer

The Modigliani and Miller theory presented in the previous question is certainly elegant, but it cannot fully explain how things actually work in real life.

We now want to look at *two basic explanations of real-life happenings*. First of all, within the same market logic, biases occur which may explain why companies borrow funds, and why they stop at a certain level. The fundamental factors from which these biases spring are *corporate taxes* (T_C) *and financial distress costs*. Their joint analysis will give birth to the 'trade-off model'.

Corporate taxes

In Question 36, our reasoning was based on a tax-free world, which of course does not exist. It would therefore be foolhardy to ignore taxation, which forces financial managers to devote a considerable amount of their time to tax optimization.

In 1963, Modigliani and Miller pushed further their initial demonstration, but this time they factored in corporate income tax (*but no other taxes*) in an economy in which companies' financial expenses are tax-deductible, but not dividends. This is pretty much the case in most countries.

The conclusion was unmistakable: once you factor in corporate income tax, there is more incentive to use debt rather than equity financing.

Interest expenses can be deducted from the company's tax base, so that creditors receive their coupon payments before they have been taxed. Dividends, on the other hand, are not deductible and are paid to shareholders after taxation.

Thus, a debt-free company with equity financing of 100 on which shareholders require a 10% return will have to generate profit of at least 15.4 in order to provide the required return of 10 after a 35% tax.

If, however, its financing is equally divided between debt at 5% interest and equity, a profit of 13.6 will be enough to satisfy shareholders despite the premium for the greater risk to shares created by the debt (e.g. 14.4%).

Operating profit		13.6
−	Interest expense	2.5
=	Pre-tax profit	11.1
−	35% tax	3.9
=	Net profit	7.2 or 14.4% of 50

Allowing interest expenses to be deducted from companies' tax base is a kind of subsidy the State grants to companies with debt. *But to benefit from this tax shield, the company must generate a profit.*

A company that continually resorts to debt will benefit from tax savings that must be factored into its enterprise value.

When corporate income taxes are levied, the enterprise value of the levered company is equal to that of an unlevered company plus the present value of the tax savings arising on the debt:[4]

$$V_L = V_U + Tax\ shield$$

Example

Take, for example, a company with an enterprise value of 100, of which 50 is financed by equity and 50 by perpetual debt at 5%. Interest expenses will be 2.5 each year. Assuming a 35% tax rate and an operating profit of more than 2.5 regardless of the year under review (an amount sufficient to benefit from the tax savings), the tax savings will be 35% × 2.5 or 0.88 for each year. The present value of this perpetual bond increases shareholders' wealth by 0.88/14.4% = 6.1 if 14.4% is the cost of equity. Taking the tax savings into account increases the value of equity by 12% to 56.1 (50 + 6.1). (See Table 1.33)

Table 1.33: Tax savings as a percentage of equity

V_D/V	k_E	Maturity of debt		
		5 years	**10 years**	**Perpetuity**
0%	10.0%*	0%	0%	0%
25%	11.5%	2%	3%	4%
33%	12.2%	3%	5%	5%
50%	14.4%	6%	9%	12%
66%	18.8%	10%	15%	18%

*Based on a β of 1.1, a 4% risk premium and a risk-free rate of 5.6%.

The longer the maturity of the debt and the larger the amount, the greater the present value of the tax savings.

[4]This is the basis of the APV method (adjusted present value).

An important question is what discount rate should be applied to the tax savings generated by the deductibility of interest expense. Should we use the cost of debt, as Modigliani and Miller did in their article in 1963, the weighted average cost of capital or the cost of equity?

Using the cost of debt is justified if we are certain that the tax savings are permanent. In addition, this allows us to use a particularly simple formula:

$$\text{Value of the tax savings} = \frac{T_C \times k_D \times V_D}{k_D} = T_C \times V_D$$

Nevertheless, there are good reasons to prefer to discount the savings at the cost of equity, since it would be difficult to assume that the company will continually carry the same debt, generate profits and be taxed at the same rate. Moreover, the tax savings accrue to the shareholders, so it should be reasonable to discount them at the rate of return required by those shareholders.

Bear in mind that these tax savings only apply if the company has sufficient earnings power and does not benefit from any other tax exemptions, such as tax loss carry forwards, etc.

Financial distress costs

We have seen that the more debt a firm carries, the greater the risk that it will not be able to meet its commitments. If the worst comes to the worst, the company files for bankruptcy; which in the final analysis simply means that assets are reallocated to more profitable ventures.

In fact, the bankruptcy of an unprofitable company strengthens the sector and improves the profitability of the remaining firms and therefore their value. Bankruptcy is a useful mechanism which helps the market stay healthier by eliminating the least efficient companies.

The public authorities would do well to apply this reasoning. Better to let a troubled sector rid itself of its lame ducks than to keep them artificially afloat, which in turn creates difficulties for the healthy, efficient firms to the point where they, too, may become financially distressed.

For investors with a well-diversified portfolio, the cost of the bankruptcy will be nil, since when a company is discontinued, its assets (market share, customers, factories, etc.) are taken over by others who will manage them better. One man's loss is another man's gain! If the investor has a diversified portfolio, the capital losses will be offset by other capital gains.

In practice, however, markets are not perfect and we all know that even if bankruptcies are a means of reallocating resources, they carry very real costs to those involved. These include:

- Direct costs:
  - redundancy payments;
  - legal fees;
  - administrative costs;
  - shareholders' efforts to receive a liquidation dividend.
- Indirect costs:
  - order cancellations (for fear they will not be honored);
  - less trade credit (because it may not be repaid);
  - reduced productivity (strikes, underutilization of production capacity);
  - no more access to financing (even for profitable projects); incalculable human costs.

One could say bankruptcy occurs when shareholders refuse to inject more funds once they have concluded that their initial investment is lost. In essence, they are handing the company over to its creditors, who then become the new shareholders. The creditors bear all the costs of the malfunctioning company, thus further reducing their chances of getting repaid.

Even without going to the extremes of bankruptcy, a highly levered company in financial distress faces certain costs that reduce its value. It may have to cut back on R&D expenditure, maintenance, training or marketing expenses in order to meet its debt payments and will find it increasingly difficult to raise new funding, even for profitable investment projects.

After factoring all these costs into the equation, we can say that:

Value of levered firm = Value of unlevered firm

+ Present value of the tax shield arising on debt

− Present value of bankruptcy costs and malfunction costs

or, as illustrated by Figure 1.39.

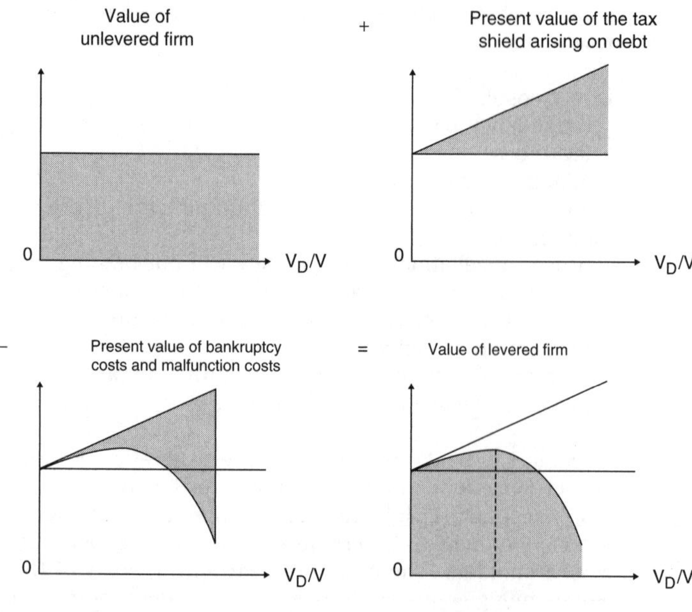

Figure 1.39: Calculating the value of a levered firm

Because of the tax deduction, debt can, in fact, create value. A levered company may be worth more than if it had only equity financing. However, there are two good reasons why this advantage should not be overstated. Firstly, when a company with excessive debt is in financial distress, its tax advantage disappears, since it no longer generates sufficient profits. Secondly, the high debt level may lead to restructuring costs and lost investment opportunities if financing is no longer available. As a result, debt should not exceed a certain level.

The same reasoning applies to the weighted average cost of capital. When a company borrows funds, its cost of capital declines thanks to the tax savings on the interest payments, but if there is a risk of default, shareholders factor the bankruptcy costs into the cost of equity. This relationship can be observed by charting a given industry's cost of capital according to its credit rating (Figure 1.40).

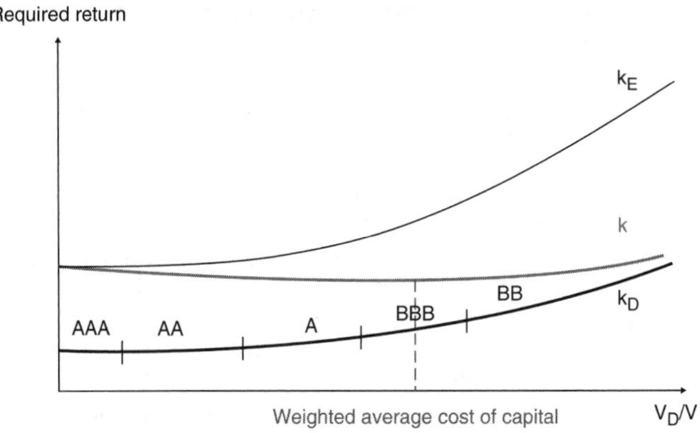

Figure 1.40: Charting a given industry's cost of capital according to its credit rating

Paradoxically, this long detour brings us back to our starting point – the conventional approach which says 'Some debt is fine, but not too much.'

The theoretical optimal debt ratio appears to be when the present value of the tax savings arising on additional borrowing is offset by the increase in the present value of financial distress and bankruptcy costs.

References and Further Reading

Almeida, D. and Philippon, T., The risk-adjusted cost of financial distress, *Journal of Finance*, **6** (62), 2557–2586, December 2007.

Altman, E., A further empirical investigation of the bankruptcy costs question, *Journal of Finance*, **39**(4), 589–609, September 1984.

Andrade, G. and Kaplan, S., How costly is financial (not economic) distress? Evidence from highly leveraged transactions that became distressed, *Journal of Finance*, 706–739, October 1998.

Barclay, S. and Smith, C., The capital structure puzzle: Another look at the evidence, *Journal of Applied Corporate Finance*, **12**(1), 8–20, Spring 1999.

Betker, B., Management's incentives, equity's bargaining power, and deviations from absolute priority in Chapter 11, *Journal of Business*, **68**, 161–183, 1995.

Cutler, D. and Summers, L., The costs of conflict and financial distress: Evidence from Texaco – Perinzoil litigation, *RAND Journal of Economics*, **19**, 157–172, Summer 1998.

Denis, D., Leveraged recaps in the curbing of corporate overinvestment, *Journal of Applied Corporate Finance*, **6**(1), 60–71, 1993.

Galai, D., Taxes, M&M propositions and government's implicit cost of capital in investment projects in the private sector, *European Financial Management*, **4**(2), 143–157, July 1998.

Grundy, B., Merton H. Miller: his contribution to financial economics, *Journal of Finance*, **56**(4), 1183–1206, August 2001.

Hennessy, C. and Whited, T., Debt dynamics, *Journal of Finance*, **3**(60), 1129–1165, June 2005.

Huizinga, H., Laeven, L. and Nicodème, G., Capital structure and international debt shifting, *Journal of Financial Economics*, 80–108, 2008.

Miller, M., Debt and taxes, *Journal of Finance*, **32**, 261–276, May 1977.

Miller, M., The M&M proposition 40 years later, *European Financial Management*, **4**(2), 113–120, July 1998.

Modigliani, F. and Miller, M., Corporate income taxes and the cost of capital: A correction, *American Economic Review*, **53**, 433–443, June 1963.

Molina, C., Are firms underleveraged? An examination of the effect of leverage on default probabilities, *Journal of Finance*, **60**(3), 1427–1459, June 2005.

Stiglitz, J., Some aspects of the pure theory of corporate finance: Bankruptcies and takeovers, *Bell Journal of Economics and Management Science*, **7**(1), 458–482, Autumn 1972.

Titman, S., The effect of capital structure on a firm's liquidation decision, *Journal of Financial Economics*, **13**, 1351–1371, 1984.

Warner, J., Bankruptcy, absolute priority and the pricing of risk debt claims, *Journal of Financial Economics*, 239–276, May 1977.

Weiss, L., Bankruptcy resolution: Direct costs and violations of absolute priority of claims, *Journal of Financial Economics*, **27**, 285–314, October 1990.

White, M., Bankruptcy costs and the new bankruptcy code, *Journal of Finance*, **36**, 477–496, 1983.

38. What are the other real-world factors that affect the capital structure decision?

Long Answer

Introducing personal taxes: a major improvement to the previous reasoning

The personal taxes paid by investors can reduce and even cancel out the advantages of deducting interest payments on corporate debt.

Let us return to the example of Question 37. We shall assume that the dividends are not taxed at the personal investor's level but that – for the sake of simplicity – the interest income is taxed at 70% at the creditors' level.

If the company has no debt financing, it will still have to generate a pre-tax profit of at least 15.4 to satisfy shareholders' required rate of return. However, if its financing is 50 debt and 50 equity, the company will need to turn in a minimum profit before taxes and interest of 19.4. This will allow it to pay 8.3 of interest to its creditors, leaving them with net revenue of 2.5 after the 70% tax, corresponding to their requested net return of 5% on 50. Corporate income tax will take out 35% × (19.4 − 8.3) = 3.9, leaving 19.4 − 8.3 − 3.9 = 7.2 for the shareholders who will get their requested 14.4% return after tax on 50. If, on the contrary, the company can only generate 15.4 instead of 19.4, there is a subtraction of value from shareholders to creditors (shareholders would get 4.6, equivalent to a 9.2% return).

Given the net expected return required by creditors – the introduction of the tax rate on interest income increases the total amount of money necessary to pay debt and subtracts resources to shareholders.

If the personal tax rate on interest income is cut to 30%, thus lower than the tax rate on corporate income, debt becomes cheaper, giving rise to (low) tax savings, although still less than Modigliani and Miller found in their 1963 article.

In 1977, Miller released a new study in which he revisited the observation made with Modigliani in 1958 that there is no one optimal capital structure. This time, however, he factored in both corporate *and* personal taxes.

Miller claimed that the taxes paid by investors can cancel out those paid by companies. This would mean that the value of the firm would remain the same regardless of the type of financing used. Again, there should be no optimal capital structure.

Miller based his argument on the assumption that equity income is not taxed, and that the tax rate on interest income is marginally equal to the corporate tax rate. But these assumptions are shaky, since in reality investors are not all taxed at the same marginal rate and both equity returns and the capital gains on disposal of shares are taxed as well. In fact, Miller's objective was to demonstrate that real life is far more complicated than the simplified assumptions applied in the theories and models. The value of the tax shield is not as big as the 1963 article would make us believe. Suppose that, in addition to the corporate income tax (T_C) there are also two other tax rates:

T_D = personal tax rate on interest income;

T_E = personal tax rate on dividends.

If we:

1. consider the cash flows net of all taxes that shareholders and creditors must pay to tax authorities;
2. sum them; and
3. rearrange terms,

the 'complete' tax shield (G) is:

$$G = \left[1 - \frac{(1 - T_C) \times (1 - T_E)}{(1 - T_D)}\right] \times V_D$$

The reader will immediately notice that if $T_E = T_D$ the tax shield turns back to the 'original' $T_C \times V_D$.

In our last example, if T_E is zero, $T_D = 30\%$ and $T_C = 35\%$, G is still positive but much lower because it equals to only 0.0714 (or 7.14%).

If we include T_E in the analysis two alternatives may be possible:

- if $T_E > T_D$ the tax shield is bigger than the basic case (i.e. the case with only corporate taxes);
- if $T_E < T_D$ the tax shield tends to be smaller than the basic case.

> *When personal taxes are introduced into the analysis, the firm's objective is no longer to minimize the corporate tax bill; the firm should minimize the present value of* all *taxes paid on corporate income (those paid by bondholders and shareholders).*

Once we factor in the tax credit granted before shareholders are taxed, the tax benefits on debt disappear although, since not all earnings are distributed, not all give rise to tax credits. Say a company has an enterprise value of 1000. Regardless of its type of financing, investors require a 6%

return after corporate and personal income taxes. Bear in mind that this rate is not comparable with that determined by the CAPM ($r_F + \beta \times (r_M - r_F)$), which is calculated before personal taxation.

Let's take a country where (realistically) the main tax rates are:

- corporate tax: 34.4%;
- tax on dividends: 12%;
- capital gains tax: 12%;
- tax on interest income: 30%.

Now let us assume that the company has an operating profit of 103. This corresponds to a cost of equity of 6% if it is entirely equity-financed.

The net return of the investor (Table 1.34), who is both shareholder and creditor of the firm, can be calculated depending on whether net debt represents 0%, 33.3%, 100% or three times the amount of equity.

The value created by debt must thus be measured in terms of the increase in net income for investors (shareholders and creditors). Our example shows that flows increase significantly only when the debt level is particularly high, well above the market average (around 33% of the enterprise value).

Miller's reasoning now becomes clearer. Table 1.35 shows that in certain countries, such as Morocco, the tax savings on corporate debt are more than offset by the personal taxes levied.

Bear in mind, too, that companies do not always use the tax advantages of debt since there are other options, such as accelerated depreciation, provisions, etc.

Table 1.34: Net return for the investor

Enterprise value	**1000**	**1000**	**1000**	**1000**
Equity	1000	750	500	250
Debt	0	250	500	750
Interest rate	–	4.5%	5.5%	8%
Operating profit	103	103	103	103
– Interest expense	0	11	28	60
= Pre-tax profit	103	92	75	43
– Corporate income tax at 34.4%	35	32	26	15
= Net profit	68	60	49	28
Personal income tax:				
On dividends / capital gains (12%)	8	7	6	3
On interest (30%)	0	3	8	18
Shareholder's net income	60	53	43	25
Shareholder's net return	6%	7.1%	8.6%	10%
Creditor's net income	0	8	20	42
Creditor's net return	–	3.2%	4.0%	5.6%
Net income for investors	60	61	63	67
Total taxes	43	42	40	36

In 2000, Graham demonstrated that the value of the tax advantage of interest expenses is around 9.7%, and it goes down to 4.3% if personal taxation of investors is also considered. Almeida and Philippon (2007) have, on the other hand, estimated the bankruptcy costs; they believe the right percentage is around 4.5% – in brief, it seems that one effect 'perfectly' compensates the other. In 2010, Van Binsbergen, Graham and Yang, and Korteweg have found similar results.

What all this amounts to is that, while taxation is certainly a key parameter in absolute terms, it is unlikely to be the determinant of capital structure.

Table 1.35: Tax rates in various countries (%)

Country	On dividends	On capital gains	On interest	On earnings
France	31.3%	31.3%	31.3%	34.4%
Germany	26.4%–28.0%	26.4%–28.0%	26.4%–28.0%	30.0–33.0%
India	0%	0% or 10%	0% to 30%	33.99%
Italy	12.5%	12.5%	12.5%–27.0%	31.4%
Morocco	10.0%	15.0%	20.0%	35.0%
Netherlands (the)	25.0%–30.0%	25.0%–30.0%	30.0%	25.5%
Spain	18.0%	18.0%	18.0%	30.0%
Switzerland	22.0%–41.0%	0.0%	22.0–41.0%	24.1%
Tunisia	0.0%	0.0%	0%–35.0%	30.0%
United Kingdom	32.5%	18.0%	40.0%	28.0%
United States	15.0%	15.0%	35.0%	39.5%

In fact, Modigliani and Miller's theory states the obvious: all economic players want to reduce their tax charge! A word of caution, however: corporate managers who focus too narrowly on reducing tax charges may end up making the wrong decisions.

Information asymmetries and the pecking order theory

The analysis of the impact of informational asymmetries on capital structure decisions requires the introduction of two new concepts: *internal capital* and *external capital*. Internal capital is represented by the cash flows generated internally or, more generically, by periodical income which is not distributed among shareholders; external capital is raised outside the firm, and can either be financial debt or equity from new shareholders.

The groups that operate within the company (directors, management, major shareholders and employees – in short, the 'insiders') normally know more about the company than all other stakeholders ('outsiders'). These asymmetries tend to penalize the company when it needs to raise funds outside. External creditors receive a smaller set of information and do not believe that insiders find it convenient to share all the information they have. This in turn may have two forms:

1. a higher cost of capital;
2. a smaller amount of capital raised (capital rationing).

It is reasonable to assume that informational asymmetries are more relevant:

- for small companies;
- in start-up phases;
- when the control of the company is in the hands of few shareholders.

Internal capital doesn't penalize the company either in terms of cost or in terms of quantity.

The major disadvantages of external capital are the additional cost of informational asymmetries and the dilution of control (for example, if shares are sold at a 'bargain price' to new shareholders or if the debt contracts introduce covenants and guarantees).

The additional costs of informational asymmetries are higher if the new external capital is a share issue. All other things being equal, new debt thus has the comparative advantage of a lower cost and volume penalization.

The evidence shows that the reaction of the market to the announcement of bond issues is:

- not necessarily negative;
- of limited amount;

- not always statistically significant, when the reaction is negative.

The reaction of share prices may even be positive if the company announces the use of additional bank debt. The reason may lie in the arm's length relationship that banks have with companies which should signal a higher quality of information. The bank may know confidential information about its client, control its liquidity or be part of their board of directors, all elements that justify a higher quality of companies that prefer to raise funds through the bank channel.

A totally different result is obtained when firms announce the issue of equity capital to new shareholders. These announcements are in fact generally viewed by the market as a bad signal and the evidence shows that the negative reaction tends to be statistically significant.

Having established that information asymmetry carries a cost, our next task is to determine what type of financing carries the lowest cost in this respect. The uncontested champion is, of course, internal financing, which requires no special procedures. Its advantage is simplicity.

Debt comes next: but only low-risk debt with plenty of guarantees (pledges) and covenants restricting the risk to creditors and thus making it more palatable to them. This is followed by riskier forms of debt and hybrid securities.

Capital increases come last, because they are automatically interpreted as a negative signal. To counter this, the information asymmetry must be reduced by means of road shows, one-to-one meetings, prospectuses and advertising campaigns. Investors have to be persuaded that the issue offers good value for money!

In an article published in 1984, Myers elaborates on a theory initially put forward by Donaldson in 1969, stating that according to the *pecking order theory, companies prioritize their sources of financing*:

- Internal financing heads their list of preferences. Companies adjust their dividend payout objectives to their investment opportunities.
- Since earnings and investment opportunities vary from year to year, companies may have to draw down their cash balances.
- If this is not enough and external financing becomes necessary, they issue risk-free debt. Credit lines are kept open to ensure that they can do so as needed.
- When a company cannot resort to traditional borrowings, it issues securities, starting with the least risky type and gradually moving up the scale.
- Lastly, when all else fails, the company issues equity.

As can be seen, although the corporate manager does not choose the type of financing arbitrarily, he does so without great enthusiasm, since they all carry the same cost relative to their risk.

The pecking order is determined by the law of least effort. Managers do not have to 'raise' internal financing, and they will always endeavor to limit intermediation costs, which are the highest on share issues.

Let's take a look to see if companies really privilege internal capital. The graph in Figure 1.41 shows the evolution of the breakdown of financing of the top worldwide 1000 listed companies between 1993 and 2010.

The histograms represent the amount of internal capital (cash flow) and external capital (new equity and the variation of the stock of debt) for the top 1000 groups representing 55% of the world equity market capitalization.

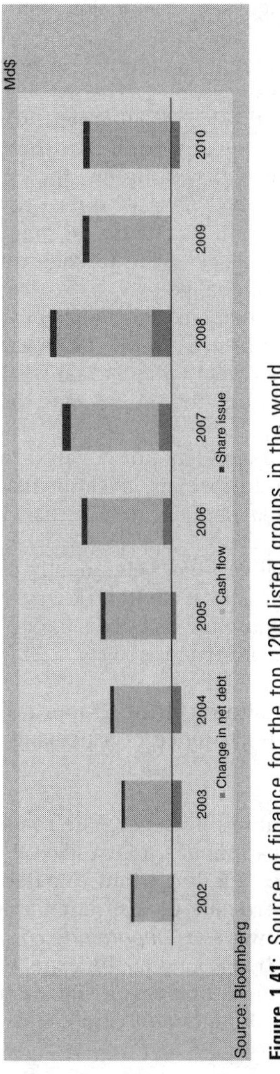

Figure 1.41: Source of finance for the top 1200 listed groups in the world

Figure 1.41 suggests three major comments:

- Internal financing has always represented the major source of companies' financing. The average incidence (94%) of internal capital is consistent with the findings of Donaldson, who suggested that the behavior of management is driven by two important factors:
  1. Firms' survival. The need for preserving the life of the company induces the management to accumulate liquidity in excess and to keep the residual borrowing capacity unchanged.
  2. Independence and self-sufficiency. The management prefers to be free to decide, regardless of external 'influences', including capital markets. An appropriate reserve of liquidity could ease the achievement of this objective.
- Internal financing has not covered the entire amount of funds required for new investments. Each period thus shows a 'financial gap' that needs to be filled with external capital.
- The financial gap has been mostly covered with debt and, if necessary, equity capital. However, the latter resource assumes a marginal role, consistent with the predictions of the pecking order model.

The evidence shown in the graph in Figure 1.41 seems to confirm the existence of a pecking order of financing choices.

A word of caution, however. The reader should never forget that internal capital has a cost like all other sources of financing. Therefore, it is important to avoid considering internal capital as a zero-cost or discretionary-cost capital. The cost of capital is always an *opportunity cost of capital*, and should be estimated by looking at the expected returns required (or obtained) by shareholders of similar (in terms of risk and duration) investments and companies.

Signaling and debt policy

Signaling theory is based on the strong assumption that corporate managers are better informed about their companies than the suppliers of funding.

This means that they are in a better position to foresee the company's future flows and know what state their company is in. Consequently, any signal they send indicating that flows will be better than expected or that risks will be lower may enable the investor to create value. Investors are therefore constantly on the watch for such signals. But for the signals to be credible there must be a penalty for the wrong signals in order to dissuade companies from deliberately misleading the market.

In the context of information asymmetry, markets would not understand why a corporate manager would borrow to undertake a very risky and unprofitable venture. After all, if the venture fails, the manager risks losing his or her job, or worse if the venture causes the company to fail. So debt is a strong signal for profitability, but even more for risk. It is unlikely that a CEO would resort to debt financing if he or she knew that in a worst-case scenario they would not be able to repay the debt.

Ross (1977) has demonstrated that any change in financing policy changes investors' perception of the company and is therefore a market signal.

It is thus obvious that an increase in debt increases the risk on equity. The managers of a company that has raised its gearing rate are, in effect, signaling to the markets that they are aware of the state of nature, that it is favorable and that they are confident that the company's performance will allow them to pay the additional financial expenses and pay back the new debt.

This signal carries its own penalty if it is wrong. If the signal is false, i.e. if the company's actual prospects are not good at all, the extra debt will create financial difficulties that will ultimately lead, in one form or another, to the dismissal of its executives. In this scheme, managers have a strong incentive to send the correct signal by ensuring that the firm's debt corresponds to their understanding of its repayment capacity.

Ross has shown that, assuming managers have privileged information about their own company, they will send the correct signal on condition that the marginal gain derived from an incorrect signal is lower than the sanction suffered if the company is liquidated.

'They put their money where their mouths are.' This explains why debt policies vary from one company to the other: they simply reflect the variable prospects of the individual companies.

> *The actual capital structure of a firm is not necessarily a signal, but any change in it certainly is.*

When a company announces a capital increase, research has shown that its share price generally drops by an average 3%. The market reasons that corporate managers would not increase capital if, based on the inside information available to them, they thought it was undervalued, since this would dilute the existing shareholdings in unfavorable conditions. If there is no pressing reason for the capital increase, investors will infer that, based on their inside information, the managers consider the share price to be too high and that this is why the existing shareholders have accepted the capital increase. On the other hand, research has shown too that the announcement of a bond issue has no material impact on share prices.

It follows that the sale of a manager's stake in the company is a very negative signal. It reveals that he has internal information indicating that the value of future flows, taking risk into account, is lower than the proceeds he expects from the sale of his investment. Conversely, any increase in the stake, especially if financed by debt, constitutes a very positive signal for the market.

This explains why financial investors prefer to subscribe to capital increases rather than buy from existing shareholders. It is also the reason why every year in the US, the UK, Italy and many other countries top managers and all directors must disclose the number of shares they hold or control in the companies they work for or of which they are board members.

Debt as a means of controlling corporate managers
Now let us examine the interests of non-shareholder executives. They may be tempted to shun debt in order to avoid the corresponding constraints, such as a higher breakeven threshold, interest payments and principal repayments. Corporate managers are highly risk averse and their natural inclination is to accumulate cash rather than resort to debt to finance investments. Debt financing avoids this trap, since the debt repayment prevents surplus cash from accumulating. Shareholders encourage debt as well because it stimulates performance. The more debt a company has, the higher its risk. In the event of financial difficulties, corporate executives may lose their jobs and the attendant compensation package and remuneration in kind. This threat is considered to be sufficiently dissuasive to encourage sound management, generating optimal liquidity to service the debt and engage in profitable investments.

The explicit cost of debt is a simple yet highly effective means of controlling a firm's management team. Large groups are well aware of the leverage this gives them and require the executives of their main subsidiaries to carry a level of 'incentive debt' which is charged to the subsidiary.

Given that the parameters of debt are reflected in a company's cash situation while equity financing translates into capital gains or losses at shareholder level, management will be particularly intent on the success of its debt-financed investment projects. This is another, indirect, limitation of the perfect markets theory:

since the various forms of financing do not offer the same incentives to corporate executives, financing does indeed influence the choice of investment.

This would indicate that a levered company is more flexible and responsive than an unlevered company. This hypothesis was tested and proven by Ofek, who shows that the more debt they carry, the faster listed US companies react to a crisis, by filing for bankruptcy, curtailing dividend payouts or reducing the payroll.

Debt is thus an internal means of controlling management preferred by shareholders.

However, the use of debt has its limits. When a group's corporate structure becomes totally unbalanced, debt no longer acts as an incentive for management. On the contrary, the corporate manager will be tempted to continue expanding via debt until his group has become too big to fail, like the Korean groups at the end of the 1990s. This risk is called 'moral hazard'.

With more empirical evidence researchers have examined if companies which have experienced a fast increase of leverage have become more efficient, as measured by profit margins and the return on invested capital.

It is the case of *leveraged buyouts* or LBOs. An LBO is the acquisition, generally by management (MBO), of all a company's shares using borrowed funds. It becomes a *leveraged buildup* if it then uses debt to buy other companies in order to increase its standing in the sector.

It is generally thought that the purpose of the funds devoted to LBOs is to use accounting leverage to obtain better returns. In fact, the success of LBOs cannot be attributed to accounting leverage, since we have already seen that this alone does not create value.

The real reason for the success of LBOs is that, when it has a stake in the company, management is far more committed to making the company a success. With management most often holding a share of the equity, resource allocation will be designed to benefit shareholders. Executives have a twofold incentive: to enhance their existing or future (in the case of stock options) stake in the capital and to safeguard their jobs and reputation by ensuring that the company does not go broke. It thus becomes a classic case of the carrot and the stick!

The results reported by Palepu (1990) show an improvement – although quite limited – of the operating efficiency of companies subjected to leveraged buyouts.

Mature, highly profitable companies with few investments to make are the most likely candidates for an LBO. Jensen (1986) demonstrated that, in the absence of heavy debt, the executives of such companies will be strongly tempted to use the substantial free cash flow to grow to the detriment of profits by overinvesting or diversifying into other businesses, two strategies that destroy value.

The only value created by debt is the fact that it forces managers to improve enterprise value.

Some questions are still looking for an answer:

- Is the capital structure influenced by the lifecycle stage the company is going through?
- Is there a role for competitors in determining the capital structure of the firm?
- Why do managers sometimes prefer to use funding as a way to send signals to financial markets?
- What is the optimal maturity structure of debt? And the optimal percentage of floating debt? How much debt issued in different currencies should a company have?
- When a company wants to move towards its chosen debt/equity mix, should it reach that leverage rapidly or gradually?

In Question 39, we shall focus on these issues to illustrate how to reach an appropriate *design* of the capital structure of a company. After having explored the bulk of the theory, the time will come to examine details.

References and Further Reading

Almeida, D. and Philippon, T., The risk-adjusted cost of financial distress, *Journal of Finance*, **6** (62), 2557–2586, December 2007.

Brounen, D., De Jong, A. and Koedijk, K. Corporate finance in Europe: Confronting theory with practice, *Financial Management*, **4**, 71–101, Winter 2004.

DeAngelo, H. and Masulis, R., Optimal capital structure under corporate and personal taxation, *Journal of Financial Economics*, **8**(1), 3–29, March 1980.

Donaldson, G., *Strategy for Financial Mobility*, Harvard Graduate School of Business Administration, 1969.

Graham, J., How big are the tax benefits of debt? *Journal of Finance*, **55**(5), 1901–1941, October 2000.

Graham, J., Taxes and corporate finance: A review, *Review of Financial Studies*, **16**(4), 1075–1129, Winter 2003.

Green, R. and Hollifield, B., The personal tax advantages of equity, *Journal of Financial Economics*, **2** (67), 175–216, February 2003.

Grundy, B. Merton, H. Miller: his contribution to financial economics, *Journal of Finance*, **56** (4), 1183–1206, August 2001.

Jensen, M., The agency costs of free cash flow, corporate finance, and takeovers, *American Economic Review*, **76**, 323–329, May 1986.

Jensen, M. and Meckling, W., Theory of the firm: Managerial behavior agency costs and ownership structure, *Journal of Financial Economics*, **3**, 305–360, October 1976.

Korteweg, A., The net benefits to leverage, *Journal of Finance*, **65**(6), 2137–2170, December 2010.

Leland, H., Agency costs, risk management and capital structure, *Journal of Finance*, **4** (53), 1213–1243, August 1998.

Miller, M., Debt and taxes, *Journal of Finance*, **32**, 261–276, May 1977.

Miller, M., The M&M proposition 40 years later, *European Financial Management*, **4**(2), 113–120, July 1998.

Molina, C., Are firms underleveraged? An examination of the effect of leverage on default probabilities, *Journal of Finance*, **60** (3), 1427–1459, June 2005.

Myers, S., Determinants of corporate borrowing, *Journal of Financial Economics*, **5**, 146–175, 1977.

Myers, S., The capital structure puzzle, *Journal of Finance*, **12**(3), 575–592, 1984.

Ofek, E., Capital structure and firm response to poor performance: an empirical investigation, *Journal of Financial Economics*, **34**(1), 3–30, August 1993.

Palepu, K., Consequences of LBO, *Journal of Financial Economics*, **27**(1), 247–262, September 1990.

Ross, S., The determination of financial structure: The incentive signaling approach, *Bell Journal of Economics*, **8**, 23–40, Summer 1977.

Van Binsbergen, J., Graham, J. and Yang, J., The cost of debt, *Journal of Finance*, **65**(6), 2089–2136, December 2010

39. How do companies design their debt funding?

Short Answer

Companies design their debt funding considering:

- the need to preserve some financial flexibility;
- the capital structure of competitors;
- the need to preserve an adequate rating; and
- the life cycle of the company.

Long Answer

The need to preserve some financial flexibility
Having and retaining flexibility is of strong concern to finance directors. They know that choice of financing is a problem to be evaluated over time, not just at a given moment; a choice today can reduce the spectrum of possibilities for another choice to be made tomorrow.

Thus, taking on debt now will reduce borrowing capacity in the future, when a major investment – perhaps foreseeable, perhaps not – may be needed. If borrowing capacity is used up, the company will have no choice but to raise fresh equity. From time to time, though, the primary market in equities is closed because of depressed share prices. If that should be the case when the company needs funds, it may have to forgo the investment.

The equity capital market may not be open for new business during a crisis, when investors prefer to stick with safer debt securities. Debt markets stay open regardless of economic conditions.

True, the markets for high-yield debt securities react as the equity markets do and may at times be closed to new issues. There are periods – such as the second half of 2001 and first half of 2002 – when the numbers of issues of shares and high-yield bonds are extremely small.

Raising money today with a share issue, however, does not foreclose another capital increase at a later time. Moreover, an equity financing today will increase the borrowing capacity that can be mobilized tomorrow.

A sharp increase in debt reduces the company's financial flexibility, whereas a capital increase augments its borrowing capacity.

> *The desire to retain flexibility prompts the company to carry less debt than the maximum level it deems bearable, so that it will at all times be in a position to take advantage of unexpected investment opportunities.*

Here we find the option concept applied to corporate finance.

In addition, the finance director will have taken pains to negotiate unutilized lines of credit with the company's bank; to have in hand all the shareholder authorizations needed to issue new debt or equity securities; and to have effective corporate communication on financial matters with rating agencies, financial analysts and investors.

Going beyond the debt–equity dichotomy, the quest for financial flexibility will require the finance director to open up different capital markets to the company. A company that has already issued securities on the bond market and keeps a dialog going with bond investors can come back to this market very quickly if an investment opportunity appears.

The proliferation of financing sources – bilateral or syndicated bank loans, securitized receivables, bonds, convertibles, shares, and so on – allows the company to enhance its financial flexibility even further. But this strategy faces two limitations:

- issues on different markets have to be big enough to ensure sufficient liquidity for investors;
- multiple disparate sources of financing (possibly at different levels with a group structure) make the capital structure more complex and harder to manage (especially during liquidity crises).

Financial flexibility has a value, although it is difficult to estimate.

We should bear in mind that the value of financial flexibility is reasonably linked to the number and the dimension of investment projects. If the company has a lot of investment opportunities and the average value of the investments is high, it should also have a high financial 'reserve'.

Capital structure of competitors

- To have higher net debt than one's rivals is to bet heavily on the company's future profitability – that is, on the economy, the strategy and so forth.
- To have higher net debt than one's rivals, other things being equal, is to be more vulnerable to a cyclical downturn, one that could lead to a shakeout in the sector and extinction of the weakest.

There is good evidence that the average capital structure of the sector is an important benchmark for the management when setting capital structure policies. Experience shows that business leaders are loath to imperil an industrial strategy by adopting a financing policy substantially different from their competitors'. If they have to take risks, they want them to be industrial or commercial risks, not financial risks. The rationale of this behavior is clear: since all companies behave similarly, the average leverage indicates the sustainable level of financial risk belonging to the same sector!

> *Our opinion is that benchmarking on competitors is not contradictory with the precepts of the trade-off model.*

Companies within the same sector – and in the same stage of the life cycle – share the same basic economic and financial characteristics. Hence, financial policies shouldn't be so different.

Industries with high volatility of cash flows and low tangible assets are those where we expect leverage to be lower. On the contrary, in sectors where flows are stable and companies can provide high collateral, the use of debt should be higher.

The choice of capital structure is not absolute but relative: the real question is how to finance the business compared with the industry average – that is, compared with the company's competitors.

However, there are at least two situations where the simple replication of what competitors do could be erroneous:

- when the sector is made up of highly heterogeneous companies; and
- when the sector is going through a restructuring phase.

With the analyses in hand, the person or body taking the financing decision will be able to do so with full knowledge of the facts. The investor will bear in mind that, statistically (and thus, for his diversified portfolio), his dream of multiplying his wealth through judicious use of debt will be the nightmare of the company in financial difficulty.

The financial success of a few tends to make one forget the failure of companies that did not survive because they were too much in debt.

Need to preserve an adequate rating

Ratings agencies have clearly gained in importance – especially in Europe – in the last 20 years, as seen in the 35% annual increase in the number of companies carrying a Moody's rating. In Europe, this is due mostly to the transition from an economy based mostly on banking intermediaries to one where the financial markets are becoming predominant.

Some companies even set rating targets (Pepsi, Diageo and Vivendi Universal, for example). This can seem paradoxical in two ways:

- although all financial communication is based on creating shareholder value, companies are much less likely to set share price targets than rating targets; and
- in setting rating targets, companies have a new objective: that of preserving value for bondholders! This is praiseworthy and, in a financial market context, understandable, but has never been part of the bargain with bondholders.

We see several possible explanations for this paradox. First of all, a debt rating downgrade is clearly a major event for a group and goes well beyond bondholder information.

A downgrade is traumatic and messy and almost always leads to a fall in the share price. So in seeking to preserve a financial rating, it is also shareholder value that management is protecting, at least in the short term.

A downgrade can also have an immediate cost if the company has issued a bond with a step-up in the coupon, i.e. a clause stating that the coupon will be increased in the event of a rating downgrade. Step-ups are meant to protect lenders against a downgrade and obviously make managers pay more attention to their debt rating.

> *A good debt rating guarantees a higher degree of financial flexibility.*

The higher the rating, the easier it is to tap the bond markets, as transactions are less dependent on market fluctuations. An investment grade company, for example, can almost always issue bonds, whereas market windows close regularly for companies that are below investment grade. The recent seizing up of the high-yield market is quite instructive, as many issues have had to be postponed. The high-yield market is similar in this respect to the equities market. Under the new Basel II banking solvency standards the highest rated companies will probably have even greater flexibility, as loans to them will require lower reserve requirements and banks will more readily agree to them.

There is a phenomenon that is even more perverse than setting a target rating: refusing to be rated or asking for a confidential 'shadow rating'. Being rated can be scary, and CFOs balance out the lack of flexibility created by the lack of rating (e.g. certain investors can no longer be tapped and the bond market is mostly closed off) with the potential lack of flexibility created by a poor rating.

In extreme cases, we have even seen companies that, in their initial rating process, tried to obtain the worst possible rating for their particular financial profile. They did this in order to gain some flexibility, i.e. some room for their situation to get marginally worse without undermining their rating. In this particular case, caution has a clear impact on value, as a lower rating means higher debt costs. But this is like an insurance premium that always looks too high until an accident strikes.

All in all, the desire of many companies to set a rating target reminds us that financial structure is above all the choice of the level of risk that shareholders choose to run and that the European debt market is becoming a real market with varied, segmented products, offered to investors who need some criteria in making their choices.

Life cycle of the company

> *It is a mistake to think that the trade-off model helps us to find an optimal leverage that doesn't change across time. The optimal capital structure is a concept that evolves from sector to sector – as discussed above – and from firm to firm.*

Let's think about startup companies. They normally:

- have a high need of equity capital because of their:
  - lower tax shield capacity;
  - high financial distress costs (low tangible assets);
  - short history;
- need additional resource for new investments whose amount normally exceeds annual depreciation.

The necessity of funding with external resources is in this case quite high since internal sources (self-financing and liquidity) are insufficient to cover the amount of new investments in fixed assets and working capital.

At the same time, they must keep an adequate level of financial flexibility for facing the uncertain competitive dynamics of evolving sectors like, for example, advanced technologies. The capital structure of startup companies must then:

- try to match assets and liabilities;
- give the company a financial reserve for absorbing unfavorable reduction of cash flows;
- allow them to exploit real market opportunities.

The evidence shows that bigger companies – living their maturity phase – tend to have higher leverage ratios, which confirms their high capacity for lowering the costs of debt thanks to their stability and higher fixed assets.

Here we see the *life cycle of financing sources*. An industrial venture is initially financed with equity. As the company becomes institutionalized and its risk diminishes, debt financing takes over, freeing up equity capital to be invested in emerging new sectors (see Table 1.36).

Similarly, in an industry with high fixed costs, a company will seek to finance itself mostly with equity, so as not to pile the fixed costs of debt (interest payments) on top of its fixed operating costs and to reduce its sensitivity to cyclical downswings. But sectors with high fixed costs – steel, cement, paper, energy, telecoms, etc. – are generally highly capital-intensive and thus require large investments, inevitably implying borrowing as well.

An industry such as retailing with high variable costs, on the other hand, can make the bet that debt entails, as the fixed costs of borrowing come on top of low fixed operating costs.

Lastly, the nature of the asset can influence the availability of financing to acquire it. (See Figure 1.42)

A highly specific asset, that is, one with little value outside of a given production process, will be hard to finance with debt. Lenders will fear that if the company goes under, the asset's market value will not be sufficient to pay off their claims.

Table 1.36: The trade-off model

	Startup	Growth	Maturity
Tax shield	Zero	Increases with earnings	High
Disciplining role of debt	Low, shareholders-managers	Increases, new external shareholders	Decreases, little new investments
Information asymmetries	High, business only an idea	Decreases, track record and credibility	Decrease, higher transparency
Financial distress costs	Very high	High	Declining
Agency costs	Very high	High	Declining
Financial flexibility	Very high	High	Low
Extended trade-off	**Costs of debt > Benefits**	**Relevant benefits from debt**	**Benefits of debt > Costs**

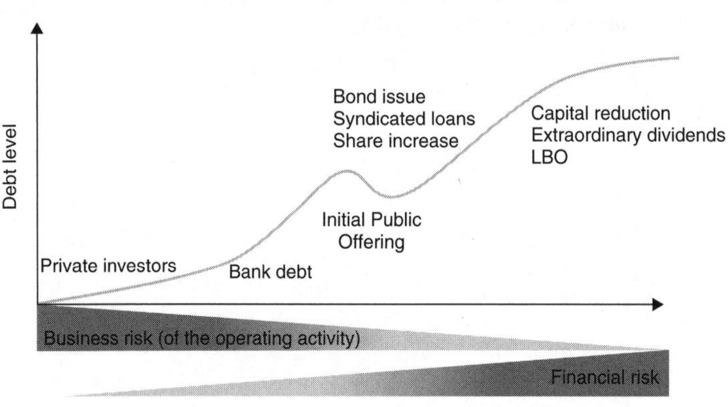

Figure 1.42: The life cycle of a company

References and Further Reading

Damodaran, A., Financing innovations and capital structure choices, *Journal of Applied Corporate Finance*, **12**, 28–39, 1999.

Hovakimian, A., Opler, T. and Titman, S., The capital structure choice: New evidence from a dynamic trade-off model, *Journal of Applied Corporate Finance*, **15**(1), 24–30, Spring 2002.

Kayhan, A. and Titman, S., Firm's histories and their capital structures, *Journal of Financial Economics*, **83**(1), 1–32, January 2007.

Kisgen, D., The influence of credit ratings on corporate capital structure decisions, *Journal of Applied Corporate Finance*, **19**(3), Summer 2007.

Leary, M. and Roberts, M., Do firms rebalance their capital structures? *Journal of Finance*, **60**(6), 2575–2619, December 2005.

MacKay, P. and Phillips, G., How does industry affect firm financial structure?, *Review of Financial Studies*, **18**(4), 1433–1466, August 2005.

Zingales, L. and Rajan, R., Debt, folklore and cross-country differences in financial structure, *Journal of Applied Corporate Finance*, **10**(4), 102–107, Winter 1998.

40. Can options be used for the analysis of the capital structure?

Short Answer

Yes, because the shareholders' equity of a levered company can be seen as a call option granted by creditors to shareholders on the company's operating assets.

Example

To keep our presentation simple, we take the example of a joint stock company in which enterprise value EV is divided between debt (V_D) and equity (V_E). We shall also assume that the company has issued only one type of debt – zero coupon bonds – redeemable upon maturity at full face value (principal and interest) for 100.

Depending on the enterprise value when the debt matures, two outcomes are possible.

- The enterprise value is higher than the amount of debt to be redeemed (e.g. EV = 120). In this case, the shareholders let the company repay the lenders and take the residual value of 20.
- The enterprise value is lower than the amount of debt to be redeemed (e.g. EV = 70). The shareholders may then invoke their limited liability clause, forfeiting only their investment, and transfer the company to the lenders who will bear the difference between the enterprise value and their claim.

Now let us analyze this situation in terms of options. From an economic standpoint, shareholders have a call option (known as a European call if it can only be exercised at the end of its life) on the firm's assets. Its features are:

- **Underlying asset** = capital employed.
- **Exercise price** = amount of debt to be reimbursed (100).
- **Volatility** = volatility of the underlying assets, i.e. the capital employed.
- **Maturity** = expiration date.
- **Interest rate** = risk-free rate corresponding to the maturity of the option.

At the expiration date, shareholders exercise their call option and repay the lenders, or they abandon it. The value of the option is no other than the value of equity (V_E).

From the shareholder's point of view, when a company borrows funds, it is selling its 'enterprise value' to its creditors, but with an option to buy it back (at the exercise price) when the debt matures. The shares of a levered company thus represent call options on the capital employed.

The lender, on the other hand, who has invested in the firm at no risk, *has sold the shareholders a put option on the capital employed*. We have just seen that in the event of default, the creditors may find themselves the unwilling owners of the company. Rather than recouping the amount they lent, they get only the value of the company back. In other words, they have 'bought' the company in exchange for the outstanding amount of debt.

The features of the put option are:

- **Underlying asset** = capital employed.
- **Exercise price** = amount of debt redeemable upon maturity (100).
- **Volatility** = volatility of the underlying asset, i.e. the capital employed.
- **Maturity** = maturity of the debt.

- **Interest rate** = risk-free rate corresponding to the maturity of the option.

The sale of this (European-style) put option results in additional remuneration for the debt-holder which, together with the risk-free rate, constitutes the total return. This is only fair, since the debt-holder runs the risk that the shareholders will exercise their put option, in other words, that the company will not pay back the debt.

The value of this option is equal to the difference between the value of the loan discounted at the risk-free rate and its market value (discounted at a rate that takes into account the default risk, i.e. the cost of debt k_D). This is the risk premium that arises between any loan and its risk-free equivalent.

All that this means is that the debt-holder has lent the company 103 at an interest rate equal to the risk-free rate. The company should have received 103, but the value of the loan is only 100 after discounting the flows at the normal rate of return required in view of the company's risk, rather than the risk-free rate.

The company uses the balance of three, which represents the price of the credit risk, to buy a put option on the capital employed. In short, the company receives 100 while the bank pays 100 for a risky claim since it has sold a put option for capital employed that the company, and therefore the shareholders, will exercise if its value is lower than that of the outstanding date at maturity. By exercising the option, the company, and thus its shareholders, discharges its debt by transferring ownership of the capital employed to the creditors.

Lending to a company is a means of investing in its assets at no risk. The lender sells the shareholders a put option at an exercise price that is equal to the debt to be repaid.

In conclusion, we see that, depending on the situation at the redemption date, one of the following two will apply:

- if $V_D < V$ the value of the call option is higher than 0, the value of the put option is zero and equity is positive; or
- if $V_D > V$ the value of the call option is zero, the value of the put option is higher than 0, and the equity is worthless.

Long Answer

Considering that the additivity rule for equity and debt applies and that there is no connection between enterprise value and the type of financing:

Enterprise value = equity + debt

Based on the preceding developments, we deduce that:

Value of equity = value of the call option on capital employed

Value of debt = present value of debt at the risk-free rate
− value of the put option

Enterprise value = value of the call option
+ present value of debt at the risk-free rate
−value of the put option

So considering the fundamental equality between put and call options we have:

Buying a call option + selling a put option
= Buying the underlying asset
+ borrowing at the risk-free rate

This underscores the relationship between the value of a call on capital employed and the value of a put on the same capital employed:

Value of equity = EV
− present value of debt at the risk-free rate
+ value of the put on capital employed

We have demonstrated that the value of a firm's equity is comparable to the value of a call option on its capital employed. The option's exercise price is the amount of debt to be repaid at maturity, the life of the option is that of the debt, and its underlying asset is the firm's capital employed.

This means that, at the valuation date, the value of equity is made up of an intrinsic value and a time value. The intrinsic value of the call option is the difference between the present value of capital employed and the debt to be repaid upon maturity. The time value corresponds to the difference between the total value of equity and the intrinsic value.

The main contribution of options theory to corporate finance is the concept of a time value for equity.

Take, for example, a company where the return on capital employed is lower than that required by investors in view of the related risk. The market value is thus lower than the book value.

If the debt were to mature today, the shareholders would exercise their put option since the capital employed is worth only 70 while the outstanding debt is 80. The company would have to file for bankruptcy. Fortunately, the debt is not redeemable today but only in, say, two years' time. By then, the enterprise value may have risen to over 80. In that case, equity will have an intrinsic value equal to the difference between the enterprise value at the redemption date and the amount to be redeemed (in our case, 80).

Today, however, the intrinsic value is zero and the present value of equity (80) can only be explained by the time value, which represents the hope that, when the debt matures two years hence, enterprise value will have raised enough to exceed the amount of debt to be repaid, giving the equity an intrinsic value.

As shown in the graphs in Figure 1.43 (a, b and c) below, a company's financial position can be considered from either the shareholders' or the creditors' standpoint.

The more economic or industrial risk on a company, the higher the volatility of its capital employed and the higher the time value of its equity. The options method is thus used to value large, risky projects financed by debt, such as the Channel tunnel, leisure parks, etc. or those with inherent volatility, such as biotech startups.

When the call option is out-of-the-money (enterprise value lower than outstanding debt), the company's equity has only

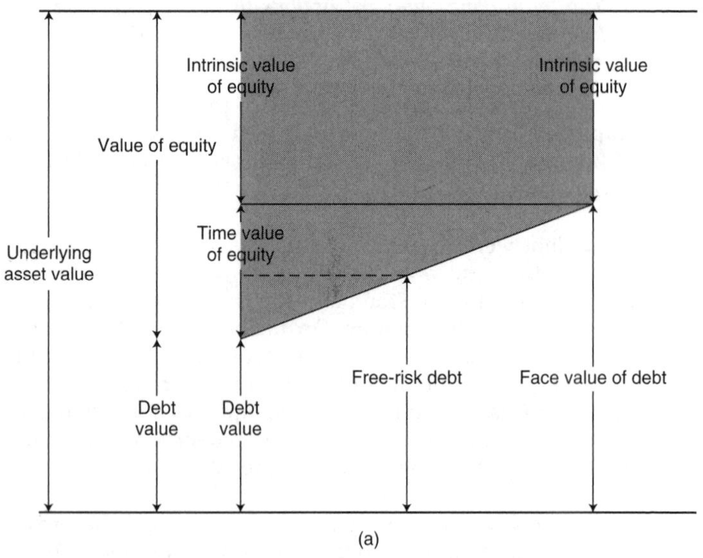

Figure 1.43: A decomposition of the underlying asset value

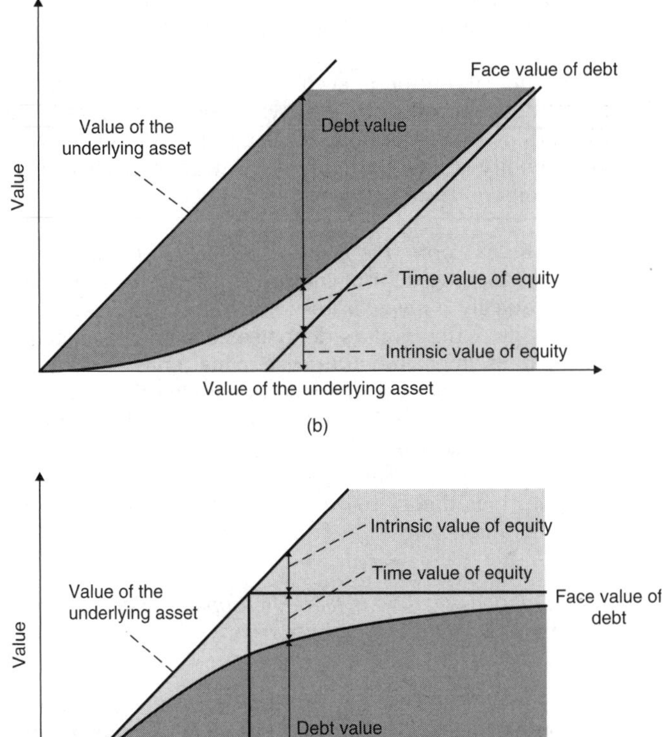

Figure 1.43: (*continued*)

time value. Shareholders hope for an improvement in the company, whose equity has no intrinsic value.

When the call option is at-the-money (enterprise value equal to debt at maturity), the time value of equity is at its highest and anything can happen. Using the options method to value equity is now particularly relevant, since it can quantify shareholders' anticipations.

When the call option is in-the-money (enterprise value higher than outstanding debt at maturity), the intrinsic value of equity quickly outweighs the time value. The risk on the debt held by the lenders decreases and becomes nearly nonexistent when the enterprise value tends towards infinity. This brings us back to the traditional idea that the higher the enterprise value, the less risk of default creditors have, and the more the cost of debt approaches the risk-free rate.

Using options theory to analyze liabilities is particularly helpful when a company is in financial distress.

> *The options method is therefore applied to companies that carry heavy debt or are very risky.*

This is why it is so important for companies in distress to reschedule debt payments, preferably at very long maturities.

Example

Consider a company that has both debt and equity financing and let us assume its debt is 100, redeemable in one year. If, based on its degree of risk, the debt carries 6% interest, the amount to be repaid to creditors one year later is 106.

Traditional theory tells us that if the firm's value is 150 at the time of calculation, the value of equity – defined as the difference between enterprise value and the value of debt – will be 150 – 100 = 50.

What happens if we apply options theory to this value?

We shall assume the risk-free rate is 5%. The discounted value of the debt + interest payment at the risk-free rate is 106/1.05, or 100.95.

The value of debt can be expressed as:

$$\text{Value of debt} = \text{Value of debt at the risk-free rate} \\ - \text{value of a put}$$

i.e. value of the put = 100.95 – 100 = 0.95.

We know that the value of equity breaks down into its intrinsic and time value:

$$\text{Value of equity} = 50 - \text{Intrinsic value} \\ = 150 - 106 = 44 \\ \text{Time value} = 6$$

You can see that, for this company with limited risk, the time value measuring the actual risk is far lower than the intrinsic value. Similarly, the value of the put, which acts as a risk premium, is very low as well.

Now, let's increase the risk to the capital employed and assume that the cost of equity required by the creditors is 15% rather than 6%, corresponding to a 10% risk premium.

The amount to be repaid in one year is thus 115.

The value of the debt discounted at the risk-free rate is 115/1.05, or 109.52. The value of the put is thus 109.52 – 100 = 9.52.

Note that the risk premium for this company is much higher than in the preceding example, reflecting the increasing probability that the company will default on its debt.

The value of equity, which is still 50, breaks down into an intrinsic value of 35 (150 – 115) and a time value of 15 (50 – 35). Since there is more risk than in our previous example, the time value accounts for a higher portion of the equity value.

References and Further Reading

Black, F. and Scholes, M., The pricing of options and corporate liabilities, *Journal of Polical Economy*, **81**, 637–654, May/June 1973.

Chesney, M. and Gibson-Asner, R., The investment policy and the pricing of equity in a levered firm: A re-examination of the contingent claim's 'valuation approach', *European Journal of Finance*, **5**, 95–107, June 1999.

Galai, D. and Masulis, R., The option pricing model and the risk factor of stock, *Journal of Financial Economics*, **33**, 53–81, 1976.

Geske, R. and Johnson, H., The valuation of corporate liabilities as compound options: A correction, *Journal of Financial and Quantitative Analysis*, **7**, 6–81, March 1979.

Hsia, C., Coherence of the modern theories of finance, *Financial Review*, Winter, 1999.

Kalotay, J., Valuation of corporate securities: Applications of contingent claim analysis, in E. Altman and M. Subrahmanyam (eds.), *Recent Advances in Corporate Finance*, Richard Irwin, 1985.

Mason, S. and Merton, R., The role of contingent claims analysis in corporate finance, in E. Altman and M. Subrahmanyam (eds.), *Recent Advances in Corporate Finance*, Richard Irwin, 1985.

Merton, R., On the pricing of corporate debt: The risk structure of interest rates, *Journal of Finance*, **29**(2), 449–470, May 1974.

Ogden, J., Determinants of the ratings and yields on corporate bonds: Tests of the contingent claim model, *Journal of Financial Research*, **10**, 329–340, 1986.

Park, S. and Subrahmanyam, M., Option features of corporate securities, in S. Figlewski, W. Silber and M. Subrahmanyam (eds.), *Financial Options. From Theory to Practice*, Richard Irwin, 1990.

Smith, C., Applications of option pricing analysis, in J. Bicksler (ed.), *Handbook of Financial Economics*, North Holland Publishing, 1979.

41. How can companies distribute their excess cash?

Short Answer

Generally, excess cash can be used for:

- dividends;
- share buybacks; and
- capital reductions.

Example – Payment of dividends

The chart in Figure 1.44 plots the share price of Unibail-Rodamco (Europe's leading listed commercial property company specialized in shopping centers in European capital cities), which on October 12th 2010, paid a special dividend of €20 per share (€1.8 bn). This distribution was financed via the undrawn credit lines.

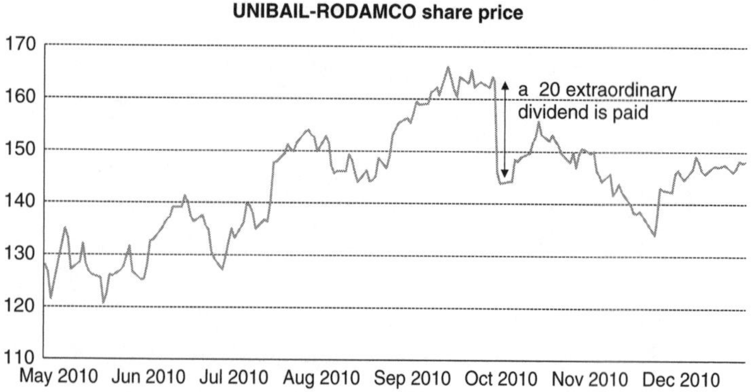

Figure 1.44: Share price of Unibail-Rodamco

This means that in a universe of markets in equilibrium, paying out more or less in dividends will have no effect on shareholder wealth.

Long Answer

Internal financing: reinvesting cash flow. Internal financing by reinvestment of cash flow enjoys an excellent image: it reduces risk for creditors and results in capital gains rather than more heavily taxed dividends for shareholders. For managers, it is a resource they can mobilize without having to go to third parties.

However, systematic reinvestment of cash flows can be dangerous. It is not appealing from a financial standpoint if it allows the company to finance investments that bring in less than the required rate of return. By doing so it would destroy value.

The trap for the unwitting is that internal financing has no explicit cost, whereas its true cost – an opportunity cost – is quite real.

Reinvesting cash flows accelerates the organic growth at a rate equal to the ROE multiplied by the earnings retention ratio (one minus the payout ratio). With constant gearing and rate of return on capital employed, the organic growth rate is the same as the growth rate of book equity and capital employed. Lastly, the rate of growth of EPS is equal to the marginal rate of return on book equity multiplied by the retention ratio.

Dividends. Within the framework of equilibrium market theory, dividend policy has little importance.

The shareholder is indifferent about receiving a dividend and letting the company reinvest the cash in assets that will earn the rate of return he or she requires. The shareholder's wealth is the same in either case.

Signaling theory interprets dividends as information communicated by managers to investors about future earnings. A rise in the dividend signals good news, a cut signals bad news.

Agency theory interprets dividends as a means of mitigating conflicts between owners and managers. Paying a dividend reduces the amount of cash that managers are able to invest without much control on the part of shareholders. On the other hand, paying a dividend aggravates conflicts between owners and lenders when the amount of that dividend is significant.

All things considered, dividend policy should be judged on the basis of the company's marginal rate of return on capital employed.

If that rate is above the weighted average cost of capital, the dividend can be low or nil because the company is creating value when it reinvests its earnings. If the marginal rate of return is below the cost of capital, shareholders are better off if the company distributes all its earnings to them.

As long as the company has opportunities to invest at a satisfactory return, managers set a target dividend payout ratio that will be higher or lower depending on whether the company has reached maturity or is still growing. Fluctuations in net earnings can be smoothed over in the per-share dividend so that it does not move erratically and send the wrong signal to investors.

The reader should not forget that, to some extent, dividend policy determines the composition of the shareholder body:

paying no dividends leads to low loyalty on the part of shareholders, who must regularly sell shares to meet their needs for cash.

A capital decrease can take the form of either a reduction in the par value of all shares via distribution to shareholders of the corresponding amount of cash, or a buyback of shares in which shareholders are free to participate or not as they see fit.

Share buybacks. A capital decrease may be undertaken for several different purposes: to return funds to shareholders when managers are unable to find investment projects meeting the shareholders' return requirements; to signal an undervalued share price; as an indirect means of increasing the percentage of control held by shareholders that do not take part in the buyback; or to distribute cash to shareholders at a lower tax cost than by paying a dividend.

Some studies show that the value of shares is much lower on the day of the repurchase than in the preceding months (by close to 3%). The drop in price could justify a repurchase, either to take advantage of the undervaluation or to prop up the share. The return over the five days following the repurchase is no different from that of shares that have not been repurchased. In other words, firms that repurchase their own shares do not benefit from information asymmetry. Accordingly, so the purpose of a share repurchase would be to stabilize market value in the event of a downward trend.

It is interesting to observe the impact of share repurchases on the liquidity of the shares. Two opposite effects are expected. On the one hand, the act of repurchasing shares itself results in an increase in the number of orders on the order book which reduces the bid–ask spread. On the other hand, however, information asymmetry (in the case of market timing) like inconsistent behavior (in the case of price support) always leads to an increase in the bid–ask spread and a reduction in liquidity. Share repurchases result in a reduction in liquidity, with the average spread rising from 2.33% before the repurchase, to 2.4% after.

> *The reduction in equity capital produces an increase in EPS if the reciprocal of the share's P/E ratio is higher than the after-tax interest rate paid on incremental debt (or forgone on short-term investments).*

But, make no mistake, this principle has only a remote association with value creation.

Debt-financed capital decreases are economically sound when they allow equity capital to be reallocated away from companies that have reached maturity and achieved predictable cash flows, towards newer companies that are still growing. They are a means of preventing overinvestment and haphazard diversification. However, they lead to value creation only if one or more of the following conditions hold:

- the added debt burden constrains managers to achieve better performance;
- the shares are bought back at a price below their true value;
- the funds returned to shareholders would have earned less than the cost of capital if kept in the company.

Choosing between dividends, share buybacks and capital reduction. Although paying dividends (ordinary or exceptional), buying back shares on the market and carrying out a capital reduction are all ways of returning funds to shareholders, they have different consequences on the various parameters of a company.

There are five key criteria used by financial managers to decide which instrument would be best suited to achieving the desired result:

1. Flexibility

   Any large, sudden change in the size of the dividend paid is always tricky. It raises questions about the company's business model and creates shareholder expectations that they'll be getting the same sort of dividend on a recurring basis. Accordingly, increasing the size of ordinary dividend payments is usually a slow process and only impacts on the company's capital structure after several years.

   Capital reductions and extraordinary dividends are, however, one-off operations, that do not raise shareholder expectations of recurrence. They are thus very well suited to returning the proceeds of the disposal of a large asset to investors (e.g. the Enel distribution network in 2004) or to modifying the company's capital structure (Bouygues in 2005).

2. Signaling

   As all financial decisions may be taken as a signal by investors, companies should think carefully about how the market will perceive the instrument chosen for returning funds to shareholders.

   The extraordinary dividend sends out the most neutral signal. By definition, extraordinary dividends are one-off rather than recurrent, and accordingly carry no implicit judgment of the value of company's share, of which they are independent. Finally, all shareholders benefit from exceptional dividends.

   On the other hand, a change in the size of the dividend or a capital reduction are received by the market as clear signals. In the first case, positive expectations are created about future profits. A company that reduces its capital is sending out a signal about the value of its shares, as no company would buy back its shares if management believed that the company was currently overvalued.

3. Impact on the shareholder base

   The ordinary and the exceptional dividend have no impact on the shareholder base as they do not alter the number of shares in the company. A capital reduction and share buybacks will, however, affect the composition of the shareholder base, since some shareholders may well decide against participating in the capital reduction or selling their shares on the market during the period when the company is buying back shares. Their share in the capital will increase. Starting in 1999, the Peugeot family steadily increased its stake in the Peugeot group from 22.7% to 29.2%, by spending €2580m buying up shares on the market. Increasing the size of the ordinary dividend, which would be difficult in a sector that is as cyclical as the automotive sector, or paying an exceptional dividend, would obviously not modify the shareholder base.

4. The impact of management stock options

   If shares are bought at a price which exceeds their market value during a capital reduction, there are often statutory provisions for adjusting the exercise price of stock options which renders the operation neutral for the holders of stock options.

   However, most laws make no such provisions in the case of payments of dividends or exceptional dividends and share buybacks on the market. As exceptional dividends may drastically reduce the value of the share, the fact that the exercise price of stock options is not automatically adjusted explains why managers are not all that keen on them.

   A partial explanation for the strong decline since 2000 in the number of US companies paying a dividend (from 66% in 1978, to 21% in 1999) is the replacement of dividends with share buybacks, probably encouraged by stock option-holding managers. Paying a dividend results in the automatic reduction of the share price by the amount of the dividend and thus reduces the expected gain on stock options by as much, as their exercise price remains fixed. Share buybacks do not impact negatively on the value of stock options in this way, and there are even those naïve enough to believe that they could drive the share price up (since shares are being bought!). Some stock option holding managers sometimes lose sight of the fact that shareholders may need cash, and if they never get a dividend, they may have to sell their shares in order to get hold of it.

5. Tax

The tax issue should obviously not be overlooked as the tax impact may differ, depending on the method used to return funds to shareholders.

When dividends are more heavily taxed than capital gains, companies have a strong incentive to give back cash to their shareholders through share buybacks rather than dividends.

In the USA, the tax rate on dividends for individual taxpayers was reduced considerably in 2003, from the marginal income tax rate to 15%. This has resulted in dividends becoming a lot more attractive again. They are now more popular than share buybacks, which in 1999 and 2000 exceeded dividend payments for the first time.

References and Further Reading

Asquith, P. and Mullins, D., The impact of initiating dividend payments on shareholders' wealth, *Journal of Business*, 77–96, January 1983.

Baker, M. and Wurgler, J., A catering theory of dividends, *Journal of Finance*, **59**, 1125–1165, June 2004.

Baker, M. and Wurgler, J., Appearing and dividends: The link to catering incentives, *Journal of Financial Economics*, **73**, 271–288, August 2004.

Bhattacharya, S., Imperfect information, dividend policy and the bird in the hand fallacy, *Bell Journal of Economics*, 259–270, Summer 1979.

Black, F., The dividend puzzle, *Journal of Portfolio Management*, 634–639, Summer 1976.

Brav, L, Graham, J., Harvey, C. and Michaely, R., Payout policy in the 21st century, *Journal of Financial Economics*, **77** (3), 483–527, September 2005.

Chay, J and Suh, J., Payout policy and cash flow uncertainty, *Journal of Financial Economics*, **93**(1), 88–107, July, 2009.

DeAngelo, H., DeAngelo, L. and Skinner, D., Are dividends disappearing? Dividend concentration and the consolidation of earnings, *Journal of Financial Economics*, **72**, 425–456, December 2004.

DeAngelo, H. and DeAngelo, L., The irrelevance of the MM dividend irrelevance theorem, *Journal of Financial Economics*, **79** (2), 293–315, 2006.

Denis, D. and Osobov, I., Why do firms pay dividends? International evidence on the determinants of dividend policy, *Journal of Financial Economics*, 2009.

Desai, M., and Fritz Foley, C., Dividend policy inside the multinational firms, *Financial Management*, 5–26, Spring, 2007.

Dittmar, A., Why do firms repurchase stocks? *Journal of Business*, **73**(3), 331–355, July 2000.

Doron, N. and Amin, Z., Dividends changes and future profitability, *Journal of Finance*, **56**, 2111–2133, December 2001.

Easterbrook, F., Two agency-cost explanations of dividends, *American Economic Review*, **74**, 650–659, September 1984.

Fama, E. and French, K., Disappearing dividends: Changing firm characteristics or lower propensity to pay? *Journal of Financial Economics*, **60**, 3–43, April 2001.

Fama, E. and French, K., Testing trade-off and pecking order prediction about dividends and debt, *The Review of Financial Studies*, **15**, 1–33, Spring 2002.

Ginglinger, E. and Hamon, J., Actual Share Repurchase, Timing and Liquidity, *Journal of Banking and Finance*, **31**(3), 915–938, 2007.

Graham, J. and Kumar, A., Do dividend clientele exist? Evidence on dividend preferences of retail investors, *Journal of Financial Economics*, **61** (3), 1305–1336, June 2006.

Grinstein, Y. and Michaeli, R., Institutional holdings and payout policy, *Journal of Finance*, **60** (3), 1389–1426, June 2005.

Grullon, G. and Michaely, R., The information content of share repurchase programs, *Journal of Finance*, **59** (2), 651–680, April 2004.

Jagannathan, M., Stephens, C. and Weisbach, M., Financial flexibility and the choice between dividends and stock repurchases, *Journal of Financial Economics*, **57**, 355–384, September 2000.

Jensen, M., Agency costs of free cash flow, corporate finance and takeovers, *American Economic Review*, **76**(2), 323–329, May 1986.

Julio, B. and Ikenberry, D., Reappearing dividends, *Journal of Applied Corporate Finance*, **16** (4), 89–100, Fall 2004.

Lambert, R., Lanen, W. and Larcker, D., Executive stock option plans and corporate dividend policy, *Journal of Financial and Quantitative Analysis*, **24**, 406–425, December 1989.

La Porta, R., Lopez-de-Silanes, F. and Shleifer, A., Agency problems and dividend policies around the world, *Journal of Finance*, **55**(1), 1–33, February 2000.

Li, W. and Lie, E., Dividend changes and catering incentives, *Journal of Financial Economics*, **80**(2), 293–308, 2006.

Lintner, J., Distribution of incomes of corporations among dividends, retained earnings and taxes, *American Economic Review*, **46**(2), 97–116, May, 1956.

Mikkelson, W. and Partch, M., Do persistent large cash reserves hinder performance? *Journal of Financial and Quantitative Analysis*, **38**, 275–294, June 2003.

Miller, M. and Modigliani, F., Dividend policy, growth, and the valuation of shares, *Journal of Business*, **34**, 411–433, January 1961.

Miller, M. and Scholes, M., Dividends and taxes, *Journal of Financial Economics*, **6**, 332–364, December 1978.

42. What are share buybacks and how do they work?

Short Answer

A company may in certain circumstances buy back its own shares and either keep them on the balance sheet or cancel them, in which case there is said to be a capital decrease or capital reduction.

Example

Table 1.37: Fifty share buybacks of European companies in 2010

	Group	2010 Share buy-backs (cm)	As % of end-of-year market capitalization	Dividends paid in 2010 (cm)	2010 share buy back and dividend paid (cm)	As % of the market (cm)
1	TELEFONICA	802	1.0%	5 218	6 020	7.6%
2	TOTAL	0	0.0%	5 093	5 093	5.4%
3	SANTANDER	172	0.2%	4 919	5 091	6.6%
4	GDF SUEZ	499	0.8%	3 257	3 756	6.2%
5	FRANCE TELECOM	2	0.0%	3 705	3 707	8.6%
6	ENI	0	0.0%	3 622	3 622	5.5%
7	SANOFI-AVENTIS	328	0.5%	3 131	3 459	5.2%
8	DEUTSCHE TELEKOM	2	0.5%	3 386	3 388	7.9%
9	ENEL	0	0.0%	2 959	2 959	8.1%
10	E ON	0	0.0%	2 858	2 858	5.8%
11	UNIBAIL-RODAMCO	0	0.0%	2 564	2 564	21.1%
12	RWE	28	0.1%	1 867	1 895	6.3%
13	BBVA	280	0.7%	1 574	1 854	4.4%
14	ALLIANZ	−6	0.0%	1 850	1 844	4.7%
15	BNP PARIBAS	47	0.1%	1 778	1 825	2.9%
16	CARREFOUR	1 025	4.1%	740	1 765	7.0%

Table 1.37: (*continued*)

Group	2010 Share buy-backs (cm)	As % of end-of-year market capitalization	Dividends paid in 2010 (cm)	2010 share buy back and dividend paid (cm)	As % of the market (cm)
17 VIVENDI	0	0.0%	1 721	1 721	7.3%
18 BASF	0	0.0%	1 561	1 561	3.6%
19 NOKIA	−1	0.0%	1 519	1 518	4.8%
20 IBERDROLA	24	0.1%	1 469	1 493	4.9%
21 SIEMENS	0	0.0%	1 388	1 388	2.0%
22 MUENCHENER RUCK.	250	1.2%	1 072	1 322	6.4%
23 REPSOL YPF	0	0.0%	1 254	1 254	5.6%
24 UNILEVER CERTS.	0	0.0%	1 254	1 254	3.7%
25 AXA	0	0.0%	1 245	1 245	3.8%
26 BAYER	0	0.0%	1 159	1 159	2.8%
27 INTESA SANPAOLO	−4	0.0%	1 124	1 120	3.8%
28 DEUTSCHE BANK	616	1.5%	465	1 081	2.6%
29 CREDIT AGRICOLE	−7	0.0%	1 039	1 032	3.9%
30 TELECOM ITALIA	−67	−0.5%	1 061	994	7.2%
31 DANONE	205	0.7%	737	942	3.3%
32 L'OREAL	0	0.0%	879	879	1.8%
33 LVMH	71	0.2%	784	855	1.8%
34 VINCI	0	0.0%	850	850	4.0%
35 SAP	220	0.5%	594	814	1.9%
36 AIR LIQUIDE	3	0.0%	609	612	2.5%
37 GENERALI	0	0.0%	545	545	2.2%
38 ANHEUSER-BUSCH INBEV	−75	−0.1%	605	530	0.8%
39 SCHNEIDER ELECTRIC	0	0.0%	530	530	2.2%
40 SAINT GOBAIN	0	0.0%	509	509	2.8%
41 CRH	0	0.0%	435	435	3.8%
42 DEUTSCHE BOERSE	0	0.0%	391	391	3.9%
43 ALSTOM	0	0.0%	364	364	3.0%
44 SOCIETE GENERALE	124	0.4%	182	306	1.0%
45 PHILIPS	−65	−0.3%	296	231	1.0%
46 DAIMLER	54	0.1%	0	54	0.1%

(*continued overleaf*)

Table 1.37: (*continued*)

Group	2010 Share buy-backs (cm)	As % of end-of-year market capitalization	Dividends paid in 2010 (cm)	2010 share buy back and dividend paid (cm)	As % of the market (cm)
47 AEGON	0	0.0%	0	0	0.0%
48 ING	−26	−0.1%	0	−26	−0.1%
49 ARCELORMITTAL	−1 027	−2.6%	873	−154	−0.4%
50 UNICREDIT	−3 916	−10.5%	550	−3 366	−9.0%
Total	−442	0.0%	75 586	75 143	4.5%

Long Answer

We know that no earnings retention policy is attractive unless the company can invest its funds at a rate of return greater than or equal to the weighted average cost of capital. Let us take the reasoning here to its logical extreme. Every euro reinvested by the company must earn at least the rate of return required by providers of funds; if it does not, value will be destroyed. Rather than destroy value, it is better to return that euro to the owners.

From a theoretical viewpoint, when a business no longer has any investment projects that are sufficiently profitable, it should not only pay out all its earnings but also return all or part of its equity capital.

Equity capital is also needed to finance the risk of the business. Without it, the company could find itself in a serious cash crisis at the first downturn in the economy. On the other hand, when the company has acquired a strategic position in its market strong enough to ensure continued profitability and value, the normal course of action is to reduce equity financing and increase debt. Free cash flow has become sure enough to support the regular fixed repayments required on borrowings.

Equity capital serves to bear business risk. When that risk appears under control, equity can normally be replaced in part by debt capital.

A capital decrease corresponding to a distribution of cash can be accomplished in a number of ways.

- **By reducing the par value of all shares**, thereby automatically reducing authorized capital.
- **By buying back shares on the open market**. The shares acquired may be cancelled and the purchase cost deducted from the par value of the repurchased shares, with any excess cost charged against distributable reserves. The repurchased shares may also be kept in treasury by the company to serve as acquisition currency or to fulfill the exercise of stock options held by employees. Lastly, they can be sold on the open market for the purpose of stabilizing the share price. If the shares are not cancelled, however, the repurchases cannot really be described as a capital decrease.

  On the company's books, repurchased shares appear on the consolidated balance sheet as marketable securities if they were acquired for the purpose of stabilizing the share price or fulfilling employee stock options. In all other cases, the purchase cost is subtracted from shareholders' equity. Under IAS and US accounting standards, repurchased shares are always deducted from consolidated equity.
- **By tender offer**. In practice, the board of directors, using an authorization that must have been granted to it at an extraordinary general meeting, makes an offer to all shareholders to buy all or part of their shares at a certain price during a certain period (usually about one month). If too many shares are tendered under the offer, the company scales back all the surrender requests in proportion. If too

few are tendered, it cancels the shares that are tendered. If management decides on a tender offer, it has the option of considering the traditional fixed-price offering or the *Dutch auction method*. In Dutch auctions, the firm no longer offers to repurchase shares at a single price, but rather announces a *range* of prices. Each shareholder thus must specify an acceptable selling price within the prescribed range set by the company. If the shareholder chooses a high selling price, he or she will increase the proceeds provided the shares are accepted by the company, but reduces the probability that shares will be accepted for repurchase. At the end of the offer period, the firm tabulates the received offers, and determines the lowest price that allows repurchasing the desired number of shares. The French food and facilities management company Sodexo used this technique in 2008, for example.

In some other European countries, a share buyback can be accomplished by issuing *put warrants* to each shareholder, each warrant giving the holder the right to sell one share to the company at a specified price.

A capital decrease changes the capital structure and thereby increases the risk borne by creditors. To protect the latter, law generally allows creditors to require additional guarantees or call their loans early, although they cannot block the operation outright.

Jagannathan et al. (2000) have measured the growth in open market stock repurchases and the manner in which stock repurchases and dividends are used by US corporations. Stock repurchases and dividends are used at different times from one another, by different kinds of firms. Stock repurchases are very pro-cyclical, while dividends increase steadily over time. Dividends are paid by firms with higher 'permanent' operating cash flows, while repurchases are used by firms with higher 'temporary', non-operating cash flows.

Repurchasing firms also have much more volatile cash flows and distributions.

Finally, firms repurchase stock following poor stock market performance and increase dividends following good performance. These results are consistent with the view that the flexibility inherent in repurchase programs is one reason why they are sometimes used instead of dividends.

Several different considerations might explain why a company would buy back its own shares.

- Absence of opportunities to invest at the required rate of return. Managers therefore pass the funds to shareholders, who take it upon themselves to find investments elsewhere that meet their requirements.
- Signaling good news (managers believe the shares are undervalued).
- Increasing financial leverage, to take fuller advantage of the corresponding tax break (not very persuasive!).
- Direct tax incentive: if the object is to transfer cash from the business to shareholders, it is more tax-efficient to buy back shares than to pay a dividend.
- Hurting creditors: buying back shares increases the risk of the business and therefore diminishes the value of its debt. Creditors may try to block it.
- Transferring value between shareholders who decline the offer for reasons of power (they want to increase their stake in the company) and shareholders who agree to sell back their shares at a price exceeding their value.

Empirical analysis confirms that share buybacks are mainly undertaken for signaling purposes. On this point, Jagganathan et al. (2000) have established that, compared with dividends, share buybacks give little indication of future earnings. Companies that raise their dividends do in fact see their earnings increase, but this is not the case when companies buy back shares. In a way, declaring a dividend represents an undertaking by the company's managers to maintain that dividend, whereas a share buyback entails no such moral commitment. Thus, cyclical businesses are more likely to use share buybacks than businesses with steady growth.

Dittmar (2000) has investigated the relation between stock repurchases and distribution, investment, capital structure, corporate control and compensation policies over the 1977–1996 period. He finds that firms repurchase stock to take advantage of potential undervaluation and, in many periods, to distribute excess capital. However, firms also repurchase stock during certain periods to alter their leverage ratio, fend off takeovers, and counter the dilution effects of stock options.

Grullon and Ikenberry (2000) argue that repurchases add value in two main ways:

1. for the tax efficiency in returning excess capital to shareholders;
2. for the signal managers send to investors about their belief that the company is undervalued.

If stock repurchase and dividends serve the same economic function, why is repurchasing popularity growing so rapidly? Basically for two reasons:

- they are more efficient tax wise in distributing excess capital; and
- they provide corporate managers with the flexibility to make small adjustments in the capital structure in order to correct perceived undervaluation of the firm's shares.

A capital decrease by itself does not reduce a company's cost of capital and thus cannot create value. At best, it can avoid value destruction by preventing the company from investing cash at less than the cost of equity.

Only if the company manages to buy back its shares at less than they are worth could it hope to create value. The theory of markets in equilibrium leaves little hope of being able to do this.

A share buyback should nowadays be regarded as a normal transaction.

The message that it signals is this: the company's managers take the shareholders' interest to heart and exceptionally, for want of adequate investment opportunities, they are paying out part of a large cash flow to avoid destroying value.

Because the announcement of a share buyback draws media attention, it probably has more impact than an increase in the dividend – even one that might signal a lasting change in the company's dividend policy.

Repurchase of shares by the company results in:

- an increase in earnings per share (accretion) whenever the reciprocal of P/E is greater than the after-tax rate of interest paid on incremental debt (or earned on short-term debt securities). If E/P is less than the rate of interest, there is a decrease in earnings per share (dilution);
- an increase in the book value of equity per share whenever book value per share before the purchase is greater than the purchase price per share.

Bear in mind that, although the calculation of the change in EPS is of interest, it is not an indicator of value creation. The real issue is not whether a capital decrease will mechanically dilute EPS, but whether:

- the price at which the shares are repurchased is less than their estimated value;

- the increase in the debt burden will translate into better performance by management; and
- the marginal rate of return on the funds returned to shareholders by the buyback was less than the cost of capital.

These are the three sources of value creation in a capital decrease.

References and Further Reading

Dittmar, A., Why do firms repurchase stocks? *Journal of Business*, **73**(3), 331–355, July 2000.

Grullon, G. and Ikenberry, D., What do we know about stock repurchases? *Journal of Applied Corporate Finance*, **13**(1), 31–51, Spring 2000.

Jagannathan, M., Stephens, C. and Weisbach, M., Financial flexibility and the choice between dividends and stock repurchases, *Journal of Financial Economics*, **57**, 355–384, September 2000.

43. What is the dilution of control in a capital increase?

Short Answer

Dilution of control is the reduction of rights in the company sustained by a shareholder for which the capital increase entails neither an outflow nor an inflow of funds.

Example

To illustrate, consider company *E* with equity capital worth €1000m split between two shareholders, *F* (80%) and *G* (20%).

If *G* sells his entire shareholding (€200m) to *H*, neither the value nor the proportion of *F*'s equity in the company is changed. If, on the other hand, *H* is a new shareholder brought in by means of a capital increase, he will have to put in €250m to obtain a 20% interest, rather than €200m as previously, since the value of equity after a capital increase of €250m is €1250m (1000 + 250). The new shareholder's interest is indeed 20% of the larger amount. Percentage interest should always be reckoned on the value including the newly issued shares.

After this capital increase has been made to the €1000m base, the value of *F*'s shareholding in the company is the same as it was (€800m) but his ownership percentage has decreased from 80% to 64% (800/1250), while *G*'s has decreased from 20% to 16%.

We see that if a shareholder does not participate in a capital increase, his percentage interest declines. This effect is called dilution.

In contrast, if the capital increase is reserved entirely for *F*, his percentage interest in the company rises from 80% to 84% (1050/1250), and the equity interest of all other shareholder(s) is necessarily diluted.

Lastly, if *F* and *G* each take part in the capital increase in exact proportion to their current shareholding, the market value of equity no longer matters in this one particular case. Their ownership percentages remain the same, and each puts up the same amount of funds for new shares regardless of the market value. This is illustrated in Table 1.38 for equity

Table 1.38: Ownership percentages

(€ million)	Value of equity in *E*	Value of shares held by *F*	Value of shares held by *G*	Value of shares held by *H*
Before capital increase	1000	800 or 80%	200 or 20%	
G sells 20% of the shares to *H* for 200	1000	800 or 80%	0 or 0% (+200)	200 or 20% (–200)
H subscribes to a cash capital increase of 250	1250	800 or 64%	200 or 16%	250 or 20% (–250)
G sells 20% of the shares to *F* for 200	1000	1000 or 100% (–200)	0 or 0% (+200)	
F subscribes to a cash capital increase of 250	1250	1050 or 84% (–250)	200 or 16%	
F and *G* subscribe to a cash capital increase of 250 in proportion to their ownership percentage at different initial values of equity (1000, 2000 and 500, respectively)	1250	1000 or 80% (–200)	250 or 20% (–50)	
	2250	1800 or 80% (–200)	450 or 20% (–50)	
	750	600 or 80% (–200)	150 or 20% (–50)	

values of €500m, €1000m and €2000m. In effect, *F* and *G* are selling new shares to themselves.

Long Answer

Returning to the example, we see that there is dilution of control – that is, reduction in the percentage equity interest of certain shareholders, whenever those shareholders do not subscribe to an issue of new shares in proportion to their current shareholding.

The dilution is greatest for any shareholder who does not participate at all in the capital increase. It is nil for any shareholder who subscribes in proportion to his or her holding.

Recall that if new shares are issued at a price significantly below their value, current shareholders will usually have pre-emptive subscription rights that enable them to buy the new shares at that price. This right of first refusal is itself tradable and can be acquired by investors who would like to become shareholders on the occasion of the capital increase.

In the absence of subscription rights, the calculation of dilution of control by a capital increase is straightforward:

$$\frac{\text{Number of new shares}}{\text{Number of new shares} + \text{Number of old shares}}$$

When the capital increase is made with an issue of pre-emptive subscription rights, this calculation no longer holds.

With a rights issue of this kind, we have to distinguish between three measures of dilution. *The most important of these is real dilution, which is equivalent to what we just now called dilution (with no modifier) in the absence of pre-emptive subscription rights.*

Any capital increase with subscription rights gives rise to *apparent dilution* (sometimes called 'overall dilution'), which is expressed by the ratio:

$$\frac{\text{Number of new shares}}{\text{Number of new shares} + \text{Number of old shares}} = \frac{N'}{N + N'}$$

In the case of a rights issue, this degree of dilution is only apparent because it is the result of two distinct transactions:

- a capital increase in the strict sense; and
- a detachment of subscription rights, which is analyzed as a distribution of bonus shares.

Subscription rights enable current shareholders to participate partially in the capital increase with no outlay of funds. As a result, the dilution of their ownership is not as great as the apparent dilution would make it appear.

We therefore need to calculate the dilution due solely to the capital increase, independently of the subscription rights mechanism. This degree of dilution is called *real dilution* and, in the analysis of the capital increase, real dilution is what we are interested in knowing.

Real dilution is the dilution of control that occurs when the capital increase is cash neutral for a shareholder who, on balance, neither pays nor receives any funds: the shareholder sells a portion of his subscription rights in order to buy new shares.

Method 1

The simplest way to calculate real dilution is to reckon on an aggregate basis rather than per share. Real dilution is then calculated as follows:

$$\text{Real dilution} = \frac{\text{Proceeds of capital increase}}{\text{Value of equity before capital increase} + \text{Proceeds of capital increase}}$$

Method 2
Regardless of the formal issue price, the existence of subscription rights ensures that the capital increase will always be subscribed at the company's market value.

Every new shareholder will have to pay the issue price and the price of one or more rights in order to obtain one new share. Therefore, to calculate real dilution eliminating the bias due to subscription rights, one need only assume that the issue price is equal to the market value of the shares.

The theoretical number n' of shares that would have been issued under these conditions is:

$$n' = \frac{\text{Proceeds of the issue}}{\text{Market value of each share}}$$

Real dilution is then equal to $n'/(N + n')$ where n' is the number of shares that would have brought in the same funds if the issue price had been equal to the market value.

Technical dilution is apparent dilution less real dilution. It is due to the distribution of 'free' bonus shares that automatically accompanies any capital increase via a rights issue.

Technical dilution represents the additional dilution attributable to the sale of subscription rights by shareholders who take the occasion of the capital increase to reduce their investment in the company.

As with any distribution of bonus shares, the various parameters of the company – EPS, dividend per share, value of the share – must be adjusted to correct for this technical aspect of the operation, which in no way changes the value of the company.

Anticipation mechanism. Take the example of a highly profitable company, entirely equity-financed, that now has investments of 100. With these investments, the company is on track to be worth 400 in four years, which corresponds to an annual rate of return on equity of 41.4%. Suppose that this company can invest an additional 100 at a rate of return similar to that on its current investments. To finance this additional capital requirement, it must sell new shares.

Suppose also that the shareholder-required rate of return is 10%.

Before the company announces the capital increase and before the market anticipates it, the value of its equity capital four years hence is going to be 400 which, discounted at 10%, is 273 today.

If, upon the announcement of the capital increase, management succeeds in convincing the market that the company will indeed be worth 800 in four years, which is 546 today, the value accruing to current shareholders is 546 – 100 = 446. There is thus instantaneous value creation of 173 (446 – 273) for the old shareholders.

The anticipation mechanism operates in such a way that new shareholders will not receive an excess rate of return. They will get only the return they require, which is 10%. If the intended use of funds is clearly indicated when the capital increase is announced, the share price *before* the capital increase will reflect the investment opportunities, and only the old shareholders will benefit from the value creation arising from them.

Some share prices that show very high P/E ratios are merely reflecting anticipation of exceptional investment opportunities. The 400 of added value in this example is already priced in. The reader will himself be able to observe companies whose share prices are at times so high that they cannot correspond to growth opportunities financed in the traditional way by operating cash flow and borrowing. The shareholders of these companies have placed a bet on the internal and external growth opportunities the company may be able to seize, as it may have done in the past, financed in part by issuing new shares.

References and Further Reading

Asquith, P. and Mullins, D., Equity issues and offering dilution, *Journal of Financial Economics*, **15**(1), 61–89, January–February 1986.

DeAngelo, H., DeAngelo, L. and Stulz, R., Seasoned equity offerings, market timing and the corporate lifecycle? *Journal of Financial Economics*, **95**(3), 275–295, February–March 2010.

Dittmar, A. and Thakor, A., Why do firms issue equity? *Journal of Finance*, **62** (1), 1–54, February 2007.

Loughran, T. and Ritter, J., The new issues puzzle, *Journal of Finance*, **50**, 23–51, March 1995.

Masulis, R. and Korwar, A., Seasoned equity offerings: An empirical investigation, *Journal of Financial Economics*, **15**(1), 91–118, January–February 1986.

44. How many different types of shareholders do we know?

Short Answer

There are (at least) seven different types of shareholders:

1. The family-owned company
2. Business angels
3. Private equity funds
4. Institutional investors
5. Financial holding companies
6. Employee-shareholders
7. Governments

Example

Table 1.39: Different types of shareholders in Europe

	Europe (%)	France (%)	Germany (%)	UK (%)	Italy (%)	Spain (%)
Free float	37	14	10	63	13	26
Family and non-listed shareholder	44	65	65	24	60	56
State	4	5	6	0	10	4
Other listed company	2	4	4	1	3	2
Financial institution	9	11	9	9	12	12
Cross shareholding	1	1	3	0	1	0
Other	3	0	3	3	1	0
By size (% with the free float as the largest shareholder)						
20 largest	45	60	45	90	35	45
50 mid-sized	29	14	10	65	8	34
50 smallest	25	8	14	42	14	36

Source: Faccio and Lang (2002).

Long Answer

The family-owned company
By 'family-owned' we mean that the shareholders have been made up of members of the same family for several generations and, often through a holding company, exert significant influence over management. This is still the dominant model in Europe.

Faccio and Lang (2002) analyzed the ultimate ownership of 5232 firms across western Europe and concluded that over 44% of firms are still family-owned. British firms are mostly widely held (63% versus 24% family-owned) and the majority of continental European firms are family-owned (except in northern Europe where ownership is more balanced).

However, this type of shareholder structure is on the decline for several reasons:

- Some new or capital-intensive industries, such as telecoms, media and energy/utilities, require so much capital that a family-owned structure is not viable. Indeed, family ownership is more suited to consumer goods, retailing, services, processing, etc.
- Financial markets have matured and financial savings are now properly rewarded, so that, with rare exceptions, diversification is a better investment strategy than concentration on a specific risk.
- Increasingly, family-owned companies are being managed on the basis of financial criteria, prompting the family group either to exit the capital or to dilute the family's interests in a larger pool of investors that it no longer controls.

Lastly, there are generally no tax incentives for a company to remain family-owned. In fact, family members who are passive investors in the company may be penalized though inheritance taxes and wealth taxes.

Business angels

Business angels are generally former executives or majority shareholders. They invest a few tens or hundreds of thousands of euros, bringing advice and their networks to help entrepreneurs to launch their companies. Some get lucky, like the business angels that financed Facebook when it was based in a Harvard University student's room. Their failure rate is very high as they invest at the most risky stage of a company's life.

Private equity funds

Today, private equity funds, financed by insurance companies, pension funds or wealthy investors, play a major role. In most cases these funds specialize in a certain type of investment: venture capital, development capital and LBOs, which correspond to different companies' different stages of maturity.

Venture capital funds focus on bringing seed capital, i.e. equity, to startups to finance their early developments, or to struggling companies, buying their debts to take them over and restructure them.

Development capital funds give an acquisitive company in a consolidating market the financial resources it needs to achieve its goals.

LBO funds invest in companies put up for sale by a group looking to refocus on its core business or by a family-held group faced with succession problems, or help a company whose shares are depressed (in the opinion of the management) to delist itself in a public to private (P-to-P) transaction. LBO funds are keen to get full control over a company in order to reap all of the rewards and also to make it possible to restructure the company as they think best, without having to worry about the interests of minority shareholders.

Some private equity funds take a minority stake in listed companies, a PIPE (private investment in public equity), helping the management to revitalize the company so as to make a capital gain. Thus, in 2007 and 2008, Wendel bought a 20% stake in Saint-Gobain.

Managed by teams of investment professionals whose compensation is linked to performance, these funds have a limited life span (no more than ten years). Before the fund is closed, the companies that the fund has acquired are resold, floated on the stock exchange or the fund's investments are taken over by another fund.

Private equity funds are playing a growing role in the economy and are a real alternative for a listing on the stock exchange. They solve agency problems by putting in place strict reporting from the management which is incentivized through management packages and the pressure of debt (LBO funds).

They also bring a cash culture to optimize working capital management and limit capital expenditure to reasonably value-creating investments. Private equity funds are ready to bring additional equity to finance acquisitions with an industrial logic. They also bring to management a capacity to listen, to advise and to exchange which is far greater than that provided by most institutional investors. They are professional shareholders who have only one aim – to create value – and they do not hesitate to align the management of companies they invest in with that objective.

Institutional investors
Institutional investors are banks, insurance companies, pension funds and unit trusts that manage money on behalf of private individuals.

Collectively they can be the longest-standing shareholder of many listed companies and play mainly a passive role. However, new regulations on corporate governance may push them to vote at annual general meetings to defeat some resolutions they do not like (share issue without pre-emption rights, voting limits, too generous stock option plans, etc).

Some of them have started to play a far more active role and are called *activity funds*. They publicly put pressure on underperforming managements, suggesting corrective measures to improve value creation. One of them, TCI, prompted the dismantling of ABN-Amro in 2007.

Financial holding companies
Large European financial holding companies such as Deutsche Bank, Paribas, Mediobanca, Société Générale de Belgique, etc. played a major role in creating and financing large groups. In a sense, they played the role of (then-deficient) capital markets.

Their gradual disappearance or mutation has led to the breakup of core shareholder groups and cross-shareholdings. Today, in emerging countries (e.g. Korea, India, Colombia) large industrial and financial conglomerates play their role (e.g. Samsung, Tata).

Employee-shareholders
Many companies have invited their employees to become shareholders. In most of these cases, employees hold a small proportion of the shares, although the majority in a few cases. This shareholder group, loyal and non-volatile, lends a

degree of stability to the capital and, in general, strengthens the position of the majority shareholder, if any, and of the management.

The main schemes to incentivize employees are:

- **Direct ownership**. Employees and management can invest directly in the shares of the company. In LBOs, private equity sponsors bring the management into the shareholding structure to minimize agency costs.
- **Employee Stock Ownership Programs (ESOPs)**. ESOPs consist in granting shares to employees as a form of compensation. Alternatively, the shares are acquired by shareholders but the firm will offer free shares so as to encourage employees to invest in the shares of the company. The shares will be held by a trust (or employee savings plan) for the employees. Such a program can include *lock-up clauses* to maintain the incentive aspect and limit flow-back. In that case the shares allocated to each employee will vest (i.e. become available) gradually over time.
- **Stock options**. Stock options are a right to subscribe to new (or existing) shares at a certain point in time.

For service companies and fast-growing companies, it is key to incentivize employees and management with shares or stock options. For other companies, offering stock to employees can be part of a broader effort to improve employee relations (all types of companies) and promote the company's image internally. The success of such a policy largely depends on the overall corporate mood. Bears Stern, the US investment bank, was one of the listed companies with the largest employee shareholdings (c. 33%) when it melted down in 2008.

Regardless of the type of company and its motivation for making employees shareholders, the reader should keep in mind that the special relationship between the company and the employee-shareholder cannot last forever. Prudent investment principles dictate that the employee should not invest too heavily in the shares of the company that pays their salaries, because in so doing they in fact compound the 'everyday life' risks they are running.

Basically, the company should be particularly fast-growing and safe before the employee agrees to a long-term participation in the fruits of its expansion. Most often, this condition is not met. Moreover, just because employees hold stock options does not mean they will be loyal or long-term shareholders. In a crisis, the employees may be keener to protect their jobs than to vote for a painful restructuring.

Governments

In Europe, governments' role as the major shareholders of listed groups is fading even if they are still playing a key role in some groups like Deutsche Telekom, EADS, EDF and ENI.

At the same time, *sovereign wealth funds* (SWFs), mostly created by emerging countries and financed thanks to reserves from staples, are gaining importance as long-term shareholders.

They are normally very financially minded, but their opacity, their size (often above €50bn or €100bn) or their strong connections with mostly undemocratic states are worrying some. The most well known SWFs are, for example, GIC and Temasek (Singapore), Adia (Abu Dhabi) and KIA (Kuwait).

References and Further Reading

Almeida, H. and Wolfenzon, D., A theory of pyramidal ownership and family business groups, *Journal of Finance*, **61**(6), 2637–2680, December 2006.

Brow, A., Wei, J., Partnoy, F. and Thomas, R., Hedge fund activism, corporate governance and firm performance, *Journal of Finance*, **63**(4), 1729–1775, August 2008.

Faccio, M. and Lang, L., The ultimate ownership of western European corporations, *Journal of Financial Economics*, **65**(3), 365–395, September 2002.

Hellwege, J, Pirinski, C. and Stulz, R., Why do firms become widely held? An analysis of the dynamics of corporate ownership, *Journal of Finance*, **62**(3), 995–1028, June 2007.

Jensen, M., Eclipse of the public corporation, *Harvard Business Review*, **67**, 61–74, September 1989.

Maury, B., Family ownership and firm performance: Empirical evidence from Western European corporations, *Journal of Corporate Finance*, **12**(12), 321–341, January 2006.

Morck, R. et al. *History of Corporate Ownership: The Rise and Fall of a Great Business Family*, NBER, 2004.

Myers, S., Outside equity, *Journal of Finance*, **55**, 1005–1037, 2000.

Villalonga, B. and Amit, R., How do family ownership, control and management affect firm value? *Journal of Financial Economics*, **2**, 385–417, May 2006.

45. Why do companies go public?

Short Answer

A stock exchange listing offers distinct benefits: it enables financial managers to access capital markets and obtain the market value for their companies.

Example

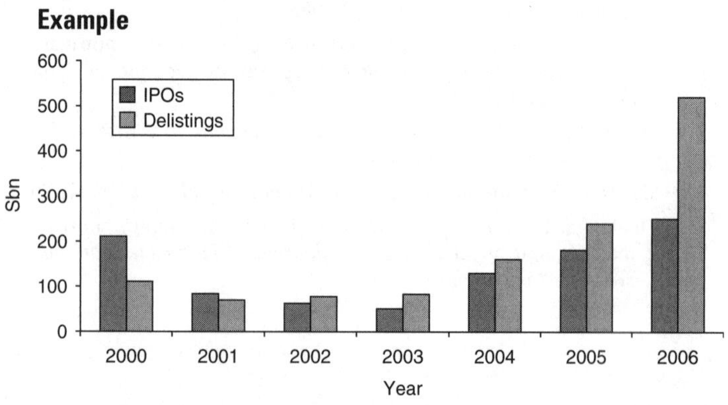

Figure 1.45: IPOs and delisting (in $bn)

Long Answer

Whether or not to float a company on the stock exchange is a question that first and foremost concerns the shareholders rather than the company. But technically, it is the company that requests a listing on the stock exchange.

When a company is listed, its shareholders' investments become more liquid, but the difference for shareholders between a listed company and a non-listed company is not always that significant. Companies listed on the market gain liquidity at the time of the listing, since a significant part of the equity is floated. But thereafter, only few shares are usually traded every day, unless the market 'falls in love' with the company and a long-term relationship begins.

An IPO is always to the advantage of the minority shareholders.

In addition to real or potential liquidity, a stock market listing gives the minority shareholder a level of protection that no shareholders' agreement can provide. The company must publish certain information; the market also expects a consistent dividend policy. If the majority shareholders sell their stake, the rights of minority shareholders are protected.

Conversely, a listing complicates life for the majority shareholder (see Figure 1.45). Liquidity gives majority shareholders the opportunity to sell some of their shares in the market without losing control of the company. Listing can also allow the majority shareholder to get rid of a bothersome or restless minority shareholder by providing a forum for the minority shareholders to sell their shares in an orderly manner. But, in return, a majority shareholder will no longer be able to ignore financial parameters such as P/E multiples, EPS, dividends per share, etc. when determining his or her strategy.

Once a majority shareholder has taken the company public, investors will judge the company on its ability to create value and communicate financial information properly.

Delisting a company to take it private again is a long, drawn-out process.

For the company, a stock market listing presents several advantages:

- *the company becomes widely known to other stakeholders (customers, suppliers, etc.).* If the company communicates well, the listing constitutes a superb form of 'free' advertising, on an international scale;
- the company can tap the financial markets for additional funding and acquire other companies, using its shares as currency. This constitutes invaluable flexibility for the company;
- *the company finds it easier to incentivize employees in the success of the company* through stock options, stock-based bonuses, etc.;
- in a group, a mother company can obtain a market value for a subsidiary by listing it, in the hope that the value will be high enough to have a positive impact on the value of the parent company's shares.

Now for the warning flags: a stock market listing does not guarantee happy shareholders. If only a small percentage of the shares are traded, or if total market capitalization is low, i.e. less than €500m, large institutional investors will not be interested, especially if the company is not included in a benchmark index. Volatility on the shares will then be relatively high because the presence of just a few buyers (or sellers) can easily drive up (or down) the share price significantly.

A company may consider a public to private move – a delisting – when the reasons why it initially decided to list its shares start to become irrelevant. It has to weigh the cost of listing against the benefits of listing when deciding whether the company should remain listed or not. This is especially the case if:

1. the company no longer needs large amounts of outside capital and shareholders themselves are able to meet any

requirements it may have. The company no longer has any ambition to raise capital on the market or to pay for acquisitions in shares;

2. the stock exchange no longer provides minority shareholders with sufficient liquidity (which is often rapidly the case for smaller companies which only really benefit from liquidity at the time of their IPO). Listing then becomes a theoretical issue and institutional investors lose interest in the share;
3. the company no longer needs the stock exchange in order to increase awareness of its products or services.

Another reason for delisting is financial. Large shareholders, whether majority shareholders or not, may consider that the price does not reflect the intrinsic value of the company. Turning a problem into an opportunity, they could offer minority shareholders an exit, thus granting a larger share of the creation of future value for themselves.

A public tender offer must be launched in order to delist a company. Delisting is possible if the majority shareholder exceeds specific ownership thresholds, above which he or she is then obliged to acquire the rest of the shares. This is known as a *squeeze-out*. In practice, this pushes minority shareholders to sell any outstanding shares. The price of the operation is analyzed very closely by the market regulator. In most countries, a fairness opinion has to be drawn up by an independent, qualified financial expert.

But let's not delude ourselves – no matter how the company's shares have performed, minority shareholders will insist that the price they're offered reflects the intrinsic value of their shares. If it doesn't, they won't tender their shares in the offer. Accordingly, it is not surprising to note that, even though there is no change in control, tender offers launched for the purpose of delisting a company are made at a premium that is equivalent to the premium paid for takeovers.

If an investor is below the squeeze-out threshold, he or she has first to launch an offer on the company's shares, hoping to go above the squeeze-out threshold so as to be able to take the company private. It is a P-to-P, public-to-private deal.

Being listed is never a dead-end because a company can become private again and come back on to the stock exchange years later.

References and Further Reading

Brau, J. and Fawcett, S., Initial public offerings: An analysis of theory and practice, *Journal of Finance*, **61**(1), 399–436, February 2006.

Pastor, L. and Veronesi, P., Rational IPO waves, *Journal of Finance*, **60**(4), 1713–1757, August 2005.

Subrahmanyam, A. and Titman, S., The going public decision and the development of financial markets, *Journal of Finance*, **54**(3), 1045–1082, June 1999.

46. How can the control of a company be strengthened?

Short Answer

Defensive measures fall into four categories:

1. Separate management control from financial control:
   - different classes of shares: shares with multiple voting rights and non-voting shares;
   - holding companies;
   - limited partnerships.
2. Control shareholder changes:
   - right of approval;
   - pre-emption rights.
3. Strengthen the position of current loyal shareholders:
   - reserved capital increases;
   - share buybacks and cancellations;
   - mergers and other tie-ups;
   - employee shareholdings;
   - shareholders' rights plan.
4. Exploit legal and regulatory protection:
   - regulations;
   - voting caps;
   - strategic assets;
   - change of control provisions.

The reader should be aware that defensive measures for maintaining control of a company always carry some costs. They are not only linked to the cost of putting in place the appropriate measures, but also to the preclusion from accessing certain financial instruments.

These costs are borne by current shareholders and ultimately by the company itself in the form of a higher cost of capital.

Long Answer

Separate management control from financial control

Different classes of shares: shares with multiple voting rights and non-voting shares As an exception to the general rule, under which the number of votes attributed to each share must be directly proportional to the percentage of the capital it represents (principle of one share, one vote), companies in some countries have the right to issue multiple voting shares or non-voting shares.

In the Netherlands and the Scandinavian countries, dual classes of shares are not infrequent. The company issues two (or more) types of shares (generally named A shares and B shares) with the same financial rights but with different voting rights.

French corporate law provides for the possibility of double voting shares but, contrary to dual class shares, all shareholders can benefit from the double voting rights if they hold the shares for a certain time.

Multiple-voting shares can be particularly powerful, as the following example will illustrate.

Example

Electrolux, the Swedish home appliance group, has 309m shares outstanding of which 9.5m are A shares carrying ten times the voting rights of the rest of the shares. Investor, a holding company of the Wallenberg family, owns 11.9% of the share capital but 28.2% of voting rights because it owns 87% of A shares. These dual class shares can appear as unfair and contrary to the principle that the person who provides the capital gets the power in a company. Some countries (Italy, Spain, the UK and Germany) have outlawed dual class shares.

Issuing non-voting shares is similar to issuing dual class shares because some of the shareholders will bring capital without getting full voting power. Nevertheless, issuing non-voting shares is a more widely spread practice than issuing dual class shares across Europe. Actually, in compensation for giving up their voting rights, holders of non-voting shares usually get preferential treatment regarding dividends (fixed dividend, increased dividend compared to ordinary shareholders, etc.). Accordingly, non-voting (preference) shares are not perceived as unfair but as a different arbitrage for the investor between return, risk and power in the company.

Holding companies Holding companies can be useful but their intensive use leads to complex, multi-tiered shareholding structures. As you might imagine, they present both advantages and disadvantages.

Suppose an investor holds 51% of a holding company, which in turn holds 51% of a second holding company, which in turn holds 51% of an industrial company. Although only holding 13% of the capital of this industrial company, the investor uses a cascade of holding companies to maintain control of the industrial company.

A holding company allows a shareholder to maintain control of a company, because a structure with a holding disperses the minority shareholders. Even if the industrial company were floated on the stock exchange, the minority shareholders in the different holding companies would not be able to sell their stakes.

Maximum marginal personal income tax is generally higher than income taxes on dividends from a subsidiary. Therefore, a holding company structure allows the controlling shareholder to draw off dividends with a minimum tax bite and use them to buy more shares in the industrial company.

Technically, a holding company can 'trap' minority shareholders; in practice, this situation often leads to an ongoing conflict between shareholders. For this reason, holding companies are usually based on a group of core shareholders intimately involved in the management of the company.

A two-tiered holding company structure often exists where:

- a holding company controls the operating company;
- a top holding company holds the controlling holding company. The shareholders of the top holding company are the core group. This top holding company's main purpose is to buy back the shares of minority shareholders seeking to sell some of their shares.

Often, a holding company is formed to represent the family shareholders prior to an IPO. For example, Portman Baela SL is a holding company formed to hold the del Pino family's stakes in Ferrovial.

Limited partnerships A limited share partnership introduces a complete separation between management and financial ownership of the company.

A limited share partnership (LSP) is a company where the share capital is divided into shares, but with two types of partners:

- several *limited partners* with the status of shareholders, whose liability is limited to the amount of their investment in the company. A limited share partnership is akin to a public limited company in this respect;
- one or more *general partners*, who are jointly liable, to an unlimited extent, for the debts of the company. Senior executives of the company are usually general partners, with limited partners being barred from the executive suite.

The company's articles of association determine how present and future executives are to be chosen. These top managers have the most extensive powers to act on behalf of the company in all circumstances. They can be fired only under the terms specified in the articles of association. In some countries, the general partners can limit their financial liability by setting up a (limited liability) family holding company. In addition, the LSP structure allows a change in management control of the operating company to take place within the holding company. For example, a father can hand over the reins to his son, while the holding company continues to perform its management functions.

Thus, theoretically, the chief executive of a limited share partnership can enjoy absolute and irrevocable power to manage the company without owning a single share.

Management control does not derive from financial control as in a public limited company, but from the stipulations of the by-laws, in accordance with applicable law. Several large listed European companies have adopted the LSP form, including Merck, Michelin and Hermès.

Control shareholder changes

Right of approval The right of approval, written into a company's articles of association, enables a company to avoid 'undesirable' shareholders. This clause is frequently found in family-owned companies or in companies with a delicate balance between shareholders. The right of approval governs the relationship between partners or shareholders of the company; be careful not to confuse it with the type of approval required to purchase certain companies.

Technically, the right of approval clause requires all partners to obtain the approval of the company prior to selling any of their shares. The company must render its decision within a specified time period. If no decision is rendered, the approval is deemed granted.

If it refuses, the company, its board of directors, executive committee, senior executives or a third party must buy back the shares within a specified period of time, or the shareholder can consummate the initially planned sale.

The purchase price is set by agreement between the parties, or in the event that no agreement is reached, by independent appraisal.

Right of approval clauses might not be applied when shares are sold between shareholders or between a shareholder, his spouse or his ascendants and descendants.

Pre-emption rights Equivalent to the right of approval, the pre-emption clause gives a category of shareholders or all shareholders a priority right to acquire any shares offered for sale. Companies whose existing shareholders want to increase their stake or control changes in the capital use this clause. The board of directors, the chief executive or any other authorized person can decide how shares are divided amongst the shareholders.

Technically, pre-emption rights procedures are similar to those governing the right of approval.

Most of the time, pre-emption rights do not apply in the case of inherited shares, liquidation of a married couple's community property, or if a shareholder sells shares to his spouse, ascendants or descendants.

Right of approval and pre-emption right clauses constitute a means of controlling changes in the shareholder structure of a company. If the clause is written into the articles of association and applies to all shareholders, it can prevent any undesirable third party from obtaining control of the company. These clauses cannot block a sale of shares indefinitely, however. The existing shareholders must always find a solution that allows a sale to take place if they do not wish to buy.

Strengthening the position of current shareholders

Reserved capital increases In some countries, companies can issue new shares on terms that are highly dilutive for the existing shareholders. For example, to fend off a challenge from activist shareholders, the Philadelphia bank, Sovereign Bank, issued 25% of its share capital to the Spanish banking group Santander in 2006.

The new shares can be purchased either for cash or for contributed assets. For example, a family holding company can contribute assets to the operating company to strengthen its control over this company.

Share buybacks and cancellations The company offers to repurchase a portion of outstanding shares with the intention of cancelling them. As a result, the percentage ownership of the shareholders who do not subscribe to the repurchase offer increases. In fact, a company can regularly repurchase shares. For example, Peugeot regularly uses this method in order to strengthen the control of the family shareholders.

Mergers and other tie-ups Mergers are first and foremost a method for achieving strategic and industrial goals. As far as controlling the capital of a company is concerned, a merger can have the same effect as a reserved capital increase, by diluting the stake of a hostile shareholder or bringing in a new friendly shareholder.

The risk of course is that the new shareholders, initially brought in to support existing management, will gradually take over control of the company.

Employee shareholdings Employee-shareholders generally have a tendency to defend a company's independence when there is a threat of a change in control. A company that has taken advantage of the legislation favoring different employee share ownership schemes can generally count on a few percentage points of support in its effort to maintain the existing equilibrium in its capital. In 2007, for example, the employee-shareholders of Eiffage rallied behind management in its effort to see off Sacyr's rampant bid. The various forms of employee share ownership include profit-sharing plans, stock option plans, capital increases reserved for employees and stock-based company pension plans. Employee savings plans almost always enjoy favorable tax treatment.

Shareholder rights plan A shareholder rights plan, colloquially known as a 'poison pill', is a type of defensive tactic used by corporations against a takeover. These plans were devised in the early 1980s as a way for directors to prevent takeover bidders from negotiating a price for sale of shares directly with shareholders, and instead forcing the bidder to negotiate with the board. Shareholder rights plans are unlawful without shareholder approval in many jurisdictions such as the UK, frowned upon in others, such as throughout the European Union, and lawful if used 'proportionately' in others including Delaware in the USA.

The typical shareholder rights plan involves a scheme whereby shareholders will have the right to buy more shares at a discount, if one shareholder buys a certain percentage of the company's shares. The plan could be triggered, for instance, when any one shareholder buys 20% of the company's shares, at which point every shareholder (except the one who possesses 20%) will have the right to buy a new issue of shares at a discount. The plan can be issued by the board as an 'option' or a 'warrant' attached to existing shares, and only be revoked at the discretion of the board of directors. A shareholder who can reach a 20% threshold will potentially be a takeover bidder. If every other shareholder will be able to buy more shares at a discount, such purchases will dilute the bidder's interest, and the cost of the bid will rise substantially. Knowing that such a plan could be called on, the bidder could be disinclined to the takeover of the corporation without the board's approval, and will first negotiate with the board so that the plan is revoked.

This type of provision is common in the Netherlands (ING or Philips), France (Pernod Ricard, Suez) and in the USA.

Legal and regulatory protection

Regulations Certain investments or takeovers require approval from a government agency or other body with vetoing power. In most countries, sectors where there are needs for specific approval are:

- media;
- financial institutions; and
- activities related to defense (for national security reasons).

Golden shares are special shares that enable governments to prevent another shareholder from increasing its stake above a certain threshold or the company from selling certain of its assets (Suez, Total, Telecom Italia, Eni and Cameroon Airlines are some examples). The legitimacy of golden shares is being questioned by EU authorities.

Voting caps In principle, the idea of limiting the right to vote that accompanies a share of stock contradicts the principle of 'one share, one vote'. Nevertheless, companies can limit the vote of any shareholder to a specific percentage of the capital. In some cases, the limit falls away once the shareholder reaches a very large portion of the capital (e.g. 50% or two-thirds).

For example, Danone's articles of association stipulate that no shareholder may cast more than 6% of all single voting rights and no more than 12% of all double voting rights at a shareholders' meeting, unless he or she owns more than two-thirds of the shares. Voting caps are commonly used in Europe, specifically in Switzerland (12 firms out of the 50 largest use them), France, Belgium, the Netherlands and Spain. Nestlé, Total, Alcatel and Novartis use voting caps. This is a very effective defense. It prevents an outsider from taking control of a company with only 20% or 30% of the capital. If the outsider truly wants to take control, he or she has to 'ante up' and bid for all of the shares. We can see that this technique is particularly useful for companies of a certain size. It makes sense only for companies that do not have a strong core shareholder.

Strategic assets Strategic assets can be patents, brand names or subsidiaries comprising most of the business or generating most of the profits of a group. In some cases the company does not actually own the assets but simply uses them under license. In other cases these assets are located in a subsidiary with a partner who automatically gains control should control of the parent company change hands. Often contested as misuse of corporate property, poison pill arrangements are very difficult to implement, and in practice are generally ineffective.

As a general matter, change of control provisions on key contracts can play the role of poison pills. These contracts can be JV agreements, distribution contracts or even bank debt contracts.

Change of control provisions Some contracts may include a clause whereby the contract becomes void if one of the control provisions over one of the principles of the contract changes. The existence of such clauses in vital contracts for the company (distribution contract, bank debt contract, commercial contract) will render its takeover much more complex.

Some *golden parachute* clauses in employment contracts allow some employees to leave the company with a significant amount of money in case of change of control.

Reference and Further Reading

Quiry, P., Dallocchio, M., Le Fur, Y. and Salvi, A., *Corporate Finance*, 3rd ed., John Wiley & Sons, 2011.

47. What are holding company and conglomerate discounts?

Short Answer

A holding company discount occurs when the market capitalization of the holding company is less than the sum of the investments it holds. A conglomerate discount occurs when the market value of the conglomerate is less than the sum of the values of the assets the conglomerate holds.

Long Answer

Holding company discount
A holding company owns minority or majority investments in listed or unlisted companies either for purely financial reasons or for the purpose of control.

> *A holding company trades at a discount when its market capitalization is less than the sum of the investments it holds.*

This is usually the case. For example, the holding company holds assets worth 100, but the stock market values the holding company at only 80. Consequently, investors who buy the holding company's stock will think they are buying something 'at a discount', because they are paying 80 for something that is worth 100. The market value of the holding company will never reach 100 unless something happens to eliminate the discount, such as a merger between the holding company and its operating subsidiary.

The size of the discount varies with prevailing stock market conditions. In bull markets, holding company discounts tend to contract, while in bear markets they can widen to more than 30%.

Here are four reasons for this phenomenon:

1. The *portfolio of assets* of the holding company is imposed on investors who cannot choose it.
2. The *free float* of the holding company is usually smaller than that of the companies in which it is invested, making the holding's shares less liquid.
3. *Tax inefficiencies.* Capital gains on the shares held by the holding company may be taxed twice: first at the holding company level, then at the level of the shareholders. Moreover, it takes time for the flow of dividends to come from the operating company up to the ultimate holding company.
4. *Administrative inefficiencies.* The holding company has its own administrative costs which, discounted over a long period, constitute a liability to be subtracted from the value of the investments it holds. Imagine a holding company valued at €2bn with administrative costs of €10m p.a. If those costs are projected to infinity and discounted at 8% p.a., their present value is €125m before tax, or 6.25% of the value of the holding company.

These factors can generally explain a statistical discount up to the 15–25% range. Beyond that, the discount is probably more indicative of a power struggle between investors and holding companies. The former want to get rid of the latter and finance the operating assets directly. The disappearance of many listed holding companies over the last few years, such as Olivetti and IFI in Italy, Eurafrance in France, Cobepa and Electrabel in Belgium or Companie Financière Michelin in Switzerland, has demonstrated how effective investor pressure can be.

Conglomerate discounts

A conglomerate is a group operating in several, diverse businesses. Whether the group combines water and telephones or missiles and magazines, the market value of the conglomerate is usually less than the sum of the values of the assets the conglomerate holds. The difference, the conglomerate discount, generally reflects investors' fears that resources will be poorly allocated.

In other words, the group might reduce emphasis on profitable investments in order to support ailing divisions in which the profitability is mediocre or below their cost of capital.

Moreover, investors now tend to prefer 'pure play' stocks so as to diversify their holdings themselves. In a conglomerate, investors cannot select the company's portfolio of assets; they are in fact stuck with the holding company's choice. As in the case of holding companies, head office costs absorb some of the value of the conglomerate. Finally, a company can suffer both a conglomerate and a holding company discount if some of the company's activities are lodged in a listed subsidiary.

A persistent conglomerate discount usually leads to a spin-off or a hostile takeover bid.

Some conglomerates are valued without a discount (General Electric, Bouygues) because investors are convinced that they are efficiently managed.

48. What are control premiums and minority discounts?

Short Answer

The control premium is the amount a buyer is ready to pay over the current market value in order to obtain the control of a company.

The minority discount is a reduction from the market value accepted by minority shareholders in order to sell their stocks.

Example

Table 1.40 shows the premiums (bid price compared to share price one month before) of public deals in Europe and the USA.

Table 1.40: Premiums of public deals in Europe and USA

	1998–2008 (%)
France	15%
Germany	11%
Italy	15%
Scandinavia	21%
Spain	15%
UK	26%
USA	27%

Source: Mergermarket.

Long Answer

There is no real control value other than strategic value.

For a long time, the control premium was a widely-accepted notion that was virtually a pardon for dispossessing minority shareholders. When a company was valued at 100 and another company was willing to pay a premium of 20 to the controlling shareholder (e.g. holding 50.01%), minority shareholders were excluded from this advantageous offer.

The development of financial markets and financial market regulations has changed this: equality among shareholders is an untouchable principle in most countries.

Shareholder agreements are a common method for expressing this principle in unlisted companies.

When control of a listed company changes hands, minority shareholders should receive the same premium as that paid to the majority shareholder.

Nevertheless, entrepreneurs often have a diametrically opposed view. For them, minority shareholders are passive beneficiaries of the fruits of all the personal energy the managers and majority shareholders have invested in the company. It is difficult to convince entrepreneurs that the roles of management and shareholders can be separated and that they must be compensated differently – and especially that risk assumed by all types of shareholders must be rewarded.

What then is the basis for this premium which, in the case of listed companies, can often lift a purchase price to 20% or 30% more than the current market price? The premium is still called a 'control premium' even though it is now paid to minority shareholders as well as to the majority shareholder.

If we assume that markets are efficient, the existence of such a premium can be justified only if the new owners of the company obtain more value from it than did its previous owners. A control premium derives from the industrial, commercial, administrative or tax synergies the new majority shareholders hope to unlock. They hope to improve the acquired company's results by managing it better, pooling resources, combining businesses or taking advantage of economies of scale. These value-creating actions are reflected in the buyer's valuation. The trade buyer (i.e. an acquirer which already has industrial operations) wants to acquire the company so as to change the way it is run and, in doing so, create value.

The company is therefore worth more to a trade buyer than it is to a financial buyer (i.e. usually a venture capitalist fund which has no operations in the industry), who values the company on a standalone basis, as one investment opportunity among others, independently of these synergies.

The peculiarity of the market for corporate control arises from the existence of synergies that give rise to strategic value.

In this light, we now understand that the trade buyer's expectations are not the same as those of the financial investor. This difference can lead to a different valuation of the company. We call this strategic value.

Strategic value is the maximum value a trade buyer is prepared to pay for a company.

It includes the value of projected free cash flows of the target on a standalone basis, plus the value of synergies from combining the company's businesses with those of the trade buyer. It also includes the value of expected improvement in the company's profitability compared to the business plan provided, if any.

Depending on whether a company belongs to one group of companies or another, it does not have the same value. Make sure you understand why this is the case. The difference in value derives from different cash flow projections, not from a difference in the discount rate applied to them, which is a characteristic of the company and identical for all investors.

The principles of value are the same for everyone, but strategic value is different for each trade buyer, because each of them places a different value on the synergies it believes it can unlock and on its ability to manage the business better than current management.

For this reason, a company's strategic value is often higher than its standalone value.

As the seller will also hope to benefit from the synergies, negotiation will focus on how the additional profitability the synergies are expected to generate will be shared between the buyer and the seller.

But some industrial groups go overboard, buying companies at twice their standalone value on the pretext that their strategic value is high or that establishing a presence in such-and-such geographic location is crucial. They are in for a rude awakening. Sometimes the market has already put a high price tag on the target company. Specifically, when the market anticipates merger synergies, speculation can drive the share price far above the company's strategic value, even if all synergies are realized. In other cases, a well-managed company may benefit little or even be hurt by teaming up with another company in the same industry, meaning either that there are no synergies to begin with or, worse, that they are negative.

We have often seen minority holdings valued with a discount, and you will quickly understand why we believe this is unjustified. A 'minority discount' would imply that minority shareholders have proportionally less of a claim on the cash flows generated by the company than the majority shareholder. This is not true.

Whereas a control premium can (and must) be justified by subsequent synergies, there is no basis for a minority discount.

In fact, a shareholder who already has the majority of a company's shares may be forced to pay a premium to buy the shares held by minority shareholders. Indeed, majority shareholders may be willing to pay such a premium if they need full control over the acquired company to implement certain synergies. For example, in 2007 the minorities of AGF were bought back by Allianz at a 9% premium over the one-month average market price.

Having said that, the lack of liquidity associated with certain minority holdings, either because the company is not listed or because trading volumes are low compared with the size of the minority stake, can justify a discount. In this case, the discount does not really derive from the minority stake per se, *but from its lack of liquidity.*

Lack of liquidity may increase volatility of the share price. Therefore investors will discount an illiquid investment at a higher rate than a liquid one. The difference in values results in a liquidity discount.

Based on our experience and on the conceptual work of corporate finance researchers, we have long been convinced that there was something almost mediaeval about minority discounts.

Three examples serve to illustrate this point of view:

1. When a group wishes to buy up the shares held by minority shareholders in one of its listed subsidiaries, in which the group has a controlling interest that exceeds 50%, the average premium payable in Europe is around 18%.
2. A shareholder with a 20% stake in a family-owned company of which he also happened to be the general manager decided to sell his shares. All of the financial investors and trade players he approached had already received a visit from the majority shareholders, who had threatened to make the life of any foolish investor who dared to buy the minority stake a misery. After three years, and because he needed to cash-in, the minority shareholder sold his stake at less than 30% of its value to the only buyer on the market, i.e. the majority family-shareholder. Did you say minority discount? 70% isn't a discount, it's a fire sale!
3. Three brothers each held a 17% stake in an industrial group. One of them wanted to sell his shares, but he no longer got along very well with his brothers. Both he and the industrial group were able to exit the capital without granting a discount at all, as the two remaining brothers, afraid of becoming minority shareholders, bought their shares at a little more than their market value, without even haggling. Not exactly a minority discount is it?

In other words, a minority discount, when it is granted, is merely the result of a power play between a seller who, for various reasons, wishes to sell and a buyer who knows he or she is the only party in a position to buy and who intends to take full advantage of this position. You can now see why we used the word 'mediaeval' earlier on. A minority discount makes no sense when the minority shareholder is reluctant or does not wish to sell and the majority shareholder wants to buy. In this situation what we see are premiums being paid.

What we should be referring to more accurately here is a *liquidity* or an *illiquidity discount*. Because the minority shareholder wishes to liquidate his or her stake, the shareholder may be forced, if in a poor position to negotiate, to make do with whatever the majority shareholder is prepared to offer. If the general manager in our third example had been able to hold out for a bit longer, he would have been able to sell his stake alongside the family and taken a share of the control premium when the family sold a controlling interest in the company four years later.

Recent events have shown that turning shares into cash can sometimes be a very costly business (Bear Stearns). Accordingly, it is very difficult to put a figure on a liquidity discount, even if rationally it can be compared to an IPO discount that penalizes shareholders wanting to liquidate their shares and is usually around 15% on average. However, the above examples show the limitations of the idea of 'average'.

49. What is a cascade structure?

Short Answer

A cascade structure is a form of ownership used in order to lever control.

Example

Figure 1.46 shows the Russian Matryushka doll like structure of the Frère Group.

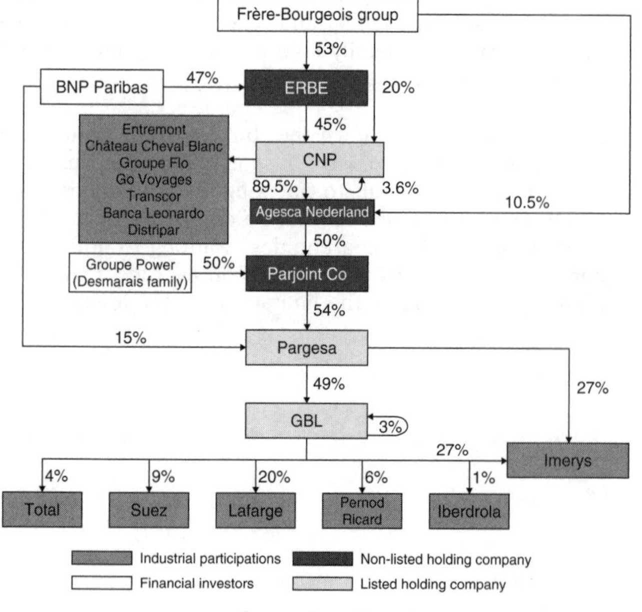

Figure 1.46: Simplified structure of the Frère Group (March 2008)

Long Answer

As a newly-minted CEO, you may be tempted to structure your group as a Russian Matryushka doll, like Groupe Arnault and LVMH or Olivetti and Telecom Italia, or like the current Albert Frère group.

At each level, it makes sense to create a new company only if it will house different businesses. The most profitable activities must be as close as possible to the controlling holding company. Otherwise, if it is the company at the bottom of the 'cascade', cash flow will have trouble reaching the controlling holding company, and shareholders will have the impression that their money is working for free!

What are the advantages and disadvantages of such a cascade structure?

The multiplier effect is maximized With capital of 100, you can control a set of businesses with a capital of 2500! Even more leverage can be obtained if intermediate structures borrow, but we strongly recommend against this practice. As they do not hold the operating assets directly and depend solely on dividends for their livelihood, borrowing would make the intermediate structures even more fragile. Remember that a chain is only as strong as its weakest link.

These cascade companies generally trade with a deep discount (between 20% and 50%) If a parent company wants to participate in its subsidiary's capital increase in order to maintain control over it, it must in turn carry out a capital increase. But because of the holding company discount, the new shares of the holding company will be issued at a heavy discount, increasing its cost of capital. In effect, the cost of capital for a parent holding company which has stock that trades at a 50% discount is twice the cost of capital of the operating subsidiary.

These structures have fallen a bit out of fashion. Investors are afraid of being caught on the least liquid and most fragile part of the ladder and suffering an accumulation of discounts.

References and Further Reading

Aggarwal, A. and Samwick, A., Why do managers diversify their firms? Agency reconsidered, *Journal of Finance*, **58**(1), 71–118, February 2003.

Boone, A., Haushalter, D. and Mikkelson, W., An investigation of the gains from specialized equity claims, *Financial Management*, 67–83, Autumn 2003.

Boot, A., Gopalan, R. and Thakor, A., The entrepreneur's choice between private and public ownership, *Journal of Finance*, **61** (2), 803–836, April 2006.

Cornell, B. and Liu, Q., The parent company puzzle: When is the whole worth less than one of the parts? *Journal of Corporate Finance*, **7**, 341–366, December 2001.

Cronqvist, H. and Nilsson, M., Agency costs of controlling minority shareholders, *Journal of Financial Quantitative Analysis*, **38**(4), 695–719, December 2003.

Hearman and Sterling, ISS, ECGI, Report on the Proportionality Principle in the European Union, 2007.

Rauh, J., Own company stock in defined contribution pension plans. A takeover defense? *Journal of Financial Ecomonics*, **81**(2), 379–410, August 2006.

50. Why is corporate governance so important?

Short Answer

Corporate governance is the organization of the control over and management of a firm. A narrower definition of corporate governance covers the relationship between the firm's shareholders and management, mainly involving the functioning of the board of directors or the supervisory board.

Example

The idea of corporate governance first arose in the 1990s and has been given a boost by the eruption of several major financial scandals in recent years (e.g. Enron, Worldcom and Parmalat).

More fundamentally, corporate governance is a natural by-product of the changing economy. For example, a change in the shareholding structure of firms (with a shift away from family-owned firms to a more widely-held shareholding structure made up of institutional and retail investors) leaves management with greater freedom. The issue of shareholder control over management has thus become more pressing. Corporate governance was first introduced at listed companies in the UK and the USA (where firms are generally more widely held) before spreading to countries where the frequent cohabitation of family shareholders and minority shareholders also raises issues of corporate governance.

Long Answer

Corporate governance is the organization of the control over and management of a firm. It covers:

- the definition of the legal framework of the firm: the organization, the functioning, the rights and responsibilities of shareholders' meetings and the corporate bodies responsible for oversight (board of directors or executive board, supervisory board);
- the rules for appointing managers and directors;
- management rules and any conflicts of interest;
- the organization of control over the management and the running of the company: internal controls, regulatory controls, auditing;
- the rights and responsibilities of other stakeholders (lenders, customers, suppliers, employees);
- the disclosure of financial information on the firm and the role and responsibility of external analysts: financial analysts, rating agencies and legal and financial advisors.

In a more narrow definition, the term 'corporate governance' is used to describe the link that exists between shareholders and management. From this point of view, developments in corporate governance mainly involve the role and functioning of boards of directors or supervisory boards.

We would suggest that corporate governance covers all of the mechanisms and procedures surrounding decisions relating to the creation and sharing of value. They concern four main areas: shareholders' rights, transparency of information, organs of management and control and the alignment of compensation.

We'd like to emphasize that corporate governance is a system that necessarily differs from one firm to the next, depending on its shareholding structure and its nationality.

Strictly speaking, it is a bit of a misnomer to refer to 'good' or 'bad' corporate governance. There is only corporate governance that in practice either inspires investors' confidence (or not) in the way in which decisions are taken within the firm, based on whether the following five principles are respected: efficiency, responsibility, transparency, fairness and ethics.

Over the years, a number of recommendations and guidelines have been added to the purely regulatory and legislative framework, in the form of reports and best practice codes (commissioned and/or drafted by employer bodies, investor associations, governments and government agencies, stock exchanges, etc. in the various European countries). It is important to note that these codes remain recommendations and guidelines only and are not legally binding laws or regulations.

We can see that the main recommendations and guidelines in terms of corporate governance all focus on key issues: transparency in the way that the board and management operate, the role, composition and functioning of the board and the exercise of shareholder power at general meetings.

Transparency

The first recommendation is for transparency in the way the company's management and oversight bodies operate.

There has been a huge increase in transparency of the way the boards of listed groups operate over the last 15 years.

Transparency surrounding the compensation of managers and directors is also recommended (Figure 1.47).

For a long time, this was a taboo subject, and most listed companies have only recently started disclosing clear figures on the compensation paid to their managers and directors.

With the granting of variable compensation or stock options, managers have a financial interest that coincides with that of shareholders, to whom they are accountable. Since stock

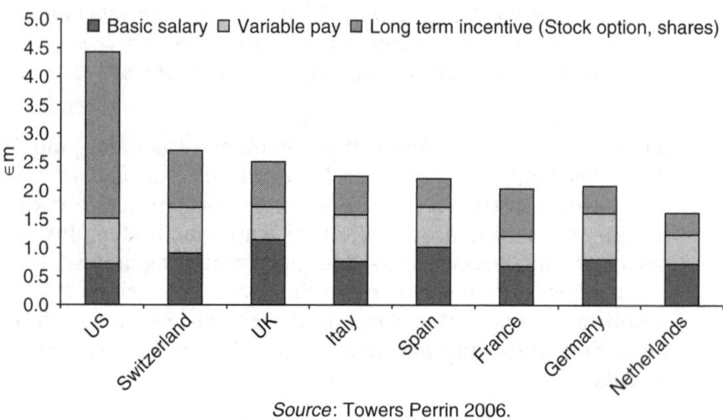

Source: Towers Perrin 2006.

Figure 1.47: Compensation for managers of groups with turnover of c. €5bn (in €m)

options are options to buy or subscribe shares at a fixed price, managers have direct financial stakes in the financial performance of their companies, i.e. the higher the share price the larger their capital gains will be. Accordingly, there is a major incentive to make decisions that will create value.

Stock options are not, however, a cure for all, as the short-term vision they encourage may sometimes tempt management to conceal certain facts when disclosing financial information and, in extreme cases, they may even consider committing fraud. This has resulted in the development of alternative products, such as the granting of free shares, the payment of part of their compensation in shares, etc.

The role of an independent board

Corporate governance codes all recommend that a firm's corporate strategy be defined by a body (board of directors or supervisory board) which enjoys a certain degree of independence from management.

Independence is achieved by limiting the number of managers who sit on the board, and by setting a minimum number of independent directors.

For example, in the UK the latest recommendation is that at least half of the directors of listed companies should be independent. There are very few companies with no or hardly any independent directors on the board. One such example is Ubisoft, the video game company, with the founding family controlling 13% of the capital and occupying six out of seven seats on the board.

The definition of the term 'independent director' is the subject of much controversy.

The Bouton report defines an independent director as follows: 'Directors are independent when they have no link of any nature whatsoever with the company, the group or management, which could compromise them in the exercise of their free will.' Even though this definition makes it clear that a member of management or a shareholder representative would not be considered as independent, it allows for a great deal of leeway, which means that deciding whether or not a director is indeed independent is not as easy as it might appear.

The importance given to the need for independent directors on the board tends to overshadow the importance of other more vital matters, such as their competence, their availability and their courage when it comes to standing up to management. These qualities are indispensable throughout the financial year, whereas their independence only becomes an issue in situations of conflict of interest, which fortunately are the exception rather than the rule.

Lawyers will surely forgive us for pointing out that the development of corporate governance has brought an end to the idea of the board of directors as an entity invested with the widest of powers, authorized to act in all circumstances, in the name of the company.

This gives the impression that the board was responsible for running the company, which was quite simply never the case. This erroneous idea put management in a position where it was able to call all of the shots. These days, boards are designed to determine the direction the company will take and to oversee the implementation of corporate strategy.

This is a much more modest mandate, but also a lot more realistic. The board is asked to come up with fewer but better goods.

The functioning of the board and the creation of directors' committees

Corporate governance codes insist on the creation of special committees which are instructed by the board to draw up reports. These committees generally include:

- **an audit committee** (inspects the accounts, monitors the internal audit, selects the external auditors);
- **a remunerations committee** (managers, sometimes directors);
- **a selections or appointments committee** (paves the way for the succession of the managing director and/or CEO, puts forward proposals for new directors);
- **a strategic and/or financial committee** (that is concerned with large capex plans, mergers and acquisitions, financing issues).

The exercise of shareholder power during general meetings
It is clear that anything that stands in the way of the exercise of shareholder power will be an obstacle to good corporate governance. Such obstacles can come in various forms:

- The existence of shares with multiple voting rights that may enable minority shareholders with only a tiny stake in the capital to impose their views by wielding their extra voting rights. One such example occurred as recently as 2004, when the Wallenberg family and Industrivärden were able to control 66% of the voting rights in Ericsson, when they held only 7.3% of the share capital, thanks to the existence of A shares (with 1000 voting rights attached to each share) and B shares (with only one voting right attached).
- The existence of preferred shares with no voting rights attached. The control held by Porsche over Volkswagen is facilitated by the existence of preferred shares with a guaranteed dividend but no voting rights attached, accounting for 27% of the share capital; the restriction of voting rights in meetings by introducing caps on the number of votes cast during general meetings. For example, at Alcatel-Lucent, a single investor cannot represent more than 8% or 16.5% of the voting rights.
- Administrative or material restrictions on exercising voting rights by proxy or by postal vote.

On the other side, making it compulsory for institutional shareholders to vote in general meetings of shareholders, or allowing shareholders to vote without having to freeze their shares a few weeks before the meeting, have clearly improved voting habits and enhanced shareholder democracy.

The *organization of power within the board* in itself is a much debated topic. The need for a body that is independent from the management of the company remains an open question.

Today, the French system is the most flexible, offering three types of organization (Table 1.41):

- **Board of directors with a chief executive officer acting also as chairman of the board**. This means that a great deal of power is concentrated in the hands of one person who is head of the board and who also manages the company. This is known as a one-tier structure and is in place at groups such as Exxon Mobil, Roche and Telefonica.
- **Board of directors with an executive or a non-executive chairman and a separate chief executive officer**. This sort of dual structure has been adopted by Infosys, Sony and Vodafone;
- **Board of directors and executive board.** This two-tier structure is in place at Peugeot, Vale and Philips.

Table 1.41: Examples of one-tier and two-tier organizations

Country	Main type of board	Separation of management and board	Employee representation on board
France	One-tier or two-tier	Optional	Can be provided for in articles of association (consultative)
Germany	Two-tier	Yes	Yes
Italy	One-tier	Optional	No
Japan	One-tier	Optional	No
Netherlands	Two-tier	Yes	Consultative
Spain	One-tier	Optional	No
Switzerland	One-tier	Optional	No
UK	One-tier	Optional	No
USA	One-tier	Optional	No

Source: Weil *et al.*, 2007.

A board on which the control and management roles are exercised by two different people should, in theory, be more effective in controlling management on behalf of the shareholders. Is this always the case in practice? The answer is no, because it all depends on the quality and the probity of the men and women involved.

Enron had a chairman and chief executive officer, and General Electric has a chief executive officer also acting as chairman of the board. The former went bankrupt in a very spectacular way as a result of fraud and the latter is seen as a model for creating value for its shareholders.

So it's much better to have an outstanding manager, and possibly even compromise a bit when it comes to corporate governance, by giving the manager the job of both running the company and chairing the board, rather than to have a mediocre manager. Even if extremely well controlled by the chairman of the board, a mediocre manager will remain a mediocre manager!

There is no straight answer to the question of whether it is best to combine the functions of management and control. Each case has to be assessed on its merits, taking into account the shareholder structure and the personality of the managers. Nothing is written in stone.

It cannot be denied that great strides forward have been taken in the area of corporate governance even if there is still progress to be made in some emerging countries with less experience in dealing with listed companies and minority shareholders. Associations of minority shareholders, or minority shareholder defense firms such as ISS or Deminor, which also provide shareholders with advice on how to vote in general meetings, have often acted as a major stimulus in this regard.

The fact that, in developed countries, many groups have simplified their structures has made this a lot easier:

- these days, it is usually only the parent company that is listed, which eliminates the possibility of conflicts of interest between the parent company and minority shareholders of its subsidiaries;
- cross-holdings between groups which used to swap directors have been unwound; and
- assets used by the group but which belong to the founders have been contributed to the group.

It's now up to researchers to determine whether this simplification was the cause or the consequence of the spread of corporate governance.

References and Further Reading

Albuquerue, R. and Wang, N., Agency conflicts, reinvestments and asset pricing, *Journal of Finance*, **63**(1), 1–40, February 2008.

Anderson, R. and Reeb, D., Founding-family ownership and firm performance: Evidence from the S & P 500, *The Journal of Finance*, **58**(3), 1301–1328, June 2003.

Baker, H. and Anderson, R., *Corporate Governance: A Synthesis of Theory, Research, and Practice*, John Wiley & Sons, 2010.

Bauer, R., Guenster, N., and Otten, R., Empirical evidence on corporate governance in Europe. The effect on stock returns, firm value and performance, *Journal of Asset Management*, **5**(2), 91–104, August 2004.

Bebchuk, L., Cohen, A. and Ferrell, A., *What Matters in Corporate Governance*, Harvard discussion paper, no. 491, September 2004.

Chara, R., *Boards that Deliver*, Jossey-Bass, 2005.

Chhaochharia, V. and Grinstein, Y., Corporate governance and firm value – The impact of the 2002 Governance Rules, *Journal of Finance*, **62**(4), 1789–1825, August 2007.

Clarke, T., *Theories of Corporate Governance*, Routledge, 2004.

Clarke, T., *International Corporate Governance: A Comparative Approach*, 2nd ed., Routledge, 2011.

Core, J., Guay, W. and Rusticus, T., Does weak corporate governance cause stock returns? An examination of firm operating performance and analysts' expectations, *Journal of Finance*, **61**(2), 655–687, April 2006.

Demsetz, H., The structure of ownership and the theory of the firm, *The Journal of Law & Economics*, **26**(2), 375–390, June 1983.

Doidge, C., Karolyi, G. and Stulz, R., Why countries matter so much for corporate governance. *Journal of Financial Economics*, **86**(1), 1–39, October 2007.

Durnev, A. and Han Kim, E., To steal or not to steal: Firm attributes, legal environment and valuation, *Journal of Finance*, **60**(3), 1461–1493, June 2005.

Fahlenbrach, R., Low, A. and Stulz, R., Why do firms appoint CEOs as outside directors?, *Journal of Financial Economics*, **97**(1), 12–32, July 2010.

Gillian, G., Recent developments in corporate governance: An overview, *Journal of Corporate Finance*, **12**(3), 381–402, June 2006.

Gompers, P., Ishii, J. and Metrick, A., Corporate governance and equity prices, *The Quarterly Journal of Economics*, **118**(1), 107–155, February 2003.

La Porta, R., Lopez de Silanes, F., Shleifer, A. and Vishny, R., Law and finance, *Journal of Political Economy*, **106**(6), 1133–1155, December 1998.

La Porta, R., Lopez de Silanes, F., Shleifer, A. and Vishny, R., Investor protection and corporate valuation, *Journal of Finance*, **57**(3), 1147–1170, June 2002.

Lipman, F., *Corporate Governance: Best Practices*, John Wiley & Sons, 2006.

Monks, R. and Minow, N., *Corporate Governance*, John Wiley & Sons, 2007.

Mork, R., *A History of Corporate Governance around the World: Family Business Groups to Professional Managers*, University of Chicago Press, 2007.

Nguyen, B., Does the Rolodex Matter? Corporate Elite's Small World and the Effectiveness of Boards of Directors, working paper, 2011.

Nguyen, B. and Nielsen, K., The value of independent directors: evidence from sudden death, *Journal of Financial Economics*, **98**(3), 550–567, December 2010.

Stulz, R. and Williamson, R., Culture, openness, and finance, *Journal of Financial Economics*, **70**(3), 313–349, December 2003.

Weil, A. *et al.*, International companions of selected corporate governance guidelines and codes of best pratice, Powerpoint presentation, March 2007.

www.boardmember.com, an information resource for senior officers and directors of publicly traded corporations.

www.ecgi.org, the website of the European Corporate Governance Institute.

www.icgn.org, the website of the International Corporate Governance Network.

www.oecd.org, the website of the OECD which devotes a large section to corporate governance issues.

51. How can companies be taken over?

Short Answer

For a *private company* the key is the art of negotiation that consists of allocating the value of the synergies expected from a merger or acquisition between the buyer and the seller.

For a *public company* the procedure is generally more complex. *Stake-building* can be the first step to acquiring control over a listed company. But it can be slow and faces the requirement of declaring the crossing of some specific thresholds. A *public offer* is the usual way to acquire a listed company. It can be in cash or in shares, hostile or friendly, voluntary or mandatory.

Example

M&A activity and means of payment (Figure 1.48)

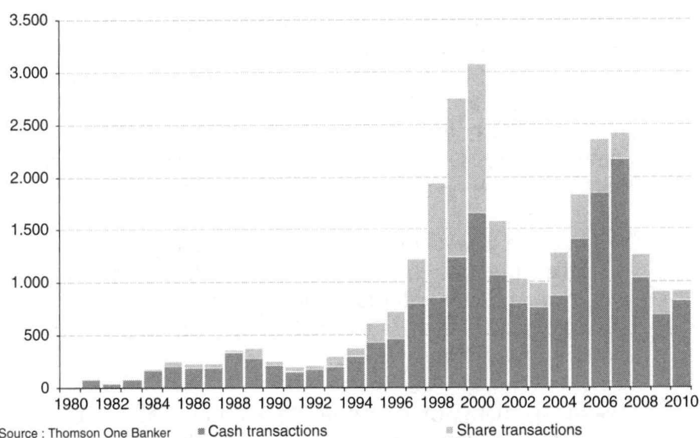

Figure 1.48: Worldwide merger activity (in €bn)

When the market is bearish, cash payments are more attractive to both parties. The seller receives cold, hard cash which will not lose value as shares might, while the buyer is reluctant to issue new shares at prices he or she considers to be a discount to the intrinsic value of the buyer's shares.

Long Answer

Private companies

There are two basic methods of conducting the negotiations for taking over a private company:

- private negotiations; and
- private auction.

Private negotiations The seller or his or her advisor contacts a small number of potential acquirers to gauge their interest. After signing a confidentiality agreement, the potential acquirers might receive an information memorandum describing the company's industrial, financial and human resource elements. Discussions then begin. It is important that each potential acquirer believes he or she is not alone, even if in reality they are. In principle, this technique requires extreme confidentiality. Psychological rather than practical barriers to the transaction necessitate the high degree of confidentiality.

To preserve confidentiality, the seller often prefers to hire a specialist, most often an investment banker, to find potential acquirers and keep all discussions under wraps. Such specialists are usually paid a success fee that can be proportional to the size of the transaction.

Strictly speaking, there are no typical negotiating procedures. Every transaction is different. The only absolute rule about negotiating strategies is that the negotiator must have a strategy.

The advantage of private negotiation is a high level of confidentiality. In many cases, there is no paper trail at all.

The discussion focuses on:

- how much control the seller will give up (and the status of any remaining minority shareholders);
- the price;
- the payment terms;
- any conditions precedent;
- representations and warranties; and
- any contractual relationship that might remain between the seller and the target company after the transaction.

As you might expect, price remains the essential question in the negotiating process. Everything that might have been said during the course of the negotiations falls away, leaving this one all-important parameter.

We now take a look at the various agreements and clauses that play a role in private negotiation:

1. *Memorandum of understanding (MOU) or letter of intent (LOI).* When a framework for the negotiations has been defined, a memorandum of understanding is often signed to open the way to a transaction. A memorandum of understanding is a moral, not a legal, obligation. Often, once the MOU is signed, the management of the acquiring company presents it to its board of directors to obtain permission to pursue the negotiations.
The memorandum of understanding is not useful when each party has made a firm commitment to negotiate. In this case, a memorandum of understanding slows down the process rather than accelerating it.

2. *Agreement in principle.* The next step might be an agreement in principle, spelling out the terms and conditions of the sale. The commitments of each party are irrevocable, unless there are precedent conditions such as approval of the regulatory authorities. The agreement in principle can take many forms.

3. *Financial sweeteners.* In many cases, specific financial arrangements are needed to get over psychological, tax, legal or financial barriers. These arrangements do not change the value of the company.
These arrangements cannot transform a bad transaction into a good one. They serve only to bring the parties to the transaction closer together.
Sometimes, for psychological reasons, the seller refuses to go below some purely symbolic value. If he or she draws a line in the sand at 200, for example, whereas the buyer does not want to pay more than 190, a schedule spreading out payments over time sometimes does the trick. The seller will receive 100 this year and 100 next year. This is 190.9 if discounted at 10%, but it is still 200 to the seller's way of thinking. Recognize that we are out of the realm of finance here and into the confines of psychology, and that this arrangement fools only those who … want to be fooled.

Private auctions In an auction, the company is offered for sale under a pre-determined schedule to several potential buyers who are competing with each other. The objective is to choose the one offering the highest price. An auction is often private, but it can also be announced in the press or by a court decision.

Private auctions are run by an investment bank in the following manner. Once the decision is taken to sell the company the seller asks an audit group to produce a *vendor due diligence* (VDD), which provides a clear view of the weak points of the asset from legal, tax, accounting and regulatory points of view, for example. The VDD is communicated to buyers later on in the process.

Meanwhile, a brief summary of the company is prepared (a 'teaser'). It is sent, together with a nondisclosure agreement, to a large number of potentially interested companies and financial investors.

In the next stage (often called 'Phase I'), once the potential buyers sign the nondisclosure agreement, they receive additional information, gathered in an information memorandum. Then they submit a nonbinding offer indicating the price, its financing, any conditions precedent and eventually their intentions regarding the future strategy for the target company.

At that point in time ('Phase II') either:

- a 'short list' of half a dozen candidates at most is drawn up. They receive still more information and possibly a schedule of visits to the company's industrial sites and meetings with management. Often a *data room* is set up, where all economic, financial and legal information concerning the target company is available for perusal. Access to the data room is very restricted, for example no photocopies can be made. At the end of this stage, potential investors submit binding offers; or
- *exclusive negotiations* are opened for a few days. For a given period of time, the potential buyer is the only candidate. At the end of the exclusive period, the buyer must submit a binding offer (in excess of a certain figure) or withdraw from the negotiations.

Together with the binding offers, the seller will ask the bidder(s) to propose a markup (comments) to the disposal agreement (called the share purchase agreement, SPA) previously provided by the seller. The ultimate selection of the buyer depends, naturally, on the binding offer, but also on the buyer's comments on the share purchase agreement.

An auction can lead to a high price because buyers are in competition with each other. In addition, it makes it easier for the seller's representatives to prove that they did everything in their power to obtain the highest possible price for the company, be it:

- the executive who wants to sell a subsidiary;
- a majority shareholder whose actions might be challenged by minority shareholders; or
- the investment banker in charge of the transaction.

Moreover, an auction is faster, because the seller, not the buyer, sets the pace. Competition sometimes generates a price that is well in excess of expectations.

However, the auction creates confidentiality problems. Many people have access to the basic data, and denying rumors of a transaction becomes difficult, so the process must move quickly. Also, as the technique is based on price only, it is exposed to some risks, such as several potential buyers teaming up with the intention of splitting the assets among them. Lastly, should the process fail, the company's credibility will suffer. The company must have an uncontested strategic value and a sound financial condition. The worst result is the one of an auction process which turns sour because financial results are not up to the estimations produced a few weeks before, leaving only one buyer who knows they are now the only buyer.

A well-processed auction can take three to five months between intention to sell and the closing. It is sometimes shorter when an investment fund sells to another fund.

The principal remaining element is the *representations and warranties clause*, particularly important because it gives confidence to the buyer that the profitability of the company has not been misrepresented. It is a way of securing the value of assets and liabilities of the target company as the contract does not provide a detailed valuation.

Representations and warranties clauses are not intended to protect the buyer against an overvaluation of the company. *They are intended to certify that all of the means of production are indeed under the company's control and that there are no hidden liabilities.*

Well-worded representations and warranties clauses should guarantee to the buyer:

- the substance of fixed assets (and not their value);
- the real nature and the value of inventories (assuming that the buyer and the seller have agreed on a valuation method);
- the real nature of other elements of working capital;
- the amount and nature of all of the company's other commitments, whether they are on the balance sheet (such as debts) or not.

Public companies For a public company, the negotiation cannot take place between two parties in the same way as for a private company. The transaction has to include minority shareholders.

Local regulations aim at protecting minority shareholders in order to develop financial markets. The main target of these regulations is to guarantee a transparent and equal treatment for all shareholders.

In order to acquire a listed company, the buyer needs to secure shares from a large number of minority shareholders.

It would be too difficult and time-consuming to acquire shares on the open market; therefore the buyer usually makes a public offer (takeover bid) to all shareholders to buy their shares.

Each country has regulations governing takeovers of companies listed on domestic stock exchanges. The degree of constraints varies from one country to another.

To succeed in acquiring a listed company the first step can be to start building a block in the company (*stake-building*). This can be done on the open market by buying shares.

In order to prevent the acquirer from taking control of a company in that way, most market regulations require investors in a listed company to publicly declare when they pass certain thresholds in the capital of a company. If the acquirer fails to declare these shares, voting rights would be lost.

It is very unusual for an acquirer to gain control of a public company without launching a public offer on the target. Such offers are made to all shareholders over a certain period of time (two to ten weeks depending on the country). Public offers can be split between:

1. **Share offers or cash offers**. Table 1.42 summarizes the criteria relevant for assessing whether a bidder wants to propose shares or cash in a public offer.

   Let's consider an example. Companies *A* and *B* have the characteristics shown in Table 1.43.

   Depending on the method used, the post-transaction situation is as shown in Table 1.44.

   Enterprise value and consolidated operating income are the same in each scenario. Economically, each transaction represents the same business combination of companies *A* and *B*.

   Financially, however, the situation is very different, even putting aside accounting issues. If *A* pays for the

Table 1.42: Criteria for assesing whether a bidder wants to propose shares or cash in a public offer

	Payment in cash	Payment in shares	Comments
Signal from buyer's point of view	Positive: buyer's stock is undervalued. Debt financing: positive signal	Negative: buyer's stock is overvalued	
Signal from seller's point of view	None	Positive: the seller is taking some of the risk of the deal	
Allocation of synergies	Target company's shareholders benefit from synergies only via the premium they receive	Target company's shareholders participate fully in future synergies	In a friendly share exchange offer, the premium might be minimal if the expected synergies are high
Psychological effects	Cash lends credibility to the bid and increases its psychological value	Payment in shares has a 'friendly' character	

(*continued overleaf*)

Table 1.42: (*continued*)

	Payment in cash	Payment in shares	Comments
Purchaser's financial structure	Increases gearing	Decreases gearing	The size of the deal sometimes requires payment in shares
Impact on purchaser's share price	After the impact of the announcement, no direct link between the purchaser's and target's share price	Immediate link between purchaser's and target's share price, maintained throughout the bid period	A share exchange offer gains credibility when the two companies' share prices align with the announced exchange ratio.
Shareholder structure	No impact unless the deal is later on refinanced through a share issue	Shareholders of the target become shareholders of the enlarged group	Sometimes, shareholders of the target get control of the new group in a share for share offer

Accounting effects	Increases EPS and its growth rate if the inverse of the target's P/E including any premium is greater than the after-tax cost of debt of the acquirer	Increases EPS if the purchaser's P/E is higher than the target's, premium included	EPS is not a real indicator of value creation
Purchaser's tax situation	Interest expense deductible	No impact, except capital gain if treasury shares are used	Taxation is not a determining factor
Seller's tax situation	Taxable gain	Gain on sale can be carried forward	
Index weighting	No change	Higher weighting in index (greater market capitalization)	In the case of a share exchange, possible rerating owing to size effect

Table 1.43: Characteristics of companies *A* and *B*

(in € m)	Enterprise value	Value of shareholder equation agreed in the merger
Company *A*	900	450
Company *B*	1000	750

acquisition in shares, the shareholders' equity of *A* is increased by the shareholders' equity of *B*. If *A* purchases *B* for cash, the value of *A*'s shareholders' equity does not increase.

It can be noted that when the target is a listed company, a 100% successful share exchange offer is financially equivalent to a legal merger.

We reiterate that our reasoning here is strictly arithmetic and we are not taking into account any impact the transaction may have on the value of the two companies. If the two companies were already correctly priced before the transaction and there are no synergies, their value will remain the same. If not, there will be a change in value. The financial mechanics (sale, share exchange, etc.) have no impact on the economics of a business combination.

This said, there is one important financial difference: an acquisition paid for in cash does not increase a group's financial clout (i.e. future investment capacity), but an all share transaction creates a group with financial means which tend to be the sum of that of the two constituent companies.

2. **Voluntary or mandatory offers**. The concept of the mandatory offer does not exist in every country. Nevertheless, in most countries, when a buyer passes a certain threshold or acquires the control of the target, he or she is required by stock exchange regulation to offer to buy back all the shareholders' shares. It is one of the founding rules of stock exchange regulations. It should be

Table 1.44: Post-transaction situation

(in € m)	*A* acquires *B* shares for cash	*A* issues new shares in exchange for *B* shares and dissolves *B*	*A* issues new shares in exchange for *B* shares and *B* becomes a 100% subsidiary of *A*	*A* issues new shares in exchange for assets and liabilities of *B*
Value of *A*'s new capital employed (now $A + B$)	1900	1900	1900	1900
Value of *A*'s shareholders' equity	450	1200	1200	1200
Percentage of *A* held by *A* shareholders	100%	37.5%	37.5%	37.5%
Percentage of *A* held by *B* shareholders		62.5%	62.5%	62.5%

noted that in the USA, there is no mandatory offer and an acquirer can buy a majority of the capital of a listed company without having to launch an offer to the minority shareholders.

Generally, the constraints for a mandatory offer are tighter than for a voluntary offer. For example, in the UK the mandatory offer will be in cash or at least a cash alternative will be provided. Obviously the conditions of the offer that the acquirer is allowed to set in a mandatory offer are limited because they are defined by the regulations.

3. **Hostile or recommended offers**. The success or failure of an offer can largely depend on the attitude of the target's management and the board of directors towards the offer.

   To maximize the chances of success, the terms of an offer are generally negotiated with the management prior to the announcement, and then recommended by the board of the company. The offer is then qualified friendly or recommended.

   In some cases, the management of the target is not aware of the launch of an offer; it is then called an *unsolicited offer*. Facing this sudden event the board has to convene and to decide whether the offer is acceptable or not. If the board rejects the offer, it becomes hostile. This does not mean that the offer will not succeed but just that the bidder will have to fight management and the current board of directors during the offer period to convince shareholders.

   In theory, a company whose shares are being secretly bought up on the stock market generally has a greater variety and number of *defensive measures* available to it than a company that is the target of a takeover bid.

   - The target company can either defend itself by embarking on an information campaign, explaining to shareholders and to the media how it will be able to create greater value in the future than the premium being offered by the predator, or it can use more active

defensive measures, such as: finding a third party ready to launch a competing takeover bid;
- launching its own takeover bid on the hostile bidder;
- getting 'friends' to buy up its shares;
- carrying out a capital increase and changing the scope of consolidation of the company;
- poison pills;
- legal action.

A *competing takeover bid* must be filed a few days before the close of the initial bid. The price offered should be at least a few percentage points higher than the initial bid. There's always the possibility that the initial bidder will make a higher bid, so there's no guarantee that the competing offer will succeed. Likewise, the *white knight* can sometimes turn gray or black when the rescue offer actually succeeds. We saw this when the German group E.On came to the 'rescue' of Endesa that was 'under attack' by the Spanish group Gas Natural and when Alcan fell into the arms of Rio Tinto.

A *share purchase* or *exchange offer* by the target on the hostile bidder, known as a *Pac-Man defense*, is only possible if the hostile bidder itself is listed and if its shares are widely held. In such cases, industrial projects are not that different given that an offer by *X* on *Y* results in the same economic whole as an offer by *Y* on *X*. This marks the start of a communications war (advertisements, press releases, meetings with investors), with each camp explaining why it would be better placed to manage the new whole than the other.

The *buying up of shares by friends* is often highly regulated and generally has to be declared to the market authority which monitors any acting in concert or which may force the 'friend' to file a counter offer!

A *capital increase or the issue of marketable securities* is often only possible if this has been authorized by the general meeting of shareholders prior to the takeover bid, because generally there won't be enough time to convene an EGM to fit in with the offer timetable. In any event, a reserved issue is often not allowed.

Poison pills are a strong dissuasive element. The negative consequences of warrants being issued for the company launching a hostile takeover bid mean that it is generally prepared to negotiate with the target – neutralization of the warrants in exchange for a higher offer price.

Legal action could be taken to ensure that market regulations are complied with or on the basis of misleading information if the prospectus issued by the hostile bidder appears to criticize the target's management. There is also the possibility of reporting the hostile bidder for abuse of a dominant position or insider trading if unusual trades are made before the offer is launched, for failing to comply with the principle of equality of shareholders or for failing to protect the interests of employees if the target has made risky acquisitions during the offer period. The real aim of any legal proceedings is to gain time for the target's management given that, in general, it takes a few months for the courts to issue rulings on the facts of a case.

However, in our view, loyal shareholders can be the best defense. What makes them loyal? Good financial performance, candid financial communication, a share price that reflects the company's value, and skilled managers who respect the principles of shareholder value and corporate governance.

References and Further Reading

Agrawal, A. and Jaffe, J., The post-merger performance puzzle, *Advances in Mergers and Acquisitions*, **1**, 7–41, 2000.

Alexandridis, G., Petmezas, D. and Travlos, N., Gains from mergers and acquisitions around the world: New evidence, *Financial Management*, **39**(4), 1671–1695, Winter 2010.

Boone, A. and Mulherin, J., How are firms sold? *Journal of Finance*, **62**(2), 847–875, April 2007.

Danielson, M. and Karpoff, J., Do pills poison operating performance? *Journal of Corporate Finance*, **12**, 536–559, June 2006.

Dong, M., Hirshleifer, D., Richardson, R. and Teoh, S., Does investors' misvaluation drive the takeover market? *Journal of Finance*, **61**(2), 725–762, April 2006.

Emery, G. and Switzer, J., Expected market reaction and the choice of method of payment for acquisitions, *Financial Management*, **28**, 73–86, Winter 1999.

Faccio, M. and Masulis, R., The choice of payment method in European mergers & acquisitions, *Journal of Finance*, **60**(3), 1345–1388, June 2005.

Hubbard, G. and Darius, P., A reexamination of the conglomerate merger wave in the 1960s, *Journal of Finance*, **54**(3), 1131–1152, June 1999.

Jensen, M. and Ruback, R., The market for corporate control: The scientific evidence, *Journal of Financial Economics*, **11**, 5–50, April 1983.

Rhodes-Kropf, M. and Viswanathan, S., Market valuation and merger waves, *Journal of Finance*, **59**(6), 2685–2718, December 2004.

Schwert, G., Hostility in takeovers: In the eyes of the beholder? *Journal of Finance*, **55**(6), 2599–2640, December 2000.

Shleifer, A. and Vishny, R., Stock market driven acquisition, *Journal of Financial Economics*, **70**(3), 295–331, December 2003.

Straska, M. and Waller, G., Do antitakeover provisions harm shareholders? *Journal of Corporate Finance*, **16**(4), 487–497, September 2010.

www.iclg.co.uk, main aspects of antitrust and takeover rules for 50 countries.

52. What are synergies?

Short Answer

Value is created only when the sum of cash flows from two companies is higher than the value of the single companies because they are both managed by the same group. This is the result of industrial synergies $(2 + 2 = 5)$, and not financial synergies, which do not exist.

Example

In order to understand the importance of synergies, we can say that approximately one out of two mergers fail because the promised synergies never materialize.

Synergies are often overestimated, their cost and time to implement underestimated.

Numerous research works have measured the value created by an M&A deal and how this value is shared between shareholders of the buyer and of the target.

They demonstrate that value is created for the target's shareholders because of the control premium paid. For the buyer's shareholders, the results are more mixed, even if they tend to show a recent improvement compared to the end of the 1990s where it was widely assumed that two-thirds of mergers were failing.

Without some resounding failures (acquisition of Chrysler by Daimler) or the AOL–Time Warner merger) which heavily bias the results, M&A deals would appear value creative because of some largely successful deals such as Santander–Abbey National, Air France–KLM, NBC–Universal.

Quality and speediness of the integration process are the key factors for successful M&A deals.

Long Answer

The peculiarity of the market for corporate control arises from the existence of synergies that give rise to strategic value.

Unless it can draw on industrial synergies, the value of a company remains the same whether it is independent or part of a large group. The financial investor does not want to pay a premium in the form of lower returns for something he can do himself at no cost by diversifying his portfolio. The existence of a control premium can be justified only if the new owners of the company obtain more value from it than did its previous owners. A control premium derives from the industrial, commercial, administrative or tax synergies the new majority shareholders hope to unlock.

The value of synergies is allocated during the negotiation phase. The seller receives more than the value for the company on a standalone basis because he or she pockets part of the value of the synergies the buyer hopes to unlock. Similarly, the buyer pays out part of the value of the synergies, but has still not paid more than the company is worth to them.

Merger synergies are not shared in the same way.

In a *cash acquisition*, selling shareholders pocket a portion of the value of synergies immediately (depending on the outcome of the negotiation). The selling shareholders do not bear any risk of implementation of the synergies.

Table 1.45: Numerical example for companies *A* and *B*

(in € m)	Sales	Net income	Book equity	Value of shareholders' equity
A	1500	15	250	450
B	5000	35	450	680

In an *all-share transaction*, however, the value creation (or destruction) of combining the two businesses will be shared according to the relative values negotiated by the two sets of shareholders. Let's consider, in Table 1.45, a numerical example with two companies *A* and *B*.

Example

Putting aside for one moment potential industrial and commercial synergies, the financial elements of the new company $A + B$ resulting from the merger with *B* are shown in Table 1.46.

Table 1.46: Financial elements of new company $A + B$

(in € m)	Sales	Net income	Book equity	Value of shareholders' equity
Group $A + B$	6500	50	700	1130

Turning our attention now to the EPS of companies *A* and *B*, we observe the following (Table 1.47):

Table 1.47: EPS of companies *A* and *B*

	Value of Shareholders' equity (€ m)	Net income (in € m)	P/E	Number of shares (million)	Earning per share
Company *A*	450	15	30	4.5	3.33
Company *B*	680	35	19.4	3.75	9.33

Let's now suppose that synergies between *A* and *B* will increase the after-tax income of the merged group by €10m from the first year onwards.

The big unknown is the credit and the value investors will ascribe to these synergies:

- 300m – i.e. a valuation based on *A*'s P/E multiple of 30;
- 194m – i.e. a valuation based on *B*'s P/E multiple of 19.4;
- 226m – i.e. a valuation based on a P/E multiple of 22.6, the average of the P/Es of *A* and *B*;
- some other value.

Two factors lead us to believe that investors will attribute a value that is lower than expected:

- *The amount of synergies announced at the time of the merger is only an estimate and the announcers have an interest in maximizing it to induce shareholders to approve the transaction.* In practice, making a merger or an acquisition work is a managerial challenge. You have to motivate employees who may previously have been competitors to work together, create a new corporate culture, avoid losing customers who want to maintain a wide variety of suppliers, etc. Experience shows that:

  - more than half of all mergers fail on this score;
  - actual synergies are slower in coming; and
  - the amount of synergies is lower than originally announced.
- *Sooner or later, the company will not be the only one in the industry to merge*. Because mergers and acquisitions tend to come in waves, rival companies will be tempted to merge for the same reasons: unlock synergies and remain competitive. As competition also consolidates, all market participants will be able to lower prices or refrain from raising them, to the joy of the consumer. As a result, the group that first benefited from merger synergies will be forced to give back some of its gains to its customers, employees and suppliers.

A study of the world's largest mergers and acquisitions shows that the P/E multiple at which the market values synergies when they are announced is well below that of both the acquiring company and the target. Based on this information, let's assume that the investors in our example value the €10m p.a. in synergies at a P/E of 12, or €120m.

The value of shareholders' equity of the new group is therefore:

$$450 + 680 + 120 = 1250\text{m}$$

Value is created in the amount of 1250 – 1130 = 120m. This is not financial value creation, but the result of the merger itself, which leads to cost savings or revenue enhancements. The €120m synergy pie will be shared between the shareholders of *A* and *B*.

At the extreme, the shareholders of *A* might value *B* at 800m. In other words, they might attribute the full present value of the synergies to the shareholders of *B*. The relative value ratio would then be at its maximum, 1.78.

The relative value ratios of 1.19 and 1.78 constitute the upper and lower boundaries of the negotiable range. If they agree on 1.19, the shareholders of *A* will have kept all of the value of the synergies for themselves. Conversely, at 1.78, all of the synergies accrue to the shareholders of *B*.

The relative value choice determines the relative ownership stake of the two groups of shareholders, *A*'s and *B*'s, in the post-merger group, which ranges from 45.6%/54.4% to 36%/64%. The difference is significant!

Determining the value of potential synergies is a crucial negotiating stage. It determines the maximum merger premium that company *A* will be willing to pay to the shareholders of *B*:

- large enough to encourage shareholders of *B* to approve the merger;
- small enough to still be value creating for *A*'s shareholders.

53. What are demergers and split-offs?

Short Answer

A *demerger* is a separation of the activities of a group: the original shareholders become the shareholders of the separated companies.

In a *split-off*, shareholders have the option to exchange their shares in the parent company for shares in a subsidiary.

Long Answer

Demerger
The transaction can be carried out by distributing the shares of a subsidiary in the form of a dividend (a *spin-off*), or by dissolving the parent company and distributing the shares of the ex-subsidiaries to the shareholders (a *split-up*). Immediately after the transaction, the shareholders of the demerged companies are the same, but ownership evolves very quickly thereafter.

Broadly speaking, studies on demergers have shown that the shares of the separated companies outperform the market, both in the short and long term.

> *In the context of the efficient markets hypothesis and agency theory, demergers are an answer to conglomerate discounts.*

In this sense, a demerger creates value, because it solves the following problems:

- Allocation of capital within a conglomerate is suboptimal, benefiting divisions in difficulty and penalizing healthy ones, making it harder for the latter to grow.
- The market values primary businesses correctly but undervalues secondary businesses.
- The market has trouble understanding conglomerates, a problem made worse by the fact that virtually all financial analysts are specialized by industry. With the number of listed companies constantly growing and investment possibilities therefore expanding, investors prefer simplicity. In addition, large conglomerates communicate less about smaller divisions, thus increasing the information asymmetry.
- Lack of motivation of managers of non-core divisions.
- Small base of investors interested by all the businesses of the group.
- The conglomerate has operating costs that add to the costs of the operating units without creating value.

Demergers expose the newly-created companies to potential takeovers. Prior to the demerger, the company might have been too big or too diverse. Potential acquirers might not have been interested in all of its businesses. And the process of acquiring the entire company and then selling off the unwanted businesses is cumbersome and risky. A demerger creates smaller, pure-play companies, which are more attractive in the takeover market. Empirically, it has been shown that demerged subsidiaries do not always outperform. This is the case when the parent company has completely divested its interest in the new company or has itself become subject to a takeover bid.

Lastly lenders are not great fans of demergers. By reducing the diversity of activities and consequently potentially increasing the volatility of cash flows, they increase the risk for lenders. At one extreme, the value of their debt decreases if the transaction is structured in such a way that one of the new companies carries all the debt, while the other is financed by equity capital only.

In practice, however, debt-holders are rarely spoiled that way. Loan agreements and bond indentures generally stipulate that, in the event of a demerger, the loan or the bonds become immediately due and payable.

Consequently they are in a position to negotiate demerger terms that are not unfavorable to them. This explains why empirical studies have shown that, on average, demergers lead to no transfer of value from creditors to shareholders.

Because of their complexity and the detailed preparation they require, demergers are less frequent than mergers.

Demerging is not a panacea. If one of the demerged businesses is too small, its shares will suffer a deep liquidity discount. And not all conglomerates are financial failures: General Electric and Bouygues are two prominent examples to the contrary.

If we wanted to be cynical, we might say that demergers represent the triumph of sloth (investors and analysts do not take time to understand complex groups) and selfishness (managers want to finance only the high-performance businesses).

But it's also the triumph of modern financial theory, which says that enterprises that bring together unrelated businesses without creating value will not stay as a group indefinitely.

Split-off

To avoid unnecessary holdings of treasury shares, the shares tendered are cancelled. A split-off is a share repurchase paid for with shares in a subsidiary rather than in cash. If all shareholders tender their shares, the split-off is identical to a demerger. If the offer is relatively unsuccessful, the parent company remains a shareholder of the subsidiary.

References and Further Reading

Anslinger, P., Klepper, S. and Subramaniam, S., Breaking up is good to do, *McKinsey Quarterly*, **1**, 16–27, 1999.

Chemmanur, T. and Yan, A. Corporate Control and Disciplining Effect of Spin-offs: A Theory of Performance and Value Improvements in Spin-offs, working paper, Boston College, January 2002.

Desai, H. and Jain, P., Firm performance and focus: Long-run stock market performance following spin-offs, *Journal of Financial Economics*, **54**(1), 75–101, October 1999.

Hege, U., Lovo, S. and Slovin, M., Equity and cash in intercorporate asset sales: theory and evidence, *Review of Financial Studies*, **22**(2), 681–714, 2009.

Krishnaswami, S. and Subramaniam, V., Information asymmetry, valuation, and the corporate spin-off decision, *Journal of Financial Economics*, **53**(1), 73–112, July 1999.

Leland, H., Financial synergies and the optimal scope of the firm: Implication for mergers spin-offs and structured finance, *Journal of Finance*, **62**(2), 765–807, April 2007.

Maxwell, W. and Rao, R., Do spin-offs expropriate wealth from bondholders?, *Journal of Finance*, **58**(5), 2087–2108, October 2003.

McKenna, M., *Methods of Divesting Assets: Straight Sales, Carve-outs, Spin-offs, Tracking Stocks and Hybrid Divestitures*, Working Paper, Stern School of Business, April 1999.

Mehrotra, V., Mikkelson, W. and Partch, M., The design of financial policies in corporate spin-offs, *Review of Financial Studies*, **16**(4), 1359–1388, Winter 2003.

Parrino, R., Spin-offs and wealth transfers: The Marriott case, *Journal of Financial Economics*, **43**(2), 241–274, February 1997.

Rosenfeld, J., Additional evidence on the relation between divestiture announcements and shareholder wealth, *Journal of Finance*, **39**(5), 1437–1448, December 1984.

Veld, C. and Veld-Merkoulova, D., Do spin-offs create value? The European case, *Journal of Banking & Finance*, **28**, 1111–1135, 2004.

54. What is a leveraged buyout?

Short Answer

A *leveraged buyout* (LBO) is the acquisition of a company by one or several private equity funds which finance their purchase mainly by debt.

Example

Take a look at the example of Elis, sold in mid-2007 by the LBO fund PAI for an enterprise value of €2.3bn (Figure 1.49). Elis generated a 2007 operating profit of €160m for sales of €930m and an EBITDA of €220m.

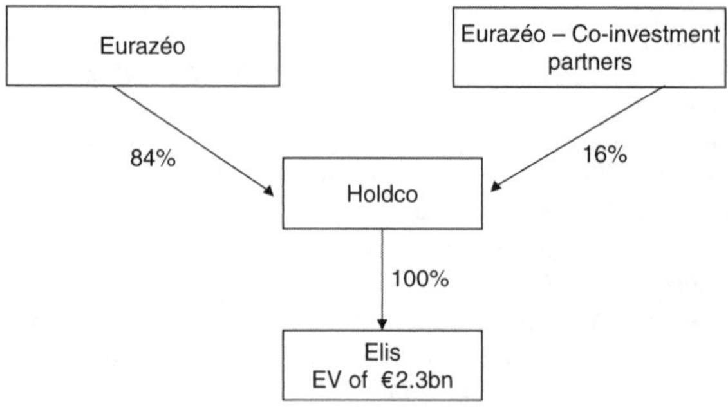

Figure 1.49: Operating profit for Elis (2007) in €bn

We assume that the pre-tax cost of debt is 7% (4% plus a 3% margin). The balance sheets are shown in Table 1.48.

Note that consolidated shareholders' equity, on a revalued basis, is now 81% lower than it was prior to the LBO.

Table 1.48: Balance sheets in €m

Elis's revalued balance sheet		**Holdco's unconsolidated balance sheet**		**Group's consolidated balance sheet**	
Operating assets €2276m	Shareholders' equity €2276m	Shares of Elis €2276m	Debt €426m	Operating assets €2276m	Debt €426m
			Shareholders' equity €1850m		Shareholders' equity €1850m

An LBO leads to a massive destruction of equity.

The profit and loss statement, meanwhile, is shown in Table 1.49.

Table 1.49: Profit and loss in €m

(in €m)	Elis	Holdco	Consolidated
Earnings before interest and tax	160	104	160
–Interest expense	0	130	–130
– Income tax at 35%	–56	0	–10
=Net income	104	–26	20

Long Answer

Leveraged buyout or LBO is the term for a variety of transactions in which an external financial investor uses leverage to purchase a company. Depending on how management is included in the takeover arrangements, LBOs fall into the following categories:

- **(Leveraged) management buyout** or **(L)MBO**, is a transaction undertaken by the existing management together with some or all of the company's employees.
- When outside managers are brought in, the transaction is called a **BIMBO**, i.e. a combination of a *buying* and a management *buyout*. This is the most common type of LBO in the UK.
- **Leveraged buildup (LBU)** describes an LBO in which the new group continues to acquire companies in its sector so as to create industrial synergies. These acquisitions are financed primarily with debt.
- **Owner buyout (OBO)** is a transaction undertaken by the largest shareholder to gain full control over the company.

The average LBO lifetime is short. Financial investors generally keep the investment for two to five years.

There are several *exit strategies*:

- **Sale to a trade buyer**. When the time has arrived for the exit of the financial buyer, either the market or the company will have had to change for a trade buyer to be interested. Galbani, the leading Italian cheese company, was sold by P/E funds in 2006 to Lactalis.
- **Stock market flotation**. This strategy must be implemented in stages, and it does not allow the sellers to obtain a control premium; most of the time they suffer from an IPO discount. It is more attractive for senior management than a trade sale. At end-2006, Hertz was listed by Clayton Dubillier & Rice, and Carlyle.
- **Sale to another financial investor**, who in turn sets up another LBO. These 'secondary' LBOs are becoming more and more common. Elis is a tertiary LBO.
- **A leveraged recapitalization**. After a few years of debt reduction thanks to cash flow generation, the target takes on additional debt with the purpose of either paying a large dividend or repurchasing shares. The result is a far more financially leveraged company.

There are different players involved in an LBO transaction.

Potential targets
The target company must generate profits and cash flows that are sufficiently large and stable over time to meet the holding company's interest and debt payments. The target must not have burdensome investment needs. Mature companies that are relatively shielded from variations in the business cycle make the best candidates: food, retail, water, building materials, real estate, cinema theaters and yellow pages are all prime candidates.

The group's LBO financing already packs a hefty financial risk, so the industrial risks had better be limited. Targets are usually drawn from sectors with high barriers to entry and minimal substitution risk. Targets are often positioned on niche markets and control a significant portion of them, like Elis.

Traditionally, LBO targets are 'cash cows' but, more recently, there has been a movement towards companies exhibiting higher growth or operating in sectors with opportunities for consolidation.

As the risk aversion of investors decreases, some private equity funds have carried out LBOs in more difficult sectors or specialized in heavy turn-around situations (Chrysler). The mid-2007 crisis and the sudden disappearance of LBOs larger than €500m is likely to prompt a return to the basics: targets with high, stable and predictable cash flows able to pay down their debt with a reasonable degree of confidence.

Sellers

Around half of all LBOs are carried out on family-owned companies (the first LBO on Elis). An LBO solves the succession problem as the majority shareholders may be reluctant to sell to a competitor, may prefer to sell to their faithful and dedicated management team, and/or the stock exchange exit may be close at that time. In 20% of cases, a large group wishing to refocus on a core business sells a subsidiary or a division via an LBO. Some sectors are so concentrated that only LBO funds can buy a target as the antitrust authorities would never allow a competitor to buy it or would impose severe disposals making such an acquisition unpalatable to many trade buyers (Pro Sieben Sat 1, in German TV).The larger transactions fall into the latter category (Hertz sold by Ford).

But more and more frequently (30%), targets are companies already under an LBO, sold by one private equity investor to another one, for the second, third or more times, such as Elis.

Finally, some listed companies that are undervalued (often because of liquidity issues or because of lack of attention from the investment community because of their size) sometimes opt for *public-to-private* (P-to-P) LBOs. In the process, the company is delisted from the stock exchange. Despite the fact that these transactions are complex to structure and generate high execution risk they are becoming more and more common thanks to the drop in market values.

LBO funds (the equity investors)
Setting up an LBO requires specific expertise, and certain investment funds specialize in them. These are called *private equity sponsors*, because they invest in the equity capital of unlisted companies.

LBOs are particularly risky because of their high gearing. Investors will therefore undoubtedly require high returns. Indeed, required returns are often in the region of 25% p.a. In addition, in order to eliminate diversifiable risk these specialized investment funds often invest in several LBOs.

To reduce their risk, LBO funds also invest alongside another LBO fund (they form a consortium) or an industrial company (sometimes the seller) with a minority stake. In this case, the industrial company contributes its knowledge of the business and the LBO fund its expertise in financial engineering, the legal framework and taxation.

Most of the private equity sponsors contribute equity for between 20% and 40% of the total financing. The Elis LBO was done at the top of the market with only 19% of equity.

Post 2007, LBOs are financed with an equity component closer to 40%. Materially, LBO funds are organized in the form of a management company that is held by partners who manage funds raised from institutional investors or high net worth individuals.

When a fund has invested nearly all of the equity it has raised, another fund is launched. Each fund is required to return to investors all of the proceeds of divestments as these are made, and the ultimate aim is for the fund to be liquidated after a given number of years.

The management company, in other words the partners of the LBO funds, is paid on the basis of a percentage of the funds invested and a percentage of the capital gains made, known as *carried interest*.

Lenders

For smaller transactions (less than €10m), there is a single bank lender, often the target company's main bank.

For larger transactions, debt financing is more complex. The LBO fund negotiates the debt structure and conditions with a pool of bankers. Most of the time, bankers propose a financing to all candidates (even the one advising the seller). This is *staple financing*.

The high degree of financial gearing requires not only traditional bank financing, but also subordinated lending and *mezzanine debt*, which lie between traditional financing and shareholders' equity. This results in a four-tier structure: traditional, secured loans called *senior debt*, to be repaid first, *subordinated* or *junior debt* to be repaid after the senior debt, mezzanine financing, the repayment of which is subordinated to the repayment of the junior and senior debt and, last in line, shareholders' equity. Sometimes, shareholders of the target grant a vendor loan to the LBO fund (part of the price of which payment is deferred) to help finance the transaction. Assets of the target can also be securitized to raise more financing. Lastly in the halcyon days of LBOs (2005 until mid-2007) other products were created but they have since disappeared.

Management of a company under an LBO

The managers of a company under an LBO may be the historical managers of the company or new managers appointed by the LBO fund. Regardless of their background, they are responsible for implementing a clearly defined business plan that was drawn up with the LBO fund when it took over the target. The business plan makes provision for operational improvements, investment plans and/or disposals, with a focus on cash generation because, as the reader is no doubt aware, cash is what is needed for paying back debts!

LBO funds tend to ask managers to invest large amounts of their own cash in the company, and even to take out loans to be able to do so, in order to ensure that management's interests are closely aligned with those of the fund. Investments could be in the form of warrants, convertible bonds or shares, providing managers with a second leverage effect, which, if the business plan bears fruit, will result in a five- to ten-fold or even greater increase in their investment. On the other hand, if the business plan fails, they will lose everything. So, only in the event of success will the management team get a partial share of the capital gains and a higher IRR on its investment than that of the LBO funds. This arrangement is known as the *management package*.

References and Further Reading

Achleitner, A., *Value creation in private equity*, Centre for Entrepreneurial and Financial Studies, Capital Dynamics, 2009.

BCG-IESE, *The advantage of persistence: how the best private-equity firms 'beat the fade'*, 2008.

Burrough, B. and Hillyar, J., *Barbarians at the Gate*, Harper Business Essentials, 2003.

Elitzur, R., Halpern, P., Kieschnick, R. and Rotenberg, W., Management incentives and the structure of management buy-outs, *Journal of Economic Behaviour and Organization*, **35**(3), 347–367, August 1998.

EVCA, *Private Equity Funds Structures in Europe*, European Private Equity and Venture Capital Association, 2006.

Guo, S., Hotchkiss, E. and Song, W., Do Buyouts (Still) Create Value, *Journal of Finance*, **66**(2), April 2011.

Jensen, M., Eclipse of the public corporation, *Harvard Business Review*, **67**, 61–74, September 1989.

Pindur, D., *Value Creation in Successful LBOs*, DUV, 2007.

Povel, P. and Singh, R., Stapled Finance, *Journal of Finance*, **65**(3), 927–953, April 2011.

www.evca.com, site of the European Private Equity and Venture Capital Association.

www.nottingham.ac.uk/business/cmbor, The Centre for Management Buy-out Research's website.

55. What is bankruptcy?

Short Answer

Bankruptcy is triggered when a company can no longer meet its short-term commitments and thus faces a liquidity crisis. This situation normally does not arise because the company has too much debt (which is the tip of the iceberg), but because it is not profitable enough.

Example

Rating agencies also estimate the probability that a company will go bankrupt in the short or long term.

When US energy giant Enron filed for bankruptcy at the end of 2001, rating agencies were criticized for not anticipating financial difficulties and warning creditors. In this case, the rating system (Figure 1.50) did not work properly.

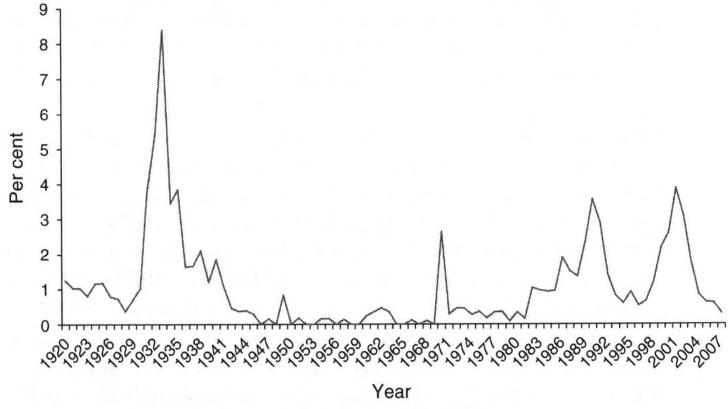

Source: moody's 2008.

Figure 1.50: Bankruptcy rate of companies rated by Moody's

Long Answer

Every economic system needs mechanisms to ensure the optimal utilization of resources. Bankruptcy is the primary instrument for reallocating means of production from inefficient to efficient firms.

Theoretically, bankruptcy shakes out the bad apples from sectors in difficulty and allows profitable groups to prosper. Without efficient bankruptcy procedures, financial crises are longer and deeper.

A bankruptcy process can allow a company to reorganize, often requiring asset sales, a change in ownership and partial debt forgiveness on the part of creditors. In other cases, bankruptcy leads to liquidation – the death of the company.

The problems generally stem from an ill-conceived strategy, or because that strategy is not implemented properly for its sector (e.g. costs are too high). As a result, profitability falls short of creditor expectations. If the company does not have a heavy debt burden, it can limp along for a certain period of time. Otherwise, financial difficulties rapidly start appearing.

Generally speaking, financial difficulties result either from a market problem, a cost problem or a combination of the two. The company may have been caught unaware by market changes and its products might not suit market demands (e.g. Smoby, producer of wooden toys and Boo.com). Alternatively, the market may be too small for the number of companies competing in it (e.g. online book sales and satellite TV platforms in various European countries). Ballooning costs compared with those of rivals can also lead to bankruptcy. Alitalia, for example, was uncompetitive against other airlines. Eurotunnel, meanwhile, spent twice the budgeted amount on digging the tunnel between France and the UK.

Nevertheless, a profitable company can encounter financial difficulties, too. For example, if a company's debt is primarily short term, it may have trouble rolling it over if liquidity is lacking on the financial markets. In this case, the most rational solution is to restructure the company's debt.

One of the fundamental goals of financial analysis as it is practiced in commercial banks, whose main business is making loans to companies, is to identify the companies most likely to go 'belly up' in the near or medium term and not lend to them.

The bankruptcy process is one of the least standardized and homogenized legal mechanisms around the world. Virtually all countries have different systems. In addition, legislation evolves rapidly.

Nevertheless, among the different procedures, some patterns can be found. In a nutshell, there are two different types of bankruptcy procedure. The process will be either 'creditor (lender) friendly' or 'debtor (company) friendly'. But all processes have the same ultimate goals although they may rank differently:

- pay-down the liabilities of the firm;
- minimize the disruptive impact on the industry; and
- minimize the social impact.

The way in which default on payment is managed in different countries (Table 1.50) modifies the percentage of the debt that creditors (and more specifically banks) are able to recover. By examining bankruptcy law in three European countries (France, Germany and the UK), Davydenko and Franks (2008) show that banks seek to tailor their loans to make the most of legislation in force. They reproduce the rankings from a now famous article that awarded France the

Table 1.50: Management of default payment in different countries

	UK	France	Germany	India	Italy	USA
Type	Creditor (lender) friendly	Debtor (borrower) friendly	Creditor (lender) friendly	Creditor (lender) friendly	Debtor (borrower) friendly	Debtor (borrower) friendly
Possible restructuring	Rare after opening of a proceeding	Yes	Yes (rare)Creditor (lender) friendly	Yes	Yes	Yes
Management can stay in place	No	Yes*	Yes*	No	‡	Yes
Lenders vote on restructuring/liquidation plan	Yes	No	Yes	Yes	Yes†	Yes

Priority rule	Proceeding charges; secured debts on specific assets; tax and social security; other secured debts; other debts	Salaries; tax, other social liabilities; part of secured debts; proceeding charges; other secured debts; other debts	Proceeding charges; secured debts; other debts	Secured debts and employees proceeding charges; tax and social liabilities; unsecured debts	Proceeding charges; preferential creditors (inc. tax and social) and secured creditors; unsecured creditors	Secured debts granted after filing; employee benefit and tax claims; unsecured debts

*Assisted by court designated trustee.

†Yes in the case of restructuring (pre-emptive arrangement) but only consultative committee in case of liquidation (fallimento).

‡No in the case of liquidation (fallimento).

lowest score for creditor protection, compared with a score of three for Germany and a maximum four points for the UK.

In France, the absolute priority given to keeping the business going and protecting jobs has the side effect of reducing creditor protection. Banks require more collateral – over 100% of the value of the debt (compared with 40% in Germany and 60% in the UK). There is very little use of mortgages as assets tend to be sold off at far below their market value once bankruptcy procedures are launched. Banks prefer personal guarantees that they can activate directly. In the UK, default on payment leads to a procedure in which first ranking creditors have a veto on all decisions made by the directors. This means that first ranking creditors obtain *de facto* control over the company. In Germany, creditors do not enjoy quite as much protection but are better off than their French equivalents, retaining some power in the restructuring of loans.

> *Notwithstanding the efforts made by banks to adapt, there is still a huge gap between recovery rates in the three countries, which are 92% in the UK, 67% in Germany and only 56% in France.*

However, it should be noted that spreads used by UK banks are higher than those used by French banks (16 base points for an equivalent loan). Davydenko and Franks attribute this to less competition between lending establishments, the result of a financial system that is dominated by markets. Moreover, by focusing on firms that have defaulted on their loans, the article fails to analyze the abilities of the three systems to prevent debtor default (such as the 'alert procedure' in France). Competition between banks and prevention of debtor default are factors that should be taken into account for a fuller comparison of the merits of legislation in place in different countries in this domain.

Depending on the severity of the bankruptcy process and in particular whether or not it allows and promotes restructurings, *two opposite inefficiencies may arise*. The process may:

- allow restructuring of an inefficient firm that destroys value. This could be an issue as such restructuring may destabilize the whole industry; or
- lead to liquidation of efficient companies. A firm can be caught in a bankruptcy procedure because of a liquidity problem. In this case, liquidation could be value destroying.

It is important to understand that not all financial difficulties lead to voluntary or court-mandated reorganization or liquidation, which is often costly, lengthy and sometimes ineffective. *The first step is usually private negotiation between the company (shareholders and/or managers) and its creditors*. The more numerous the company's sources of funding – common shareholders, preferred shareholders, convertible bond holders, creditors, etc. – the more complex the negotiations.

Barring private negotiation, the potential conflicts between the various parties necessitate the intervention of a judge.

The business plan submitted by the company in financial distress is a key element in estimating its ability to generate the cash flows needed to pay off creditors.

A restructuring plan requires sacrifices from all stakeholders. It generally includes a recapitalization, often funded primarily by the company's existing shareholders, and renegotiation of the company's debt. Creditors are often asked to give up some of their claims, accept a suspension on interest payments and/or reschedule principal payments.

Creditors and shareholders are naturally at odds with each other in a restructuring. To bring them all on board, the renegotiated debt agreements sometimes include *claw back provisions*, whereby the principal initially foregone will be repaid if the company's future profits exceed a certain level. Alternatively, creditors might be granted share warrants. If the restructuring is successful, warrants enable the creditors to reap part of the benefits.

To succeed, financial restructuring must always be accompanied by operational restructuring.

Only financial restructuring will enable the company to return to profitability. As part of the effort to improve productivity, operational restructuring is very likely to involve headcount reductions. Certain businesses might be sold or discontinued. Note that restructuring a company in difficulty can sometimes be a vicious circle. Faced with a liquidity crisis, the company must sell off its most profitable operations. But as it must do so quickly, it sells them for less than their fair value. The profitability of the remaining assets is therefore impaired, paving the way to new financial difficulties.

Bankruptcy generates both *direct* (court proceedings, lawyers, fees, etc.) and *indirect* costs (loss of credibility *vis-à-vis* customers and suppliers, loss of certain business opportunities, etc.). These costs have an impact on a company's choice of financial structure.

Financial distress will generate conflict between shareholders and creditors (agency theory), and conflict among creditors (free rider issues).

References and Further Reading

Altman, E., Financial ratios, discriminant analysis and the prediction of corporation bankruptcy, *Journal of Finance*, **23**, 589–609, September 1968.

Berkovitch, E. and Israel, R., Optimal bankruptcy laws across different economic systems, *Review of Financial Studies*, **12**(2), 347–377, Summer 1999.

Bris, A., Welch, I. and Zhu, N., The costs of bankruptcy: Chapter 7 liquidation versus Chapter 11 reorganization, *Journal of Finance*, **61**(3), 1253–1306, June 2006.

Claessens, S. and Klapper, L., *Bankruptcy Around the World – Explanation of its Relative Use*, World Bank Development Research Group, July 2002.

Davydenko, S. and Franks, J., Do bankruptcy codes matter? A study of defaults in France, Germany, and the UK, *Journal of Finance*, **63**(2), 565–608, April 2008.

Djankov, S., Hart, O., McLiesh, C. and Shleifer, A., *Debt Enforcement Around the World*, ECGI, working paper 147/2007, December 2006.

McConnell, J. and Denis, D., *Corporate Restructuring*, Edward Elgar Publishing, 2005.

Molina, C. and Preve, L., Trade receivables policy of distressed firms and its effect on the costs of financial distress, *Financial Management*, **38**(3), 663–686, Autumn 2009.

Moody's, *Bankruptcy & Ratings: A Leveraged Finance Approach for Europe – UK versus France and Germany*, Moody's Global Credit Research, March 2000.

Zhang, G., Emerging from Chapter 11 bankruptcy: Is it good news or bad news for industry competitors?, *Financial Management*, **39**(4), 1719–1742, Winter 2010.

56. What do we mean by cash flow management?

Short Answer

Cash flow management is the traditional role of the treasury function. A treasurer's job is to perform the following tasks:

- forecast trends in the credit and debit balances of the company's accounts;
- keep inactive funds to a minimum;
- invest excess cash as efficiently as possible; and
- finance borrowing requirements as cheaply as possible.

Example

From the treasurer's standpoint, the balance of cash flows is not the same as that recorded in the company's accounts or that shown on a bank statement. An example can illustrate these differences.

A, a company headquartered in Amsterdam, issues a check for €1000 on 15th April to its supplier *R* in Rotterdam. Three different people will record the same amount, but not necessarily on the same date:

- *A*'s accountant, for whom the issue of the check theoretically makes the sum of €1000 unavailable as soon as the check has been issued.
- *A*'s banker, who records the €1000 check when it is presented for payment by *R*'s bank. He then debits the amount from the company's account based on this date.
- *A*'s treasurer, for whom the €1000 remains available until the check has been debited from the relevant bank account. The date of debit depends on when the check is cashed in by the supplier and how long the payment process takes.

There may be a difference of several days between these three dates, which determines movements in the three separate balances.

Cash management based on value dates is built on an analysis from the treasurer's standpoint. The company is interested only in the periods during which funds are actually available. Positive balances can then be invested or used, while negative balances generate real interest expense.

Long Answer

The *cash budget* includes not only the cash flows that have already taken place, but also all the receipts and disbursements that the company plans to make. These cash inflows and outflows may be related to the company's investment, operating or financing cycles.

The cash budget, showing the amount and duration of expected cash surpluses and deficits, serves *two purposes*:

- to ensure that the credit lines in place are sufficient to cover any funding requirements; and
- to define the likely uses of loans by major categories (e.g. the need to discount based on the company's portfolio of trade bills and drafts).

Planning cash requirements and resources is a way of adapting borrowing and investment facilities to actual needs and, first and foremost, a way of managing a company's interest expense. It is easy to see that a better rate loan can be negotiated if the need is forecast several months in advance. Likewise, a treasury investment will be more profitable over a pre-determined period, during which the company can commit not to use the funds.

The cash budget is a forward-looking management chart showing supply and demand for liquidity within the company.

It allows the treasurer to manage interest expense as efficiently as possible by harnessing competition not only among different banks, but also with investors on the financial markets.

Different budgets may cover different forecasting horizons for the company. Budgets can be used to distinguish between the degree of accuracy users are entitled to expect from the treasurer's projections.

Companies forecast cash flows by major categories over long-term periods and refine their projections as cash flows draw closer in time. Thanks to the various services offered by banks, budgets do not need to be 100% accurate, but can focus on achieving the relevant degree of precision for the period they cover.

An annual cash budget is generally drawn up at the start of the year based on the expected profit and loss account which has to be translated into cash flows. The top priority at this point is for cash flow figures to be consistent and material in relation to the company's business activities. At this stage, cash flows are classified by category rather than by type of payment.

These projections are then refined over periods ranging from one to six months to yield rolling cash budgets, usually for monthly periods. These documents are used to update the annual budgets based on the real level of cash inflows and outflows, rather than using expected profit and loss accounts.

Day-to-day forecasting represents the final stage in the process. This is the basic task of all treasurers and the basis on which their effectiveness is assessed. Because of the precision required, day-to-day forecasting gives rise to complex problems:

- it covers all the movements affecting the company's cash position;
- each bank account needs to be analyzed;
- it is carried out on a value date basis;
- it exploits the differences between the payment methods used;
- as far as possible, it distinguishes between cash flows on a category-by-category basis.

Table 1.51 summarizes these various aspects.

The various payment methods available raise complex problems and may give rise to uncertainties that are inherent in day-to-day cash forecasting. There are two main types of uncertainty:

- Is the forecast timing of receipts correct?
- When will expenditure give rise to actual cash disbursements?

From a cash budgeting standpoint, payment methods are more attractive where one of the two participants in the transaction possesses the initiative both in terms of setting up the payment and triggering the transfer of funds. Where a company has this initiative, it has much greater certainty regarding the value dates for the transfer (Table 1.52).

The treasurer's experience is invaluable, especially when it comes to forecasting the behavior of customers (payment dates) and of creditors (collection dates for the payment methods issued).

Zero cash is the nirvana of corporate treasurers, which keeps interest expense down to a bare minimum.

Even so, this aim can never be completely achieved. A treasurer always has to deal with some unpredictable

Table 1.51: Problems of day-to-day forecasting

	BANK No. 1				
	Account value dates				
	Monday	**Tuesday**	**Wednesday**	**Thursday**	**Friday**
Bills presented for payment					
Checks issued					
Transfers issued					
Standing orders paid					
Cash withdrawals					
Overdraft interest charges paid					
Sundry transactions					
(1) TOTAL DISBURSEMENTS					

	BANK No. 1				
	Account value dates				
	Monday	**Tuesday**	**Wednesday**	**Thursday**	**Friday**
Customer bills presented for collection					
Checks paid in					
Standing orders received					
Transfers received					
Interest on treasury placements					
Sundry transactions					
(1) TOTAL RECEIPTS					
(2) − (1) = DAILY BALANCE ON A VALUE DATE BASIS					

movements, be they disbursements or collections. The greater the number or volume of unpredictable movements, the more imprecise cash budgeting will be and the harder it is to optimize. That said, several techniques may be used to improve cash management significantly.

Table 1.52: Payment methods and initiatives

	Initiative for setting up transfer	Initiative for completing the fund transfer	Utility for cash budgeting
Check	Debtor	Creditor	None
Paper bill of exchange	Creditor	Creditor	Helpful to both parties insofar as the deadlines are met by the creditors
Electronic bill of exchange	Creditor	Creditor	
Paper promissory note	Debtor	Creditor	
Electronic promissory note	Debtor	Creditor	
Transfer Debit	Debtor	Debtor	Debtor

Behavioral analysis

The same type of analysis as performed for payment methods can also yield direct benefits for cash management. The company establishes collection times based on the habits of its suppliers. A statistical average for collection times is then calculated. Any deviations from the normal pattern are usually offset where an account sees a large number of transactions.

Intercompany agreements

Since efficient treasury management can unlock tangible savings, it is normal for companies that have commercial relationships to get together to maximize these gains.

Lockbox systems

Under the lockbox system, the creditor asks its debtors to send their payments directly to a PO Box that is emptied regularly by its bank. The funds are immediately paid into the banking system, without first being processed by the creditor's accounting department.

When the creditor's and debtor's banks are located in the same place, checks can easily be cleared on the spot. Such clearing represents another substantial time saving.

Checking bank terms

The corporate treasurer's role in investing the company's cash is nevertheless somewhat specific because the purpose of the company is not to make profits by engaging in risky financial investments. This is why specific products have been created to meet this criterion (Table 1.53).

The treasurer cannot decide to make an investment without first estimating its amount and the duration. Any mistake will mean the treasurer is forced to choose between two alternatives:

- either having to resort to new loans to meet the financial shortage created if too much cash was invested, thus generating a loss on the difference between lending and borrowing rates (i.e. the interest rate spread); or
- having to retrieve the amounts invested and incur the attendant penalties, lost interest or, in certain cases such as bond investments, risk of a capital loss.

Since corporate treasurers rarely know exactly how much cash they will have available for a given period, their main concern when choosing an investment is its liquidity – that is, how fast can it be converted back into cash. For an investment to be cashed in immediately, it must have an active secondary market or a redemption clause that can be activated at any time.

Table 1.53: Investment products

Investment products with no secondary market	Secondary market investment products
Interest bearing current accounts	Treasury bills and notes
Time deposits	Certificates of deposit
Cash certificates	Money-market or cash mutual funds
Repos (repurchase agreements)	Securitization vehicles
Securities lending	Bonds
	Equity

The corporate treasurer's *first* concern in investing cash is liquidity. Of course, if an investment can be terminated at any time, its rate of return is uncertain since the exit price is uncertain. A 91-day Treasury bill at a nominal rate of 4% can be sold at will, but its actual rate of return will depend on whether the bill was sold for more or less than its nominal value. However, if the rate of return is set in advance it is virtually impossible to exit the investment before its maturity since there is no secondary market or redemption clause, or if there is, only at a prohibitive cost.

The treasurer's *second* concern – security – is thus closely linked to the first. Security is measured in terms of the risk on the interest and principal.

References and Further Reading

Bates, T., Kahle, K. and Stulz, R., Why do US firms hold so much more cash than they used to do?, *Journal of Finance*, **64**(5), 1985–2021, October 2009.

Bragg, S., *Treasury Management: the practitioner's guide*, John Wiley & Sons, 2010.

Cooper, R., *Corporate Treasury and Cash Management*, Palgrave Macmillan, 2003.

Detragiache, E., Garella, P. and Guiso, L., Multiple versus single banking relationships: Theory and evidence, *Journal of Finance*, **55**(3), 1133–1161, June 2000.

European Central Bank, Statistics on payments – Data for 2009, September 2010.

Faulkender, M. and Wang, R., Corporate financial policy and the value of cash, *Journal of Finance*, **61**(4), 1957–1990, August 2006.

Opler, T., Pinkowitz, L., Stulz, R. and Williamson, R., The determinants and implications of corporate cash holdings, *Journal of Financial Economics*, **52**, 3–46, 1999.

Van den Wierlen, L., *International Cash Management*, 2nd ed., Riskmatrix, 2006.

www.treasurers.org, website of the Association of Corporate Treasurers

57. How many types of financial risks do companies face?

Short Answer

There are five main categories of financial risk:

- Market risk;
- Liquidity risk;
- Counterparty or credit risk;
- Operating risks;
- Political, regulatory and legal risks.

Long Answer

Risks can generally be classified into three major categories:

- **Risk fundamentally linked to market changes** (interest and exchange rates, raw material prices). The likelihood of occurrence of fundamental risk, i.e. the probability that the market will move against the interests of the company, is mechanically close to 50%. The intensity of the loss will depend on the volatility of the market in question.
- **Volatility risk** is a risk that materializes during an exceptional year (fire in a hypermarket). This sort of risk should always be covered.
- **Disaster risk** materializes once a century (for example the explosion at the BP oil refinery in Texas City) but it can have a very high level of intensity. It is difficult to cover and it is not unusual for the risk of a disaster occurring to be only partially covered, or not covered at all, given the fact that it is very unlikely to occur.

The key features of risk are:

- *intensity of the possible loss* on the amount of the exposure; and
- *frequency*, i.e. the likelihood of this loss occurring.

Risks run by companies can be split into five categories:

Market risk is exposure to unfavorable trends in product prices, interest rates, exchange rates, raw material prices or stock prices.

Market risk occurs at various levels:

- a position (a debt, for example, or an expected receipt of revenue in foreign currencies, etc.);
- a business activity (purchases paid in a currency other than that in which the products are sold, etc.); or
- a portfolio (short- and long-term financial holdings).

Liquidity risk, i.e. the impossibility at a given moment of meeting a debt payment, because:

- the company no longer has assets that can rapidly be turned into cash;
- a financial crisis (e.g. a market crash) has made it very difficult to liquidate assets, except at a very great loss in value; or
- it is impossible to find investors willing to offer new funding.

Counterparty or credit risk. This is the risk of loss on an outstanding receivable or, more generally, on a debt that is not paid on time. It naturally depends on three parameters: the amount of the debt, the likelihood of default and the portion of the debt that will be collected in the event of a default.

Operating risks are risks of losses caused by errors on the part of employees, systems and processes, or by external events:

- risk of deterioration of industrial facilities (accident, fire, explosion, etc.) that may also cover the risk of a temporary halt in business;
- technological risk: is the company in a position to identify or anticipate the arrival of new technology which will make its technology redundant?
- climate risks that may be of vital importance in some sectors, such as agriculture (how can cereal growers protect their harvests from the vagaries of the weather?) or the leisure sector (what sort of insurance should producers of outdoor concerts take out?);
- environmental risks: how can I ensure that I'm in a position to protect the environment from the potentially harmful impact of my activity? Am I in a position to certify that I comply with all environmental statutes and regulations in force?

Political, regulatory and legal risks are risks that impact on the immediate environment of the company and that could substantially modify its competitive situation and even the business model itself.

58. How can companies hedge financial risks?

Short Answer

Financial risk management comes in four forms:

- self-hedging;
- locking in prices or rates for a future transaction;
- insurance; and
- immediate disposal of a risky asset or liability.

Long Answer

Self-hedging

Self-hedging is only a strategy for hedging against risk in the true sense of the word when it is deliberately chosen by the company or when there is no other alternative (uninsurable risks). It can be structured to a greater or lesser extent. At the other extreme, we get risk taking (no hedging after the risk has been analyzed) and the setting up of a captive insurance scheme.

Self-hedging consists, in fact, in not hedging a risk. This is a reasonable strategy but mainly for large groups. Such groups assume that the law of averages applies to them and that they are therefore certain to experience some negative events on a regular basis, such as devaluations, customer bankruptcy, etc. Risk thus becomes a certainty and, hence, a cost. Self-hedging is based on the principle that a company has no interest in passing on the risk (and the profit) to a third party. Rather than paying what amounts to an insurance premium, the company provisions a sum each year to meet claims that will inevitably occur, thus becoming its own insurer.

The risk can be diminished, but not eliminated, by natural hedges. A European company, for example, that sells in the USA will also produce there, so that its costs can be in dollars rather than euros. It will take on debt in the USA rather than in Europe, to set dollar-denominated liabilities against dollar-denominated assets.

Self-hedging is a strategy adopted by either irresponsible companies or a limited number of very large companies who serve as their own insurance company!

One sophisticated procedure consists in setting up a *captive insurance* company, which will invest the premiums thus saved to build up reserves in order to meet future claims. In the meantime, some of the risk can be sold on the reinsurance market.

Setting up a captive insurance scheme is a complex operation, which takes the company into the realms of insurance. A captive insurance company is an insurance or reinsurance company that belongs to an industrial or commercial company, whose core business is not insurance. The purpose of the company's existence is to insure the risks of the group to which it belongs. This sort of setup sometimes becomes necessary because of the shortcomings of traditional insurance:

- some groups may be tempted to reduce risk prevention measures when they know that the insurance company will pay out if anything goes wrong;
- coverage capacities are limited and some risks are no longer insurable, for example gradual pollution or asbestos related damage;
- good risks end up making up for bad risks.

The scheme works as follows: the captive insurance company collects premiums from the industrial or commercial company and its subsidiaries, and covers their insurance losses. Like all insurance companies, it reinsures its risks with international reinsurance companies. A captive insurance setup has the following advantages:

- much greater efficiency (involvement in its own loss profile, exclusion of credit risk, reduction of over insurance, tailor-made policies);
- access to the reinsurance market;
- greater independence from insurance companies (pitting them against each other);
- reduction in vulnerability to cycles on the insurance market;
- possibility of tax optimization; and
- spreading the impact of losses over several financial years.

There is also the option of alternative risk financing. Well-known for their fertile imaginations, insurers have come up with products that make it possible to spread the impact of insurance losses on the income statement. The insured pays an annual premium and, if a loss occurs, the premium is adjusted, if necessary, to cover the cost of the loss. IFRS has killed off these products, which did not transfer risk but merely allowed the consequences of a loss to be spread over several financial years. Under the new accounting standards, the accounting treatment of these products has wiped out their major advantage, but they are back, albeit in hybrid forms.

Locking in prices or rates for a future transaction
Forward transactions can fully eliminate risk by locking in now the price or rate at which a transaction will be done in the future. This costs the company nothing but does prevent it from benefiting from a favorable shift in price or rates.

Forward transactions sometimes defy conventional logic, as they allow one to 'sell' what one does not yet possess or to 'buy' a product before it is available. However, they are not abstractions divorced from economic reality. As we will show, forward transactions can be broken down into the simple, familiar operations of spot purchasing or selling, borrowing and lending.

Forward currency transactions Let us take the example of a US company that is to receive 100m in euros in three months.

Let's say the euro is currently trading at \$1.5198. Unless the company treasurer is speculating on a rise in the euro, he wants to lock in today the exchange rate at which he will be able to sell these euros. So he offers to sell euros now that he will not receive for another three months. This is the essence of the forward transaction. Although forward transactions are common practice, it is worth looking at how they are calculated.

The transaction is tantamount to borrowing today the present value in euros of the sum that will be received in three months, exchanging it at the current rate and investing the corresponding amount in dollars for the same maturity.

Assume A is the amount in euros received by the company; N, the number of days between today and the date of receipt; $R€$, the euro borrowing rate; and $R\$$, the dollar interest rate.

The amount borrowed today in euros is simply the value A, discounted at rate $R€$:

$$PV = A/(1 + (R€ \times N/360))$$

This amount is then exchanged at the RS spot rate and invested in dollars at rate $R\$$. Future value is thus expressed as:

$$PV = RS \times PV \times (1 + (R\$ \times N/360))$$

Thus:

$$FV = A \times RS \times \frac{1 + R\$ \times \frac{N}{360}}{1 + R€ \times \frac{N}{360}}$$

The forward rate (*FR*) is that which equalizes the future value in euros and the amount *A*. Thus:

$$FV = A \times RS \times \frac{1 + R\$ \times \dfrac{N}{360}}{1 + R€ \times \dfrac{N}{360}}$$

If $RS = \$1.5198$, $N = 90$ days, $R\$ = 3.03\%$ and $R€ = 4.38\%$, we obtain a forward selling price of $1.5147.

A forward purchase of euros, in which the company treasurer pledges to buy euros in the future, is tantamount to the treasurer's buying the euros today while borrowing their corresponding value in dollars for the same period. The euros that have been bought are also invested during this time at the euro interest rate.

The forward exchange rate of a currency is based on the spot price and the interest rate differential between the foreign currency and the benchmark currency during the period covered by the transaction.

In our example, as interest rates are higher in euros than in dollars, the forward euro-into-dollar exchange rate is lower than the spot rate. The difference is called swap points. Swap points can be seen as compensation demanded by the treasurer in the forward transaction for borrowing in a high-yielding currency (the euro in our example), and investing in a low-yielding currency (the dollar in our example) up to the moment when the transaction is unwound. More generally, if the benchmark currency offers a lower interest rate than the foreign currency, the forward rate will be below the sport rate. Currency *A* is said to be at a discount *vis-à-vis* currency *B* if *A* offers higher interest rates than *B* during the period concerned.

Similarly, currency *A* is said to be at a premium *vis-à-vis* currency *B* if interest rates on *A* are below interest rates on *B* during the period concerned.

As in any forward transaction, treasurers know at what price they will be able to buy or sell their currencies, but will be unable to take advantage of any later opportunities.

For example, if a treasurer sold his €100m forward at $1.5147, and the euro is trading at $1.5500 dollars at maturity, he will have to keep his word (unless he wants to break the futures contract, in which case he will have to pay a penalty) and bear an opportunity cost equal to $0.0353 per euro sold.

Forward-forward rate and FRAs Let us say our company treasurer learns that his company plans to install a new IT system, which will require a considerable outlay in equipment and software in three months. His cash flow projections show that, in three months, he will have to borrow €20m for six months.

On the euro money market, spot interest rates are as shown in Table 1.54.

Table 1.54: Spot interest rates on the euro money market

3 months	21/4% – 25/16%
6 months	21/4% – 25/16%
9 months	25/16% – 23/8%

How can the treasurer hedge against a rise in short-term rates over the next three months?

Armed with his knowledge of the yield curve, he can use the procedures discussed below to lock in the six-month rate as it will be in three months.

He decides to borrow €20m today for nine months and to reinvest it for the first three months. Assuming that he works directly at money market conditions, in nine months he will have to pay back:

$$20 \times (1 + 23/8\% \times 9/12) = €20.35625\text{m}$$

But his three-month investment turns €20m into:

$$20 \times (1 + 21/4\% \times 3/12) = 20.11250$$

The implied rate obtained is called the forward-forward rate and is expressed as follows:

$$T(3.6) = ((20.35625–20.11250)/20.11250) \times (12/6) = 2.424\%$$

Our treasurer was thus able to hedge his exchange rate risk but has borrowed €20m from his bank, €20m that he will not be using for three months. Hence, he must bear the corresponding intermediation costs. His company's balance sheet and income statement will be affected by this transaction.

Now let's imagine that the bank finds out about our treasurer's concerns and offers him the following product:

- in three months' time, if the six-month (floating benchmark) rate is above 2.424% (the guaranteed rate), the bank pledges to pay him the difference between the market rate and 2.424% on a pre-determined principal;
- in three months' time, if the six-month (floating benchmark) rate is below 2.424% (the guaranteed rate), the company will have to pay the bank the difference between 2.424% and the market rate on the same pre-determined principal.

This is called a forward rate agreement, or FRA. An FRA allows the treasurer to hedge against fluctuations in rates, without the amount of the transaction being actually borrowed or lent.

If, in three months' time, the six-month rate is 2.5%, our treasurer will borrow €20m at this high rate but will receive, on the same amount, the pro-rated difference between 2.5% and 2.424%. The actual cost of the loan will therefore be 2.424%. Similarly, if the six-month rate is 1.5%, the treasurer will have borrowed on favorable terms, but will have to pay the pro-rated difference between 2.424% and 1.5%.

The same reasoning applies if the treasurer wishes to invest any surplus funds. Such a transaction would involve an FRA lending, as opposed to the FRA borrowing described above.

The notional amount of an FRA is the theoretical amount to which the difference between the guaranteed rate and the floating rate is applied. The notional amount is never exchanged between the buyer and seller of an FRA. The interest rate differential is not paid at the maturity of the underlying loan but is discounted and paid at the maturity of the FRA.

An FRA is free of charge but, of course, the 'purchase' of an FRA and the 'sale' of an FRA are not made at the same interest rate. As in all financial products, a margin separates the rate charged on a six-month loan in three months' time, and the rate at which that money can be invested over the same period of time.

Banks are key operators on the FRA market and offer companies the opportunity to buy or sell FRAs, with maturities generally shorter than one year.

Swaps To swap something means to exchange or trade it for something else. In its broadest sense, a swap is an exchange of financial assets or flows between two entities during a certain period of time. Both operators must, of course, believe the transaction to be to their advantage.

'Swap' in everyday parlance means an exchange of financial flows (calculated on the basis of a theoretical benchmark called a notional) between two entities during a given period of time. Such financial flows can be:

- currency swaps without principal;
- interest rate swaps (IRS);
- currency swaps with principal.

Unlike financial assets, financial flows are traded over the counter with no impact on the balance sheet, and allow the parties to modify the exchange or interest rate terms (or both simultaneously) on current or future assets or liabilities.

Interest rate swaps are a long-term portfolio of FRAs (from one to 15 years).

As with FRAs, the principle is to compare a floating rate and a guaranteed rate and to make up the difference without an exchange of principal. Interest rate swaps are especially suited for managing a company's long-term currency exposure.

Figure 1.51 shows the interest rate swap. That is: Fixed rate – Fixed rate – Floating rate = – Floating rate tantamount to our company's borrowing the notional at a floating rate for the duration of the swap without its lenders seeing any change in their debts. After the first year, if the variable benchmark

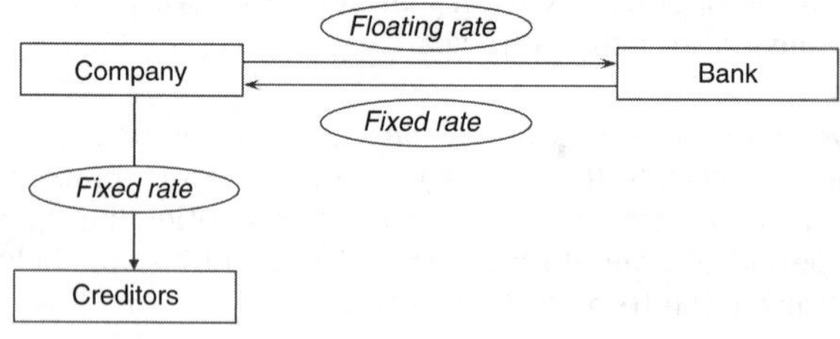

Figure 1.51: Interest rate swap

rate (Libor, Euribor, etc.) is 6%, the company will have paid its creditors an interest rate of 7%, but will receive 1% of the swap's notional amount. Its effective rate will be 6%.

The transaction described is a swap of fixed for floating rates, and all sorts of combinations are possible:

- swapping a fixed rate for a fixed rate (in the same currency);
- swapping floating rate one for floating rate two (called benchmark switching);
- swapping a fixed rate in currency one for a fixed rate in currency two;
- swapping a fixed rate in currency one for a floating rate in currency two;
- swapping a floating rate in currency one for a floating rate in currency two.

These last three swaps come with an exchange of principal, as the two parties use different currencies. This exchange is generally done at the beginning and at the maturity of the swap at the same exchange rate. More sophisticated swaps make it possible to separate the benchmark rates from the currencies concerned.

Insurance Insurance allows companies to pay a premium to a third party, which assumes the risk if that risk materializes. If it doesn't, companies can benefit from a favorable trend in the parameter covered (exchange rate, interest rates, solvency of a debtor, etc.).

> *Conceptually, insurance is based on the technique of options; the insurance premium paid corresponds to the value of the option purchased.*

An option gives its holder the right to buy or sell an underlying asset at a specified price on a specified date, or to forego this right if the market offers better opportunities.

Options are an ideal management tool for company treasurers, as they help guarantee a price while still leaving some leeway. But, as our reader has learned, there are no miracles in finance and the option premium is the price of this freedom. Its cost can be prohibitive, particularly in the case of companies operating businesses with low sales margins.

Major international banks are market makers on all sorts of markets. Below we present the most commonly used options.

- Currency options

Currency options allow their holders to lock in an exchange rate in a particular currency, while retaining the choice of realizing a transaction at the spot market rate if it is more favorable. Of course, the strike price has to be compared with the forward rate and not the spot rate. Banks can theoretically list all types of options, although European-style options are the main ones traded.

While standardized contracts are listed, treasurers generally prefer the over-the-counter variety, as they are more flexible for choosing an amount (which can correspond exactly to the amount of the flow for companies), dates and strike prices. Options can be used in many ways. Some companies buy only options that are far out of the money and thus carry low premiums; in doing do, they seek to hedge against extreme events such as devaluations. Other companies set the strike price in line with their commercial needs or perhaps their anticipations.

Given the often high cost of the premium, several imaginative (and risky) products have been developed, including look back options, options on options and barrier options.

Look back options can be used to buy or sell currencies on the basis of the average exchange rate during the life of the option. The premium is thus lower, as less risk is taken by the seller and the volatility of the underlying is below its average.

Average strike options can be used to buy or sell currencies on the basis of the average exchange rate during the life of the option. The premium is thus lower, as less risk is taken by the seller and the buyer has a lower potential.

Options on options are quite useful for companies bidding on a foreign project. The bid is made on the basis of a certain exchange rate, but let's say the rate has moved the wrong way by the time the company wins the contract. Options on options allow the company to hedge its currency exposure as soon as it submits its bid, by giving it the right to buy a currency option with a strike price close to the benchmark rate. If the company is not chosen for the bid, it simply gives up its option on option. As the value of an option is below the value of the underlying asset, the value of an option on an option will be low.

Barrier options are surely the most frequently traded exotic products on the market. A barrier is a limit price which, when exceeded, knocks in or knocks out the option (i.e. creates or cancels the option). This reduces the risk to the seller and thus the premium to the buyer. For example, if the euro is trading at $1.5, US company treasurers who know they will have to buy euros in the future can ensure that they'll get a certain exchange rate by buying a euro call at $1.46, for example; and then, to reduce the premium, placing the knock out barrier at $1.35. If the euro falls below $1.35 at any time during the life of the option, treasurers will find themselves without a hedge (but the market will have moved in their direction and at that moment the futures price will be far below the level at which they bought their options).

- Interest rate options

The rules that apply to options in general obviously apply to interest rate options. For the financial market, the exact nature of the underlying asset is irrelevant to either the design or valuation of the option. As a result, many products are built around identical concepts and their degree of popularity is often a simple matter of fashion.

A *cap* allows borrowers to set a ceiling interest rate above which they no longer wish to borrow and they will receive the difference between the market rate and cap rate.

A *floor* allows lenders to set a minimum interest rate below which they do not wish to lend and they will receive the difference between the floor rate and the market rate.

A *collar* or *rate tunnel* involves both the purchase of a cap and the sale of a floor.

This sets a zone of fluctuation in interest rates below which operators must pay the difference in rates between the market rate and the floor rate and above which the counterparty pays the differential. This combination reduces the cost of hedging, as the premium of the cap is paid partly or totally by the sale of the floor.

Swaptions are options on swaps, and can be used to buy or sell the right to conclude a swap over a certain duration. The underlying swap is stated at the outset and is defined by its notional amount, maturity and the fixed and floating rate that are used as benchmarks.

Barrier interest rate options are similar to barrier currency options:

- either the option exists only if the benchmark rate reaches the barrier rate; or
- the option is knocked in only if the benchmark rate exceeds a set limit.

The presence of barriers reduces the option's premium. Company treasurers can combine these options with other products into a custom-made hedge.

- Confirmed credit lines

In exchange for a commitment fee, a company can obtain short- and medium-term confirmed credit lines from banks, on which they can draw at any time for their cash needs. A confirmed credit line is like an option to take out a loan.

- Credit insurance

Insurance companies specializing in appraising default risk guarantee companies payment of a debt in exchange for a premium equivalent to about 0.3% of the nominal.

• Credit derivatives

Credit derivatives emerged in 1995 and have taken off since then. They are used to unlink the management of a credit risk on an asset or liability from the ownership of that asset or liability.

Developed and used first of all by financial institutions, credit derivatives are beginning to be used by major industrial and commercial groups. The purpose of these products is mainly to reduce the credit risk on some clients, which may account for an excessive portion of the credit portfolio. They can also be used to protect against a negative trend in margins on a future loan. Companies are marginal players on this market (less than 10% of volume).

Credit derivatives work very much like interest-rate or currency options. Only the nature of the risk covered is different – the risk of default or rating downgrade instead of interest rate or currency risk. The most conventional form of credit derivative is the credit default swap. In these agreements one side buys protection against the default of its counterparty by paying a third party regularly and receiving from it the pre-determined amount in the event of default.

The credit risk is thus transferred from the buyer of protection (a company, an investor, a bank) to a third party (an investor, an insurance company, etc.) in exchange for some compensation.

Credit derivatives are traded over the counter and play the same economic role as an insurance contract.

Meanwhile, a second category of derivatives has developed which is not an 'insurance' type product but a 'forward' type of product. Using these, companies can, from the start, set the spread of a bond to be issued in the future. The spread of an issue is thus bought and sold at a preset level. And, of course, wherever forward purchasing or selling exists, financial intermediaries will come up with the corresponding options. We thus end up with an insurance product called an option on future spreads!

• Political risk insurance

Political risk insurance is offered by specialized companies, such as Unistrat-Coface, Hermès and AIG, which can cover 90–95% of the value of an investment for as long as 15 years in most parts of the world. Risks normally covered include expropriation, nationalization, confiscation and changes in legislation covering foreign investments. Initially the domain of public or quasi-public organizations, political risk insurance is increasingly being offered by the private sector.

Disposal of a risky asset or liability

Outright disposal is a last-gasp measure that obviously does not unlink the ownership of the asset (or liability) from the management of its risk. Measures include securitization, defeasance and non-recourse factoring.

References and Further Reading

Adam, T. and Fernando, C., Hedging, speculation and shareholder value, *Journal of Financial Economics*, **81**(2), 283–309, August 2006.

Brown, G., Managing foreign exchange risk with derivatives, *Journal of Financial Economics*, **60**(2–3), 401–448, May 2001.

Brown, G. and Bjerre Toft, K., How firms should hedge, *The Review of Financial Studies*, **15**, 1283–1324, Autumn 2002.

Fauklender, M., Hedging or market timing? Selecting the interest rate exposure of corporate debt, *Journal of Finance*, **60**(2), 187–243, May 2001.

Mackay, P. and Moeller, S., The value of corporate risk management, *Journal of Finance*, **62**(3), 1379–1419, June 2007.

Vickery, J., How and why do small firms manage interest rate risk? *Journal of Financial Economics*, **87** (2), 446–470, 2008.

Chapter 2

Topics

50 years of research in finance

Considerable progress has been made in research into finance over the last 50 years.

During the 1950s, two very fertile areas for research were financial markets and corporate finance.

- In **1952**, Harry Markowitz developed his portfolio theory, by demonstrating mathematically that diversification was to the investor's advantage, as it reduced risk for the same level of returns (or improved returns for the same level of risk).
- In **1958**, Franco Modigliani and Merton Miller opened up a field of research into corporate finance, by demonstrating that, if markets are efficient, there is no optimal financial structure that will minimize the cost of capital, and accordingly, maximize enterprise.

Since then, huge strides forward have been taken, mainly in the field of capital markets, with a strong emphasis on mathematics, a result of the educational backgrounds of the researchers – Modigliani the economist and Markowitz the statistician.

- In **1964**, William Sharpe demonstrated that there are no portfolios that can systematically beat the market, and that the return that should be required on any financial security is linked to the risk-free interest rate and the market risk of the security via the famous 'beta' coefficient, thus creating the capital asset pricing model (CAPM).
- In **1970**, Eugene Fama elaborated the theory of market efficiency. Since all new information is immediately integrated into share prices, it is impossible to predict future share price movements.

• In **1972**, Fisher Black and Myron Scholes introduced the formula used for valuing options which is named after them.

• In **1977**, Richard Roll proved that it was not possible to demonstrate that the CAPM was false. However, together with Stephen Ross, he came up with a more general model, the Arbitrage Pricing Theory, which has not, as yet, really taken off.

In the late 1970s, the reintroduction of the human element into economic models that had turned out to be highly reductionist, opened up new areas of research which have proved to be very fruitful:

• **Signal theory**, based on the work of Stephen Ross, challenges the premise that information is shared by all at the same time and at no cost. He shows that on the contrary, some financial decisions (borrowing, paying dividends, etc.) are not necessarily taken on the basis of their own merits, but in order to pass on new information to the market in a way that is credible.

• **Agency theory,** based on the work of Michael Jensen, challenges the premise that the company is a black box in which all stakeholders are working together to maximize value for shareholders. Some financial decisions (borrowing, diversifying, listing, distributing dividends, etc.) are not necessarily taken on the basis of their economic convenience, but in order to ensure as much overlap as possible with the interests of shareholders, managers and creditors.

• Finally, in the 1990s, **behavioral finance** suggested that *homo economicus*, who constantly minimizes and maximizes everything, is probably a mythical figure. Behavioral finance looks at what impact the factoring in of the partial rationality of the individual has. Richard Thaler and Hersh Sherfin have shown that there are pockets of inefficiency, but that these are not deep enough for arbitrage gains to be made on a systematic and lasting basis.

Ten deadly mistakes in corporate finance

In both our professional and academic experience we have come across certain mistakes rather frequently. We list some of them below hoping we'll get rid of them once and for all!

1. Believing that growth in earnings per share (EPS) is equivalent to creating value

As it is difficult to measure the value created by an acquisition, share buyback, merger, capital increase, etc., the EPS impact is often used as a measure of value creation. However, there is a link between EPS accretion and value creation, or between EPS dilution and value destruction, only under three conditions. Before discussing them, let's consider a virtual example. Let's imagine that the software company SAP (2006e P/E ratio of 27) has decided to merge with Barclays bank (P/E of 10) on the basis of current share prices. As SAP's P/E is higher than Barclays, its EPS will increase automatically after this transaction, by 88%. Does this mean that the merger has created value, based on this yardstick? Of course not! If there is value creation, it will be due to synergies, and in this case, we don't see much in the way of synergies ... Incidentally, looking at things from the other side, i.e. Barclays' EPS, the impact would be completely different: 28%. So when is an improvement in EPS an indicator of value creation?

1. **When earnings growth of the merged entity is more or less the same as previously**. Clearly, in our hypothetical SAP-Barclays merger, this is not the case: SAP projects 19% earnings growth as a standalone entity, vs. 10% for Barclays. The new group's growth rate would be between the two (given the absence of synergies) and, in this case, 12%.

This is not the same as 19%! Please note that the higher SAP expected growth rate in EPS explains its higher P/E ratio.

2. **When the risk of operating assets after the merger is more or less the same as before the merger.** In our example, this is doubtful. Generally speaking, however, this can be true when two companies in the same sector and with the same positioning merge, Autostrade and Abertis, for example. This is much less true for Mittal (basic steel) and Arcelor (high value steel).

3. **When the new group's financial structure doesn't change substantially with the transaction**, as this helps ensure that financial risk is the same after the transaction as before. Moreover, it is well known that debt leverage raises EPS but does not create value; otherwise, all companies would have leveraged up long ago and we'd all be rich!

2. Believing that merger synergies can be valued on the basis of the average of the two companies' P/Es

There are two reasons that can be used for justifying why synergies cannot be estimated using the average P/E of the new group:

1. Synergies announced at the moment of the merger are only an estimate, and the people who have announced them have every interest in giving rather high figures to push shareholders to approve the deal. Moreover, the technical execution of a merger or any other link-up carries its own complications, such as making employees of formerly competing firms work together, creating a new culture, trying to keep from losing clients who wish to maintain diversity in suppliers, etc. Experience shows that more than one merger out of two fails from this point of view and that synergies actually generated are weaker than announced, and take longer to show up.

2. Sooner or later, the merged group has to pass on some of the synergies to its customers, staff and suppliers. M&A tends to come in waves, and competitors will be encouraged to follow suit, in order to generate synergies that allow them to remain competitive. Ultimately, all companies will be able to lower their prices, or refrain from raising them, and it is the end customer who will benefit.

3. Believing that the debt/equity ratio is the best measure of debt-repayment capacity

Financial leverage is often used to assess a company's debt level and its ability to meet its debt obligations. However, this approach has become completely archaic! A company does not pay off its debts with its equity but with its cash flow. Even in the event of liquidation, equity provides a cushion of security only if the company is able to sell its assets at their book value, which, in practice, is almost never the case.

If you ask a banker what the highest debt possible for a target company is he or she will surely answer expressed in terms of the net debt/EBITDA or net debt/cash flow ratio, as these ratios are good indicators of a company's ability to generate enough cash flow to pay off its debt.

Unilever, for example, has leverage of more than 130%, which may seem huge. However, when examining the company more carefully, we observe that its net debt is equivalent to just one and a half years of EBITDA!

At the other extreme, Rémy Cointreau has leverage of 0.6, but its debt is equivalent to 3.6 times its EBITDA.

4. Confusing apparent and real cost of a source of financing and comparing the costs of financing while forgetting differences in risk

When investment bankers 'sell' a convertible bond issue, they always highlight the 'insignificant' (or even 'non-existent'!) cost of this source of financing. Indeed, it is true that companies pay a very low rate of interest on a convertible bond, and its (apparent!) cost of financing is below the risk-free rate.

However, the accounting cost is only an 'illusion', as its low level is cancelled out by the ultimate risk of dilution. And CFOs are not usually duped, but it is hard sometimes to resist the temptation of low annual cash costs, especially when the materialization of the risk (i.e. the issue of shares at a price below the current share price, thus leading to shareholder dilution) occurs only years later.

Thus, a distinction should be made between the apparent cost of a source of financing, i.e. the annual cash cost, and its real cost, which includes the entire ultimate cost, including deferred coupons, redemption premium, expected increase in share price, etc.

Moreover, cost of the product must reflect the risk incurred. Obviously, issuing shares has a higher real cost than issuing convertible bonds (the difference can range from 4% to 10%). In buying new shares, the investor hopes for a good return, but the company is under no obligation to pay a dividend or to reimburse the investor. Such flexibility comes at a cost: the company must pay out a coupon and guarantee repayment of the debt.

However, we are not suggesting here that all sources of financing are equivalent and that it doesn't really matter which type is chosen. A convertible bond, for example, can be the best choice for a company whose cash flow is currently small but is expected to grow strongly in the future.

5. Forgetting the risk to profitability

This will be obvious to our readers (at least, we hope!), but in light of recent events, it is always worth pointing out. After all, finance is nothing more than risk, return and value. The value of a product can only be determined when risk and required return are known.

When financial markets are doing well, as in 1999 and 2000, investors have an unfortunate tendency to overlook risk. The big losses suffered by equity investors in 2001 and 2002 were merely the materialization of risk. The more a portfolio was invested in TMT stocks, the greater the risk was. The losses suffered were not an injustice, but simply a reminder of common sense.

What is true for investors is also true for companies. Some company treasurers thought they were doing well by investing some of their company's cash in Parmalat commercial paper, which offered much more attractive returns than other Italian industrial companies ... and for good reason!

6. Believing that increasing the leverage raises share value

Leverage is an accounting reality: if a company carries debt and its return on capital employed (ROCE) is greater than its cost of debt, then its return on equity (ROE) is greater than its ROCE. This leverage formula is based on an accounting tautology and therefore must be correct. From a financial point of view, however, ROCE and ROE are of very limited interest. As they are accounting-based concepts, they do not reflect risk and in no way should they be the company's sole objective. Otherwise, they could lead to unwise decisions.

For it is easy, as we have seen, to improve ROE by leveraging up, but the company then faces greater risk: something that is not reflected in accounting terms. Hence, if ROE increases with leverage, the required rate of return will rise commensurately and no value will have been created.

There are, nonetheless, two special cases where we believe that leverage can actually contribute to the value creation:

1. In an **inflationary economy**. This was what happened in the 1960s, when debt was a stratagem that was especially well suited to a strong-growth environment. There are two components to this strategy: heavy investment to expand industrial assets and narrow margins to win market share and keep those assets busy. Obviously, ROCE is low (because of low margins and heavy investment), but the debt that is inevitably incurred (because weak margins produce insufficient operating cash flow to cover all investment in the business) results in increased leverage and inflates ROE. This is all the more so when the real cost of debt is low or even negative because of inflation, and creditors are reimbursed with devalued currency. However, ROE is quite unstable and can drop suddenly when growth in the business slows.

This was the strategy used typically by Moulinex and it allowed the company to achieve dominance on its market and to 'flatten out the learning curve', but this was also the source of later difficulties. With the beginning of the 1980s and the return to positive real interest rates, i.e. far above the inflation rate, most companies successfully improved their ROE while reducing debt and hence leverage. This is only possible via a strong improvement in ROCE, i.e. by improving asset rotation (e.g. by reducing inventory levels) and profit margins. This has been the strategy of Peugeot throughout the last two decades and more recently of Volkswagen.

2. **When using heavy leverage**, in particular for companies having been bought out in an LBO. But beware: we are not suggesting that improving ROE through leverage creates value, or that tax savings are a real source of value creation. Heavy debt, however, tends to make managers especially efficient, so that the company can use its cash flow to meet its heavy debt-servicing obligations, at the price of constantly having its back to the wall. It is therefore the improvement in ROCE that creates value.

7. Believing that raising the dividend increases the value of the stock

If this was true, companies would long ago have raised their payout to 100% (or even higher) and investors would all be rich and happy!

Mathematical models do not necessarily provide a clear picture right off the bat. In the Gordon and Shapiro model, for example, the value of stock whose dividend grows at a constant rate is:

$$\text{Value of stock} = \text{Payout} \times \text{EPS}/(\text{Required rate of return} - \text{Dividend growth rate})$$

Intuitively, it would seem that if the payout rises, the value of the stock should also rise. However, this means forgetting the negative indirect impact on the company, which, having fewer financial resources at its disposal because of its higher dividend, will be forced to curtail its investments and grow more slowly. The two effects end up cancelling each other out, and the value of the stock remains constant.

That said, there appear to be two ways in which raising the dividend can indeed create value:

- If the company increases its dividend to return to its shareholders cash that it does not or no longer needs and that it would otherwise invest at a rate below its cost of capital. This is especially true for cash-rich companies such as Microsoft and GlaxoSmithKline. Scientific studies show clearly that raising the dividend leads to gains in the share price.
- If the company uses this to signal that its economic situation is healthier than the investment community believes. Such a signal is all the more credible as it demonstrates management's confidence in its future, since it has given up a rare and precious resource – cash!

8. Believing that structuring a corporate finance transaction is possible without a preliminary complete financial analysis

Would a doctor ever write out a prescription without first examining and diagnosing the patient? Would a tailor make a suit without first taking the customer's measurements? Of course not!

Similarly, a financial analysis of the company is the first and essential step of any solid basis of reasoning. To forget this is to end up with a haphazard strategy that would only hit the mark by coincidence.

In our experience novices often recoil in horror before a financial analysis, not knowing where to begin or end. They are likely to make mainly descriptive remarks, without trying to tie them together and check for their internal consistency and without trying to figure out which is the cause and which is the effect.

Financial analysis is not just some vague comments on the P&L, balance sheets or some ratios. Financial analysis is an investigation that must be followed to its logical conclusion and whose parts are not isolated but inter-linked. The main questions financial analysts must answer are these: Does this make sense? Is this consistent with what I've already established, and, if not, why not? Analysts must ask themselves several questions and will seek the answers in an accounting document that they do not comment on as such, but which serves as a source of raw materials.

The analyst is like a modern-day Sherlock Holmes or Miss Marple, on the lookout for a logical chain of events, as well as disruptive elements that could signal problems.

The principle that will guide the analyst in learning and understanding the company is this: 'creating value requires investments that must be funded and must be sufficiently profitable'.

Indeed, a company cannot long survive if it is unable to attract a steady stream of customers that want to buy its products or services at a given price allowing it to generate a sufficient operating profit.

So the first thing that the analyst must examine is how the company achieves its financial margins. The first thing a company needs is investment in two forms: acquisition of equipment, buildings, patents, subsidiaries, etc., and to build up working capital. And these investments obviously have to be financed, either through equity or through banking or other financial debt.

After studying the three above elements – margins, investments and financing – the analyst can calculate the company's profitability, in terms of ROCE or ROE.

The analyst will then have completed the work and can answer the simple questions that motivated it, i.e. is the company able to meet the commitments that it has taken on with its creditors? Is it able to create value for its shareholders?

9. Believing that actual return can long be kept above the required rate of return

Economists (and experience) tell us that no such situation is infinitely sustainable. A company's ROCE will sooner or later converge gradually towards its cost of capital. This is the law of diminishing returns. A return that is above the required rate of return, when factoring in risk, will naturally attract competitors or the attention of competition watchdogs (see the Microsoft case). Sooner or later, deregulation and technological progress will make net ROCE vanish. Or, as an old adage says: 'there are no impregnable fortresses, there are only fortresses that are poorly attacked!'.

True, the real economy is less fluid than financial markets and it takes longer for its efficiency to show up, but in our view, it inevitably does. After all, the returns of Air Liquide and Coca-Cola did indeed converge towards their cost of capital!

10. Believing that calculation replaces reflection

What a fabulous tool Excel is! But what a trap it is for serious reflection!

Mathematicians have made major contributions to finance (through portfolio management, the CAPM, valuing of options, etc.), but finance is not just mathematics. Consider the two following examples:

- Three years ago, the Chinese market traded at an average P/E of 10, a risk-free rate of 5%, and an estimated 5% risk premium. Given the Chinese growth rate (GDP rose 9% in volume in 2007) the above numbers were clearly inconsistent, even though they may have been mathematically correct. Such high growth rates, with a market P/E of just 10 are impossible without the discounting rate being far above the European rate (about 9%), where P/Es were about 17 with weaker growth than in China. In short, the risk premium was financially wrong, even if it was mathematically correct. A discounting rate of about 15% was much more justified, and this is the one that Chinese investors apply themselves to their companies; otherwise P/Es would have been 30 and not 10!
- The beta of a low-cost airline like easyJet or Ryanair is significantly higher than for a mainstream carrier like Air France or Lufthansa, which draw most of their earnings from business passengers. This calculation may be mathematically correct, but what a mistake from a financial point of view! Of the two types of airlines, which is more exposed to the state of the economy? Naturally, the mainstream carrier, whose cash flows accentuate fluctuations in the economy, while those of low-cost airlines are much less exposed.

In short, in finance, constantly keep in mind the Aretha Franklin song: *Think*.

Five mistakes in corporate valuation

In the current economic climate, we'd like to draw your attention to some mistakes that may have serious consequences for the overall quality of your estimates.

1. The value of debt

When calculating the value of capital employed and the value of equity, whether using the DCF method or comparative methods, financial debts must be factored in at their market value and not at their book value.

Most of the time, for companies that are solvent and/or for which market conditions have not changed substantially since their debts were issued, there is little difference between their market and their book value.

Under IFRS or US GAAP, these calculations are easy to do, as companies now provide the estimated value of their debts in the notes to their accounts.

For example, in Figure 2.1 are the values of some groups' bonds that are maturing in 2013, as a percentage of the normal value.

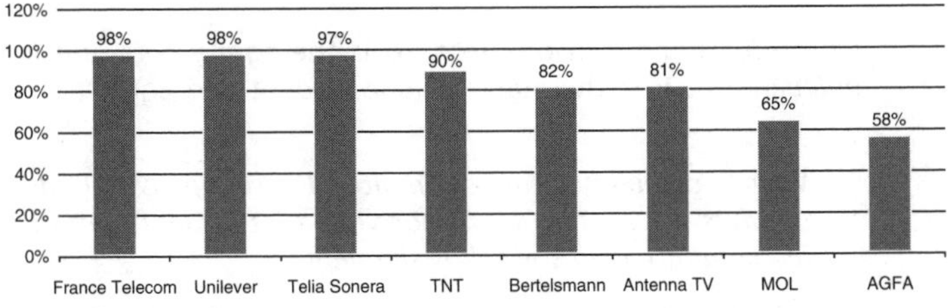

Figure 2.1: Values of groups' bonds maturing in 2013

Ford has \$154bn in financial debt on its balance sheet, compared with a market value of \$122bn, which is a difference of \$32bn, six times the group's market capitalization of \$5.5bn, and we won't mention the situation at General Motors before its bankruptcy!

2. Debt beta

Along the same lines, the assumption that the debt beta (β) could be considered as equal to zero (which is the key feature of risk-free debt) should be frequently considered unacceptable.

However, this is one of the assumptions made for calculating the unlevered β using the simplified formula:

$$\beta = \frac{\beta_{\mathrm{E}}}{1 + \dfrac{V_{\mathrm{D}}}{V_{\mathrm{E}}}}$$

Since the full formula is:

$$\beta = \frac{\beta_{\mathrm{E}} + \beta_{\mathrm{D}} + \dfrac{V_{\mathrm{D}}}{V_{\mathrm{E}}}}{1 + \dfrac{V_{\mathrm{D}}}{V_{\mathrm{E}}}}$$

where β_{D} is the β of the debt, β_{E} is the equity beta and β the *unlevered* β. V is the market value of debt and equity.

When a company's capital employed is relatively volatile, and thus risky, and/or it is carrying a lot of debt, part of this volatility is absorbed by the debt.

This explains why the value of the debt can differ from its book value, and accordingly, why the debt β frequently is different from zero.

In these circumstances, assuming that the β_D is zero, as frequently happens, can be an error. It results in a generalized undervaluation of the volatility and market risk of the capital employed. Unlevered β is then only determined by the β of equity, as the share of volatility that has been absorbed by the debt has disappeared from the computation.

To illustrate this, we use data from April 2009 to calculate the cost of capital of various groups (Table 2.1), assuming alternatively a zero β_D or an estimate of it.

Table 2.1: Cost of capital of various groups

Group	Unlevered β with $\beta_D = 0$	Unlevered β with $\beta_D \neq 0$
Enel	0.38	0.48
Lafarge	1.06	1.18
Office Depot	1.95	1.06
Pernod Ricard	0.84	1.92
Stora Enso	0.72	0.90
Valeo	0.95	1.02

3. The risk-free rate in emerging countries

There are currently countries in which the government borrows at higher interest rates than the most highly rated issuers of corporate debt in the country (Ukraine, for example). This creates a problem when determining the risk-free rate.

In general, the government is assumed (and observed) to issue debt at a rate that is deemed to be the risk-free rate, because the government, unlike private companies and investors, has the power to raise taxes to pay down its debts.

We were recently confronted with this difficulty and we decided to use, as the risk-free rate in our estimates, the rate of interest on a bank loan that was recently granted to a group that was carrying little debt and that had a solid economic model. Even though it wasn't a risk-free rate, it was at least the lowest interest rate in the country in which the group operates.

4. The pension deficit and other related issues

It is quite correct to consider the net difference between the value of pension assets and the present value of a company's commitments as an element of net debt. It can even be said to be recommended since the amount of the pension fund provision on the balance sheet is disconnected from economic and financial reality, given the prevailing accounting principles.

However, just because this figure is zero or low, you shouldn't just move rapidly on to the next valuation issue. You should always be suspicious of small differences between two large numbers.

> *Assets used to hedge commitments are essentially invested in shares, while the commitments themselves have the same quality as bonds. So a small difference between those two amounts could turn into a big gap if the stock market suddenly plummets. It will also have an impact on the* β_U.

We were recently confronted with the case of a company whose past results and business plan showed little sensitivity to the economic situation, which led us to expect that its β_U would be low. However, the calculation, which factored in a small amount of pension deficit net of pension assets, yielded a figure close to one.

Once the nature of the hedging assets was factored in, the β_U fell to 0.6. Part of the volatility evidenced by the β_E of this company was not explained by the volatility of capital employed, but by the volatility of the portfolio of pension assets made up mainly of shares, structurally financed by debt, like in any good hedge fund!

5. Performance of equity betas

If the economic and financial crisis had had the same impact on all firms, the βs would have remained stable.

But, as can be seen every day, the impact has been far greater on some sectors (banking, construction, automobile and aeronautic) than it has been on others (food, health, etc.).

However, as the market β has remained the same, and by construction equal to one, the β of firms that have been less impacted have, on the contrary, fallen (see Table 2.2).

Table 2.2: The β of less impacted companies

	Equity β computed from June 2005 to June 2007	Equity β computed from July 2007 to June 2009
Société Générale	1.32	1.57
ADP	0.57	1.02
Peugeot	0.96	1.26
L'Oreal	0.76	0.55
Danone	0.84	0.60

Accordingly, if you use a current market risk premium to estimate today's value of a share, as we recommend, it would be a good idea to update your betas!

If you don't, your estimated rate of return will be too low for the riskiest shares and too high for those that are less risky.

With an equity market risk premium that rose from 3% in June 2007 to 6.7% in October 2009, the extra return expected by the shareholders of Danone compared with the risk-free interest rate has increased by 60%, from 2.5% to 4.0%, and nearly tripled for Peugeot, rising from 2.9% to 8.4%.

M&A: Six mistakes to be avoided[1]

1. Don't apply the cost of capital of the bidder to the target firm

- The cost of capital used in a takeover should reflect the risk of the investment, not the risk profile of the bidding company.
- Risky businesses cannot become safe only because the bidder operates in a safe business!

2. Pay attention to the rules of thumb

- Daily corporate valuation is full of rules of thumb. We believe that the reader would better avoid spending too much time on them, especially after having made tremendous efforts in keeping the estimates as objective and scientific as possible! Here are a couple of examples:
  - It is quite common to add ad hoc premiums for brand name control as well as to subtract discounts for liquidity, minority stakes and so on.
  - The target company should be considered cheap if it trades at below some prevailing multiples – e.g. seven times EBITDA, 15 times earnings, market values below book values.

3. Don't go for cliché

- Through time, acquirers have tried to justify the high premiums paid for their acquisitions using

[1]This topic has been written by Massimo Mariani, Associate Professor of Corporate Finance, Jean Monnet University, Italy.

cliché – 'synergies' during the 1980s, 'strategic considerations' in the 1990s and 'real options' in the last decade, or a sum of all of them!
- Even if all of the above elements may actually have value, the reader should never forget that their contributions to value creation must be clearly stated and correctly estimated. Corporate valuation and M&A activity are not about dreams!

4. Don't be too conformist

- It is quite common to justify acquisitions with two arguments:
  - A lot of other companies in the same sector are doing acquisitions. External growth is prevailing over organic growth.
  - The transactions occurring in the current merger wave represent the key driver of our estimate when valuing possible target companies. Even if our internal 'traditional' estimates suggest lower values.

- The mere fact that your competitors are doing bad acquisitions (overpaying for them) is not a good reason to join the group! Your company may be operating in a value destroying sector; thus, differently from what other companies are doing, it may be time for you to consider shrinking and/or to continue focusing the strategy on the internal growth.

5. Don't let pride be more important than common sense

- If companies define their objective in a bidding fight as winning the auction, the bidder will get the best result. But beware the winner's curse (the bidder may end up realizing they have overpaid the target).

- The premiums paid should only reflect expected synergies, control issues and strategic considerations. They should never reflect the self-esteem of the management of the acquiring firm.
- The opinions of banks on the value of the deal are worth nothing. Never forget that investment bankers make their money on the *size* of the deal and not on its *quality*.
- M&A is not a 'macho game'. Managers are frequently too willing to fight out acquisitions with other people's money! And investment bankers are all ready to act as lemmings.

6. In M&A, external circumstances may be against the bidder

- Companies willing to do acquisitions often do so because they need to grow fast (and hopefully at low cost). Although it is true that mature companies can buy rapidly growing firms to push up their earnings, the key issue is always 'at what price' this objective can be achieved. If external growth turns out to be expensive, the company is actually destroying value for its shareholders.
- Dont forget that, on average, the stock prices of acquiring firms fall on the date of the acquisition announcement by 3–4%: a remarkable decrease.
- When a company decides to grow through acquisitions of public firms, the chances are against it because it almost always has to pay the market price plus a premium. Think about it: it is not *who* you buy that determines the final success of an M&A transaction, it is *how much* you pay for the target. The odds can improve when you grow by buying private companies, where you assess the *intrinsic* value of the target and you are less likely to fall into bidding wars. In addition, there are real constraints on private firms that may be removed when the takeover occurs.

Rating agencies

Rating agencies have clearly gained in importance in Europe in the last 20 years, as shown by the 35% annual increase in the number of companies carrying a Moody's rating.

This is obviously due mostly to the transition of continental Europe from an economy based mostly on banking intermediaries to one where the financial markets are becoming predominant.

CFOs can no longer shield themselves from this additional consideration. Ratings are even becoming one of their main concerns. Financial decisions are taken based partly on their rating impact; or, more precisely, decisions that have a negative rating impact will be adjusted accordingly.

Some companies even set rating targets (e.g. Vivendi Universal, PepsiCo). This can seem paradoxical in two ways:

- Although all financial communication is based on creating shareholder value, companies are much less likely to set share price targets than rating targets.
- In setting rating targets, companies have a new objective: that of preserving value for bondholders! This is praiseworthy and, in a financial market context, understandable, but has never been part of the bargain with bondholders.

We see several possible explanations for this paradox:

- **A downgrade is clearly a major event for a company that goes well beyond bondholder information**. A downgrade is traumatic and messy and almost always leads to a fall in the share price. Thus, by preserving a financial rating, it is also shareholder value that management is protecting, at least in the short term.

• **A downgrade can also have an immediate cost if the company has issued a bond with a step-up in the coupon**, i.e. a clause stating that the coupon will be increased in the event of a rating downgrade. Step-ups are meant to protect lenders against a downgrade and obviously make managers pay more attention to their debt rating.

• **A good debt rating guarantees some financial flexibility**. The higher the rating, the easier it is to tap the bond markets, as transactions are less dependent on market fluctuations. An investment grade company, for example, can almost always issue bonds, whereas market windows close regularly for companies that are below investment grade. The seizing up of the high-yield market over the last few months is quite instructive here, as many issues have had to be postponed. The high-yield market is similar in this respect to the equities market. Under the new Basel II banking solvency standards the highest rated companies will probably have even greater flexibility, as loans to them will require lower reserve requirements and banks will more readily lend to them.

• **Some banks sell the concept of lower cost of capital (and, thus, enhanced value) as a function of rating** – for example, obtaining the lowest possible cost of capital for a BBB rating. This is based on the tax savings brought about by financing costs but, beginning with a certain level of debt, the savings are cancelled out by the discounted value of the cost of bankruptcy. Readers who know us well know that we are not great fans of this argument. For it seems difficult to maintain that companies rated BBB can be valued significantly higher than others. The average company rating is closer to A, after all, and major groups such as Nestlé and AstraZeneca, which have stable cash flows, do not try to play leverage, preferring to hold onto their very strong rating. Similarly, setting out to obtain the best rating possible is getting things backwards! This minimizes the cost of debt, but so what? If it also requires an exorbitant level of equity, the cost of capital has not necessarily been reduced.

> *There is a phenomenon that is even more perverse than setting a target rating: refusing to be rated or asking for a confidential 'shadow rating'.*

Being rated can be scary, and CFOs balance out the lack of flexibility created by the lack of rating (e.g. certain investors can no longer be tapped and the bond market is mostly closed off) with the potential lack of flexibility created by a poor rating.

In extreme cases, we have even seen companies that, in their initial rating process, tried to obtain the worst possible rating for their particular financial profile. They have done this in order to gain some flexibility, i.e. some room for their situation to get marginally worse without undermining their rating. In this particular case, caution has a clear impact on value, as a lower rating means higher debt costs. But this is like an insurance premium that always looks too high until an accident strikes.

All in all, the desire of many companies to set a rating target reminds us that financial structure is above all the choice of the level of risk that shareholders choose to run and that the European debt market is becoming a real market with varied, segmented products, offered to investors who need some criteria in making their choices.

Credit scoring

Credit scoring is an analytical technique used to assign a rating that has been boosted by the requirements of the Basel II capital requirements for banks.

The basic idea is to prepare ratios from companies' accounts that are leading indicators (i.e. two or three years ahead) of potential difficulties. Once the ratios have been established, they merely have to be calculated for a given company and cross-checked against the values obtained for companies that are known to have run into problems or have failed. Comparisons are not made ratio by ratio, but globally. The ratios are combined in a function known as the Z-score that yields a score for each company. The equation for calculating Z-scores is as follows:

$$Z = a + \sum_{i=1}^{n} \beta_i \times R_i$$

where a is a constant, R_i the ratios, β_i the relative weighting applied to ratio R_i and n the number of ratios used.

Depending on whether a given company's Z-score is close to or a long way from normative values based on a set of companies that ran into trouble, the company in question is said to have a certain probability of experiencing trouble or remaining healthy over the following two or three year period. Originally developed in the USA during the late 1960s by Edward Altman, the family of Z-scores has been highly popular, the latest version of the Z'' equation being:

$$Z'' = 6.56\,X1 + 3.26\,X2 + 6.72\,X3 + 1.05\,X4$$

where: X1 is working capital/total assets; X2 is retained earnings/total assets; X3 is operating profit/total assets; X4 is shareholders' equity/net debt.

If Z'' is less than 1.1, the probability of corporate failure is high, and if Z'' is higher than 2.6, the probability of corporate failure is low, the gray area being values of between 1.1 and 2.6. The Z''-score has not yet been replaced by the Zeta score, which introduces into the equation the criteria of earnings stability, debt servicing and balance sheet liquidity.

The MKV firm (bought by Moody's in 2002) also developed its proprietary scoring model founded on an optional approach.

Scoring techniques represent an enhancement of traditional ratio analysis, which is based on the isolated use of certain ratios. With scoring techniques, the problem of the relative importance to be attached to each ratio has been solved because each is weighted according to its ability to pick out the 'bad' companies from the 'good' ones.

That said, scoring techniques still have a number of drawbacks.

Some weaknesses derive from the statistical underpinnings of the scoring equation. The sample needs to be sufficiently large, the database accurate and consistent and the period considered sufficiently long to reveal trends in the behavior of companies and to measure its impact.

The scoring equation has to be based on historical data from the fairly recent past and thus needs to be updated over time. Can the same equation be used several years later when the economic and financial environment in which companies operate may have changed considerably? It is thus vital for scoring equations to be kept up to date.

The design of scoring equations is heavily affected by their designers' top priority, i.e. to measure the risk of failure for small and medium-sized enterprises. They are not well suited for any other purpose (e.g. predicting in advance which companies will be highly profitable) or for measuring the risk of failure for large groups. Scoring equations should thus be used only for companies whose business activities and size is on a par with those in the original sample.

Scoring techniques, a straightforward and rapid way of synthesizing figures, have considerable appeal. Their development may even have perverse self-fulfilling effects. Prior awareness of the risk of failure (which scoring techniques aim to provide) may lead some of the companies' business partners to adopt behavior that hastens their demise. Suppliers may refuse to provide credit, banks may call in their loans, customers may be harder to come by because they are worried about not receiving delivery of the goods they buy or not being able to rely on after-sales service, etc.

Behavioral finance: are investors really rational?

1. Market anomalies: stumbling stones or lightning conductors?

Modern finance is based largely on the assumption that investors are rational people. This assumption has been very useful for simplifying the facts and designing models that have evolved, especially during the 20 years between 1950 and 1970, when IT capacities were far below what they are today. This assumed rationality of all of the players on the market gives rise to the theory of market efficiency. Efficient markets are generally defined as markets on which it is possible for resources to be allocated exactly where and when they are needed and at a lower cost. From a more micro-economic point of view, the informational efficiency of markets has been formulated by Eugene Fama as follows: changes in share prices do not depend on previous prices (low efficiency). All relevant information is taken into account in the formation of prices (semi-strong efficiency) and those holding private information cannot take advantage of it (strong efficiency).

A slew of financial research since the 1960s consisted in testing the efficiency of markets, probably the most tested hypothesis in finance. Some observations seem to contradict market efficiency. The following anomalies have been noted:

Excessive volatility. Common sense lies at the base of the first challenge to market efficiency. How can markets be so volatile? New information on, say, Google does not arrive every second, yet its share price changes from one minute to the next. There would seem to be a 'noise' effect that impacts on the basic value of the share.

Dual listed stocks and closed-end fund securities. Dual listed stocks are shares in twin companies that are listed on two different markets, with identical dividend payments. Nevertheless, the prices of the two stocks may differ over a long period. Similarly, the value of closed-end fund securities (made up only of listed stocks) can be listed over a long period at a discount or a premium to net asset value. Standard discounts applied to conglomerates do not explain the size of the discount on certain funds, and even less so the premiums on others! It is interesting to note that these premiums or discounts compared to the intrinsic value can last over the long term, which explains why arbitrage (something simple to implement) becomes complex for any investor that does not have a very long-term investment period.

Calendar effect. Certain studies highlight the fact that returns on financial securities may depend on the day of the week or the month in the year. Stocks seem to perform less well on Mondays than on other days, and returns in January are higher than in other months (this phenomenon is especially true for smaller firms). For each of these observations, reasons that are backed by investor rationality are put forward. Nevertheless, it does appear that the anomalies are not clear enough for profitable arbitrage to be carried out, given the amount of transaction costs.

Weather anomalies. It has been noted that returns on shares are higher when the weather is fine than when it rains. But here again, although the statistics of these observations are significant, they are not a sufficient basis for arbitrage.

Accordingly, there would appear to be a body of evidence that implies that the theory of efficient markets is partially invalid. Eugene Fama, the high supporter of efficient markets, defends the theory doggedly. For him, the observation of anomalies can largely be explained by the methodology used.

Fama especially challenges observations of systematic over- or under-reactions of markets noted by other economists.

If we do arrive at the conclusion that the theory of efficient markets is (at least partially) invalid, it then becomes necessary (i) to understand what it was in the initial modeling that did not correspond to reality and (ii) to attempt to develop a new modeling of investor behavior that is closer to reality.

2. Investor behavior

What if the initial assumption underlying modern theory was a false assumption: are investors really rational (i.e. do they act in a consistent manner in order to maximize returns)? Behavioral finance uses an innovative method for testing this assumption. Experiments have been carried out in order to determine the real behavior of investors faced with a choice.

The results of certain psychological experiments can be applied to finance. For example, some tests seem to prove that individuals answer questions put to them by making mental associations or taking short: a number between zero and 100 is chosen at random in front of a sample of people who are then asked to guess whether the number of African countries is higher or lower than the number drawn, and then to guess how many countries there actually are in Africa. It is interesting to note that the average number of countries given by people in the different samples to the last question depends on the initial number drawn. This example demonstrates the fact that investor decisions can be influenced (independently of fundamental choices to be made).

A typology of experiments that is also used to appreciate the attitude of investors to financial products involves giving a sample of individuals a choice between several lotteries (the gains on which are associated with probabilities) with or without a financial risk. Here we see a direct link with psychology. The field of behavioral finance has in fact been developed by financiers and psychologists in tandem. The results of these studies undermine some of the basic assumptions of investor rationality. The following behaviors can be cited:

1. Losses do not have the same weight of gains. Investors seem to prefer taking risks when there is a strong probability of loss (a probability of 50% of losing 100 rather than the certainty of losing 50), but they prefer to plump for a lower gain when the probability is high (certainty of gaining 50 rather than having one chance in two of gaining 100).
2. If the probability gap is narrow, individuals will choose the lottery offering the highest possibility of gain, but if there is a wide probability gap, they will take a close look at the expected gain. This generates a number of paradoxes. It is possible to prefer A to B and B to C, but to prefer C to A. For a financier, this means preferring BNP Paribas to Fortis, Fortis to Mediobanca, but Mediobanca to BNP Paribas! This observation is the sort of thing that can drive an asset manager crazy!

3. Impact on the market

The irrationality of some investors does not really represent a problem if the anomalies can be quickly corrected by arbitrage and if there is a rapid return to efficiency. Additionally, the presence of irrational investors among market players does not necessarily mean that markets are inefficient, especially if the trades made by these investors set each other off, or if rational investors can use arbitrage to bring about a return to balanced prices.

Nevertheless, some of the anomalies we've looked at (dual listing, closed-ended funds) last over the long term, which is proof that the inefficiency of markets cannot systematically be corrected by arbitrage. Some even seem to prove that the market systematically over- (or under-) reacts to some information. The super-performance of a share (or a portfolio) tends to follow on an under-performance, and vice versa.

4. Implications

It's very easy to criticize, but a lot harder to come up with something better. What is important is that we don't throw out the baby with the bathwater, by exploding the theory of markets in equilibrium, with all the consequences that that would entail (no more CAPM, impossible to value financial products).

What we need are suggestions for a more complete framework for finance. Existing models put forward by economists are, in our view, of partially limited use in their current state (especially for corporate finance). They focus on the first line of reasoning: model the behavior of investors in order to determine whether they get anything useful out of it and to identify how they understand financial products. This is just the first step in the reconstruction of a model, which goes as far as the valuation of shares. So, we're not quite there yet. But Rome wasn't built in a day and we'll keep a close eye on developments in the field of behavioral finance, waiting with some impatience for the direct applications thereof to corporate finance.

Investors are human beings, not computers, and are thus sensitive and irrational, and that's the way it should be. Can we model irrationality without making it disappear? And if behavioral finance manages to do that, won't it be a sort of pyrrhic victory?

But while we wait, we'd like to draw a quick parallel with physics. The theory of gravity remains valid, even though it has been proved to be defective at both the macro and micro level, by the theory of relativity and quantum theory. So we'll just soldier on for another few years with the theory of markets in equilibrium as our guide, at the risk of appearing old-fashioned, but our rational opinion is that this is a risk worth taking!

References and Further Reading

Chan, H. and Singal, V., Role of speculative short-term sales in the price formation: the case of the week-end effect, *Journal of Finance*, April 2003.

Hirshleifer, J. and Shumway, F., Good day sunshine: stock returns and the weather, *Journal of Finance*, June 2003.

www.behaviouralfinance.net, this site provides a very comprehensive list of all of the research on the subject and includes a large number of articles.

Micro-finance: helping the poor

The aim of all financial systems is to facilitate relationships between agents who have surplus capital at their disposal and agents in need of capital. It has been demonstrated that this function improves the general well-being of any society. On the whole, banks and financial markets fulfill this role very well by providing financing and/or investment opportunities to large numbers of corporations and ordinary people, especially in countries with Western-style economies, but also in countries such as China, Turkey and the Gulf States.

Like any organization, financial markets and banking systems have running costs (customer solicitation, analysis of loan applications, structuring of loans, providing of funds, management of repayments, bad debts and disputes). When these costs rise above a certain threshold, the intermediation service they cover becomes prohibitively expensive – we know of one financial intermediary that was asking for a fee equivalent to 80% of funds raised in an IPO of a firm with sales of €1.6m on the Paris OTC market!

So, there will always be some economic agents, the very poorest, who are *de facto* excluded from the official financial system which is just not interested in them. The paradox is that they are probably no less solvent in real terms than other borrowers and additionally, a portfolio of loans to the poor would be more diversified, and thus less risky for investors. Muhammad Yunus, the founder of the Grameen Bank in Bangladesh, who was awarded the 2006 Nobel Peace Prize, has provided concrete evidence to confirm this.

It is true that the emergence of credit scoring techniques, followed by on-line borrowing over the Internet have helped to lower the breakeven point on loans, but there is a level below which the market system just cannot go. Also, not everyone has access to the Internet or to a long list of credit references.

Given this situation, the emergence of a financial system specifically tailored to meet the needs of potential borrowers who have always been ignored by the traditional financial system was inevitable. It is known as micro-finance. Originally, micro-finance was a specifically created financial system and not an extension of traditional services offered by banks. Banks had, in fact, always wrongly assumed that very poor borrowers would have a much higher than average loan default.

Micro-finance is thus aimed at people who do not have access to traditional financial systems, in other words, at the very poorest members of society. This definition covers a large section of the population in emerging economies as well as the most underprivileged members of Western societies. Micro-finance works on the basis of the same logic as the traditional system. The difference lies in the size of the loans granted. The average amount of a micro-loan in Asia or Africa is around €300 (and can be for as little as €10), in eastern Europe it is usually just over €1000 and in western Europe around €2500.

There are over 1275 micro-finance institutions (MFIs) in the world that provide financing to over 100 million homes (source: Micro-finance Information Exchange, figures are from 10,000 institutions and 130 million borrowers according to PlaNet Finance). The sector is experiencing strong growth (Figure 2.2), with a ten-fold increase in the number of borrowers in ten years.

Micro-loans are generally used to finance small investments made by small businesses or rural homes. Loans are generally very short term (a protection for lenders) but may be renewed, with the possibility of larger loans for responsible borrowers who meet their repayments. Borrowers often

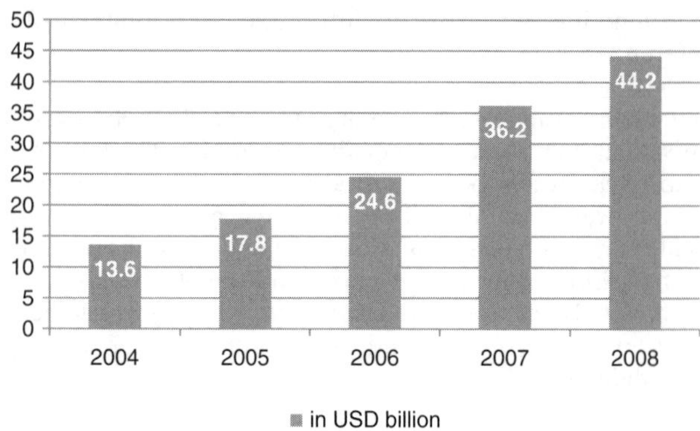

Figure 2.2: Growth in micro-finance volume worldwide.
Source: Microfinance Information Exchange (MIE)

organize themselves into solidarity groups, which enables them to guarantee the repayment of the loan.

Obviously, micro-finance does not purport to be able to solve all of the economic problems of emerging countries on its own. It is not the responsibility of MFIs to finance the infrastructure that is necessary for a country to develop. Micro-finance should thus complement other development initiatives. It is, however, undeniable that micro-finance helps to improve the living conditions of the very poorest members of society and to kick-start economic development.

The relationship between development aid and micro-finance is not that clear cut and defining micro-finance within traditional finance is not all that easy either. Even though recovery rates are very high (compared with recovery rates on traditional loans), operating costs of MFIs are, per euro lent, obviously much higher than for traditional loans:

- the number of loan applications to be processed is much larger;
- provision of services is more complicated (widely dispersed populations, etc.).

So, notwithstanding relatively high interest rates (although much lower than interest rates charged by money-lenders and usurers), very few MFIs are profitable (around 200). A lucky thing it is then that most MFIs are not-for-profit organizations (associations and foundations)!

Most MFIs are financed by entities which are not required to be economically profitable such as governments (development agencies, etc.), international organizations (EU, World Bank, etc.) or NGOs (see Figure 2.3). Traditional banks moving onto the micro-finance market generally have to sacrifice some of their profits which they justify on the grounds of corporate responsibility and ethics.

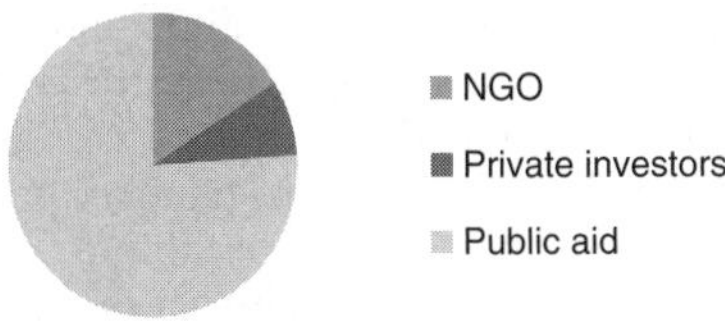

Figure 2.3: MFI financing. *Source: Micro-finance Information Exchange (MIE)*

As some countries develop economically (this is especially the case in Latin America), MFIs are becoming more profitable and some even go as far as changing their status from not-for-profit organizations to traditional banks.

We could well see a natural shift from micro-finance to traditional finance and from traditional finance (banks) to micro-finance. Even though there are clearly links between the two, we do not believe that such a shift would be either natural or desirable.

Any attempt to be more profitable will have contradictory effects on the micro-finance sector:

- greater financial efficiency for players, greater access to resources and accordingly greater involvement; and
- the solicitation of a more profitable client base (which will be more urban), with average loans for higher amounts, which would deny a section of the population access to financing.

Even though attempts to achieve a certain financial independence (covering costs with interest made) could be a goal which would guarantee the continued existence of the system, the future of micro-finance is not to become part and parcel of the traditional finance system. Its future is to plow its own furrow by sticking to its initial aims and by continuing to assist individuals in a meaningful way to 'enrich themselves through their work and their savings' (repaying a loan is a form of saving). Thanks to micro-finance, poorer clients can now hope that one day, they'll be able to gain access to the traditional financial system with all of its advantages, although they will of course also have to accept all of its unavoidable running costs. In the long term, the best proof of the success of micro-finance will be its disappearance, when it eventually runs out of clients. Unfortunately, we may have to wait quite a while yet until that happens.

Project finance

Project financing is used to raise funds for large-scale projects with costs running into the hundreds of millions of euros, such as oil extraction, mining, oil refineries, purchase of methane tankers, the construction of power plants or creation of works of art.

Lenders base their decision to extend such financing on an assessment of the project itself rather than the borrower, and on the projected cash flows generated by the project that will repay the credit. They rely on the project's assets as collateral for the debt.

This type of financing was first used in the early 1930s by American banks to extend financing to oil prospectors who could not offer the guarantees required for standard loans.

The banks drew up loan contracts in which a fraction of the oil still in the ground was given as collateral and part of the future sales were set aside to repay the loan.

With this financial innovation, bankers moved beyond their traditional sphere of financing to become more involved, albeit with a number of precautions, in the actual risk arising on the project.

But it is all too easy to become intoxicated by the sophistication and magnitude of such financial structures and their potential returns. Remember that the bank is taking on far more risk than with a conventional loan, and could well find itself at the head of a fleet of super oil tankers or the owner of an amusement park of uncertain market value. Lastly, the parent company cannot completely wash its hands of the financial risk inherent to the project, and banks will try to get the parent company financial guarantee, just in case.

When considering project financing, it is essential to look closely at the professional expertise and reputation of the contractor. The project's returns and thus its ability to repay the loan often depend on the contractor's ability to control a frequently long and complex construction process in which cost overruns and missed deadlines are far from rare. Project financing is not just a matter of applying a standard technique. Each individual project must be analyzed in detail to determine the optimal financing structure so that the project can be completed under the best possible financial conditions.

The financiers, the future manager of the project and the contractor(s) are grouped in a pool taking the form of a company set up specifically for the project. This company is the vehicle for the bank financing.

Clearly, project financing cannot be applied to new technologies which have uncertain operating cash flows, since the loan repayment depends on these cash flows. Similarly, the operator must have acknowledged expertise in operating the project, and the project's political environment must be stable to ensure that operations proceed smoothly. Only thus can investors and banks be assured that the loan will be repaid as planned.

Risks on large projects arise during three quite distinct stages:

- when the project is being set up;
- during construction; and
- during operations.

Contrary to appearances, risks arise as soon as the project is in the planning stage. Analyzing a major project can require several years, considerable expertise and numerous technical and financial feasibility studies. All this can be quite costly. At this stage, the actors involved are not sure that the project will actually materialize. Moreover, when there is a call for tenders, the potential investors are not even sure that their bid will be retained.

But, of course, the greatest risk occurs during construction, since any loss can only be recouped once the facilities are up and running!

Some of the main risks incurred during the construction phase are:

- **Cost overruns or delays**. Such risks can be covered by a specific insurance that can make up for the lack of income subject to the payment of additional premiums. Any claims benefits are paid directly to the lenders of the funds, or to both borrowers and lenders. Another method is for the contractor to undertake to cover all or part of any cost overruns and to pay an indemnity in the event of delayed delivery. In exchange, the contractor may be paid a premium for early completion.
- **Non-completion of work**, which is covered by performance bonds and contract guarantees, which unconditionally guarantee that the industrial unit will be built on schedule and with the required output capacity and production quality.
- **'Economic upheavals' imposed by the government** (e.g. car factories in Indonesia or dams in Nigeria) and arbitrary acts of government, such as changes in regulations.
- **Natural catastrophes** that are not normally covered by conventional insurance policies.

As a result, the financing is released according to expert assessments of the progress made on the project. Risk exposure culminates between the end of construction and the start of operations.

At this point, all funds have been released but the activity that will generate the flows to repay them has not yet begun and its future is still uncertain. Moreover, a new risk emerges when the installations are delivered to the client, since they must be shown to comply with the contract and the client's specifications. Because of the risk that the client may refuse to accept the installations, the contract usually provides for an independent arbitrator, generally a specialized international firm, to verify that the work delivered conforms with the contract.

Once the plant has come on stream, anticipated returns may be affected by:

- **Operating risks *per se***: faulty design of the facilities, rising operating or procurement costs. When this occurs, the profit and loss account diverges from the business plan presented to creditors to convince them to extend financing. Lenders can hedge against this risk by requiring long-term sales contracts, such as:
  - take *or* pay: these contracts link the owner of the facilities (typically for the extraction and/or transformation of energy products) and the future users whose need for it is more or less urgent. The users agree to pay a certain amount that will cover both interest and principal payments, irrespective of whether the product is delivered and of any cases of *force majeure*;
  - take *and* pay: this clause is far less restrictive than take or pay, since clients simply agree to take delivery of the products or to use the installations if they have been delivered and are in perfect operating condition.
- **Market risks**. These risks may arise when the market proves smaller than expected, the product becomes obsolete or the conditions in which it is marketed change. They can be contained, although never completely eliminated, by careful study of the sales contracts, in particular the revision and cancellation clauses which are the linchpin of project financing, as well as detailed market research.

- **Foreign exchange risks,** usually eliminated by denominating the loan in the same currency as the flows arising on the project or through swap contracts (see above).
- **Abandonment risk,** which arises when the interests of the industrial manager and the bankers diverge. For example, the former may want to bail out as soon as the return on capital employed appears insufficient, while the latter will only reach this conclusion when cash flow turns negative. Here again, the project financing contract must lay down clear rules on how decisions affecting the future of the project are to be taken.
- **Political risks**, for which no guarantees exist but which can be partly underwritten by state agencies.

Corporate finance in Europe: confronting theory with practice

Many studies have highlighted the fundamental differences between the structure and organization of markets and financial systems in the USA and Europe.

Stretching the stereotype, we could say that in the USA, market relationships are usually between a wide shareholder base and managers, while in Europe the tendency is more towards privileged relationships between dominant institutions and large controlling shareholders, often members of the company's founding family.

These differences have major repercussions in terms of corporate governance, and ultimately, on the development of financial markets in these countries. They are also likely to have significant repercussions on the financial practices of companies in Europe and in the USA. A team of Dutch researchers carried out a study on a sample of European companies, seeking to add to an American study. The results they obtained on a sample of 313 responses returned by the Finance Directors of UK, Dutch, German and French companies confirm our received ideas of how corporate finance is practiced. The main results of the research are discussed below.

The authors noted that the European companies that responded to their survey did not all have the same goals, with goals differing from country to country. British and Dutch companies all gave great importance to shareholder value as a decision-making criterion, while far fewer French and German companies saw shareholder value in this light.

The favorite investment decision-making criterion of the majority of European Finance Directors is the payback criterion. This criterion does not factor in the time value of cash flows or cash flows after the date on which the investment is recovered. In the USA, the payback criterion was only ranked third, behind IRR (internal rate of return) and NPV (net present value). The dominance of this investment decision-making criterion in Europe is more pronounced in smaller companies, in companies with older senior managers who have not done MBAs, and in unlisted companies.

Among the companies basing their investment decision-making on NPV criteria, European companies mainly use the CAPM (capital asset pricing model) for calculating the cost of capital, although not quite as often as their US counterparts. Here again, large companies and listed companies rely on this method more often than other companies.

European companies, like their US counterparts, rarely consider risk factors that are specific to the investment projects in question, such as interest rate risk, foreign exchange risk, etc. Only French companies, and to a lesser degree German ones, say that they adjust the discounted cash flow rate to recent stock market performances and to the risk of fluctuations in the price of raw materials. Finally, European companies only make minor adjustments to the cost of capital required for international projects, which goes against the theory and against common sense.

The authors also looked at choices of capital structure (debt to equity ratio) made by the financial directors of European companies. They looked at the relevance of the two main theories on which decisions relating to capital structure are based. The first is the static trade-off theory, which postulates that each company has a target capital structure which depends on tax advantages relating to debt and bankruptcy costs. The second is the pecking order theory which suggests that, as a result of information asymmetry between managers and the capital markets, companies have an order of preference for the various sources of capital for financing their investment projects. Internal resources are preferable to debt, which in turn is preferable to equity.

European companies, and especially French and British companies, would appear to set an optimal target capital structure slightly more frequently than their US counterparts. Furthermore, the criteria generally relied on for setting a target capital structure (debt-related tax breaks, bankruptcy costs) would not appear to have such a tangible influence on determining the optimal capital structure in the USA. The results obtained provide only a little support for the trade-off theory in Europe.

The pecking order theory would appear to be rejected in Europe, in the same way that the US study showed it was in the USA. The behavior of European finance directors reveals a preference for internal sources of financing relative to debt and equity.

The underlying motivation for this behavior is not linked to information asymmetry between managers and capital markets, but the determination to hold onto the company's flexibility and its ability to finance its investments autonomously. This should not come as much of a surprise to our readers.

More or less stating the obvious, the authors show that the larger the companies, the greater their preoccupation with the creation of shareholder value, and the more they will rely on sophisticated methods for their investment decision making, aware that arguments in favor of a choice of financial structure based on tax considerations have never been very convincing.

Capital markets: some useful definitions

Book-building

Book-building is a technique used to place securities on the market. It is the process whereby the bank marketing the offering gets to know investors' intentions regarding the volumes and prices they are prepared to offer for the security.

Bought deal

A bought deal takes place when a bank buys the securities from the seller or issuer and then re-sells them to investors. The remaining unsold securities go onto the bank's balance sheet. Bought deals are used most often for transactions such as block trades of already existing shares or a bond issue.

Claw-back

A claw-back clause allows the securities allocated to one class of investors to be reallocated to other classes of investors, should the structure of actual market demand (retail, institutional, etc.) differ from that planned originally.

Flow-back

Flow-back is the excessive sale of securities immediately after their placement.

Greenshoe

A greenshoe is an option granted by the seller or issuer to the bank to buy at the price of offering a number of supplementary shares over and above the number offered to investors.

Lock up
A shareholder who has sold a large number of shares or a company which has issued new shares is frequently required not to proceed with a supplementary sale or issue of shares for a given period called the lock up period. Most of the time this lasts between three and nine months.

One-on-one
Private meetings between the CEO or the CFO of a company and one of its (large) shareholders or potential investors are one-on-ones. Most of them take place during road shows.

Overhang
Overhang is a problem caused by fear that the arrival of a large number of shares on the market will depress the share price.

Road show
A road show is a meeting of the company's management with potential investors. It usually takes place as a part of a placement of a company's securities.

Warm up
Warm up sessions are meetings of investment banks with investors to test the latter's sentiment. Warm up meetings are especially important when the size of an issue is large.

Transaction multiples: before and during the crisis[2]

We have examined the effects of the current economic and financial crisis on transaction multiples. The aim of the analysis is threefold:

1. to assess to what extent multiples are affected by crisis, assuming that corporate transactions should generally occur at a lower price during a downturn and multiples be consequently lower;
2. to highlight if crisis produces differentiated effects in various countries and financial systems;
3. to test if multiples are also affected by the circumstance that companies may or may not be listed on stock markets.

Sample composition

We have examined two years: 2006 and 2008, unanimously considered, respectively, as an expansion and a depression year. We have used *three enterprise value (EV) transaction multiples*: EV/Sales; EV/EBITDA; EV/EBIT. These multiples are: among the most frequently employed; frequently available for troubled and young companies; relatively difficult to manipulate and not as volatile as net earnings multiples.

We have considered only European countries with a minimum number of 25 annual transactions for both years: France, Germany, Italy, Netherlands, Spain and UK. They have been divided into two groups, according to the financial system: *bank-based system* (France, Germany, Italy and Spain); *market-based system* (Netherlands and UK). Table 2.3 summarizes the sample characteristics.

---

[2]This topic has been written by Massimo Mariani, Associate Professor of Corporate Finance, Jean Monnet University, Italy.

Table 2.3: Sample criteria

Time period	From 1/01/2006 – 31/12/2006 and from 1/01/2008 – 31/12/2008
Countries	Buyer: EURO – Area Target: France, Germany, Italy, Netherlands, Spain, UK
Min number of annual deals per country	2006 – 25 2008 – 25
Deal type	Acquisition, Institutional buyout, MBI, MBO, Merger
Sector	Financial sector is excluded
Percentage of stake	Final stake min = 5 max = 100
Percentage of acquisition	Listed companies: min 2% Private companies: min 5%

The final sample comprises 511 deals in 2006 and 457 in 2008.

Deal multiples by country

Table 2.4 provides evidence of the deal multiples by country and by financial system.

The results show a *decrease of the median values of the multiples* from 2006 to 2008. The trend is generalized and does not substantially change with the different multiples used (–22.4% for EV/SALES, –13.7% for EV/EBITDA and –18.6% for EV/EBIT). Almost all countries behave similarly, with the sole exception of the increasing EV/Sales in the UK and the EV/EBITDA and EBIT in Spain.

The downward trend is evenly spread among the seven sectors considered in the analysis (Table 2.5). The results show that

Table 2.4: Deal multiples by target country

	EV/SALES			EV/EBITDA			EV/EBIT		
	2006	**2008**	**Δ**	**2006**	**2008**	**Δ**	**2006**	**2008**	**Δ**
France	1.01	1.00	−**2.3**%	9.04	8.05	−**10.2**%	13.01	11.06	−**11.5**%
Germany	1.03	0.08	−**41.3**%	8.05	7.03	−**14.6**%	14.04	11.06	−**19.9**%
Italy	1.03	1.01	−**22.0**%	9.03	7.00	−**24.2**%	13.02	10.03	−**22.4**%
Spain	1.07	1.04	−**18.8**%	10.01	10.03	3.2%	15.07	17.00	8.1%
BANK BASED ECONOMIES	1.03	1.00	−**20.4**%***	9.04	7.09	−**15.5**%***	13.09	11.07	−**16.1**%***
Netherlands	1.06	0.05	−**67.5**%	8.01	5.05	−**31.7**%	16.02	7.07	−**52.0**%
UK	1.03	1.05	17.3%	10.01	9.06	−**4.8**%	13.04	11.05	−**13.8**%
MARKET BASED ECONOMIES	1.04	0.07	−**47.1**%***	9.02	6.06	−**28.7**%***	15.00	8.07	−**41.8**%***
MEDIAN (AVERAGE OF) OF COUNTRIES			−**22.4**%***			−**13.7**%***			−**18.6**%***

***,** *: *tests respectively significant at the 1%, 5%, 10% levels.*

Table 2.5: Deal multiples by target sector

	EV/SALES			EV/EBITDA			EV/EBIT		
	2006	**2008**	**Δ**	**2006**	**2008**	**Δ**	**2006**	**2008**	**Δ**
Basic materials	1.16	0.0646	−**19.7**%	8.01	6.08	−**15.5**%	11.06	10.07	−**7.8**%
Consumer goods	1.16	0.0618	−**23.6**%	7.09	6.07	−**14.6**%	13.01	10.08	−**17.5**%
Healthcare	2.15	0.0646	−**56.9**%	12.05	8.02	−**34.4**%	21.00	11.09	−**43.4**%
Industrial goods	0.0597	0.0576	−**4.1**%	8.01	6.09	−**14.2**%	12.04	9.04	−**24.4**%
Services	0.0924	1.32	−**23.9**%	10.07	8.02	−**24.3**%	16.05	12.07	−**23.1**%
Technology	1.14	0.0667	−**15.8**%	11.06	8.03	−**28.2**%	17.00	11.09	−**30.0**%
Utilities	0.1458	1.43	−**50.8**%	95	8.05	−**9.7**%	15.01	14.02	−**6.2**%

the decrease is generalized and characterizes all the sectors: mainly healthcare (–43% of EBIT multiple) and technology (–30%), to a lesser extent utilities (–6.2%) and the basic materials (–7.8%). It is interesting to note that investors seem to penalize more mildly sectors with stable growth, lower volatility of earnings changes, lower R&D and incidence of intangible assets (utilities and basic materials, as well as consumer goods). These elements are consistent with the idea that investors become risk-averse during downturns, thus penalizing more intensely companies whose strategic and business risk are relatively high.

Deal multiples and target turnover

The sample has then been divided into seven classes according to the turnover of the target firm, with the aim of exploring to what extent multiples change with the size of the target company (Table 2.6). Each class of values contains an adequate number of firms (the minimum being discretionary set at 25 transactions).

While in 2006 the two smallest size classes contain the highest number and frequency of transaction (together

Table 2.6: Number of deals by target turnover (€000)

	2006	%	2008	%
0 – 10,000	114	22%	73	16%
10,000 – 50,000	141	28%	94	21%
50,000 – 150,000	88	17%	75	16%
150,000 – 300,000	37	7%	49	11%
300,000 – 1,000,000	62	12%	66	14%
1,000,000 – 5,000,000	36	7%	72	16%
>5, 000, 000	33	6%	28	6%
TOTAL	**511**	**100%**	**457**	**100%**

covering 50% of the entire sample of transactions), class density changes in 2008, because the number of transactions involving bigger targets increases substantially (the three top classes covering 36% of the entire sample). The shift toward bigger transactions could be at least partially explained with a 'flight to safety' of the M&A activity in downturns. During a crisis, investors generally increase their risk aversion and become more reluctant to consider risky transactions like small deals. *Ceteris paribus*, the bigger the size of the target company, the lower the riskiness of the potential deal tends to be. Bigger companies have higher market shares, are more diversified, have more bargaining power with stakeholders (clients, suppliers) and are generally less leveraged than small companies. All elements that, in turmoil, are positively considered by equity investors.

An additional factor concerning big size deals is provided in Table 2.7, where it can be observed that the *bigger the target size the higher the 'discount' applied by the market*. If we consider the EV/Sales of the two biggest dimension classes, the discount applied on bigger scale transactions is in fact substantially higher than the one applied on smaller deals.

A possible reason for this behavior is probably given by the high difficulty of financing big deals during a credit crunch, in turn forcing the need to offer an economic incentive in terms of lower multiples. This rationale is particularly grounded in this crisis, which has determined a dramatic credit squeeze for companies and investors, thus also reducing the possibility of structuring transactions involving the acquisition of relevant equity stakes of big companies.

The evidence of a 'big size discount' effect is further reinforced if we consider the content of Figure 2.4. It contains the regression analysis of the EV/EBITDA for 2006 and 2008 against the logarithm of the target turnover, and it has the aim of checking the statistical significance of the relationship between multiples and deal sizes.

Table 2.7: Deal multiples by target turnover

	EV/SALES			EV/EBITDA			EV/EBIT		
	2006	**2008**	**Δ**	**2006**	**2008**	**Δ**	**2006**	**2008**	**Δ**
0–10,000	1.09	1.08	−**2.8**%**	13.03	10.09	−**18.1**%**	21.01	17.00	−**19.2**%**
10,000–50,000	1.01	1.00	−**14.1**%**	8.07	8.09	2.6%	12.08	13.06	6.9%
50,000–150,000	1.01	1.00	−**4.7**%**	8.08	7.07	−**13.3**%**	13.05	11.00	−**18.2**%**
150,000–300,000	0.09	0.08	−**12.3**%**	8.09	7.07	−**25.5**%***	13.05	9.01	−**33.0**%***
300,000–1,000,000	1.04	0.08	−**38.1**%***	9.08	7.05	−**24.6**%***	13.09	10.07	−**23.3**%**
1,000,000–5,000,000	1.09	0.05	−**70.4**%***	11.03	6.05	−**42.4**%***	16.09	9.06	−**43.2**%***
>5,000,000	2.06	0.05	−**78.2**%***	10.02	6.03	−**33.2**%***	52.2	12.06	−**75.8**%***

***,**,*: *tests respectively significant at the 1%, 5%, 10% levels.*

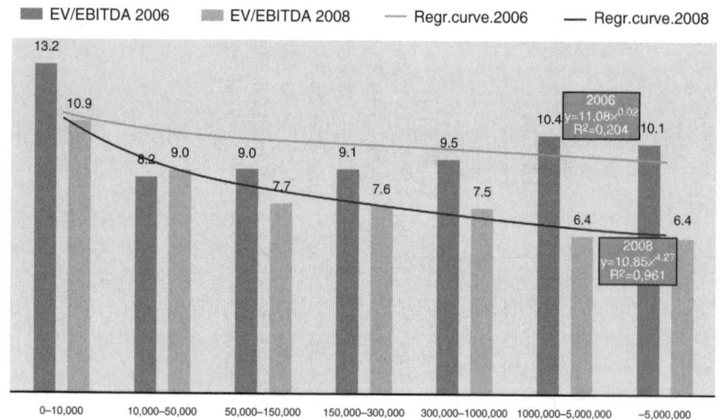

Figure 2.4: EV/EBITDA by target turnover

The regression line (and equation) shows that *multiples were strongly affected by the size of the target company* in 2008, while this effect was weaker in 2006. A possible interpretation is that investors could become more selective in choosing their target during a crisis, penalizing small deals (which occur at higher multiples) while favoring big deals (carried out at lower multiples). In times of stock market frenzy, conversely, the market euphoria could push investors to be less selective and/or the credit market to offer investors more resources for financing bigger scale transactions (thus reducing the need of a size discount on big deals).

Deal multiples and stock market listing

An additional objective is to examine to what extent multiples are also affected if the target is either a listed or privately held company. The assumption here tested is that transactions involving privately held companies could be penalized more intensely during a crisis, by applying to them a higher discount because of their lower *liquidity*. Liquidity could in fact be a key element of the transactions especially during downturns, as investors perceive the difficulties arising when investing in companies whose shares cannot be freely traded on a stock market.

Table 2.8 shows that the sample of transactions is balanced between listed and unlisted companies and the frequency of these two classes does not change from one year to the next.

Table 2.8: Target ownership status

	2006	%	**2008**	%
Listed	219[1]	43	203	44
Privately held	292	57	254	56
TOTAL	**511**	**100**	**457**	**100**

[1] This figure includes also companies delisted after 2006 (91 cases).

As shown in Table 2.9, EV multiples have decreases for both groups of companies. However, it is possible to observe that *multiples of listed companies decrease less markedly than those of private companies* (–0.4% vs. –28.5% for the EBITDA multiple). A similar behavior occurs for the other two multiples considered in the analysis, the EBIT multiples and the Sales multiple). The first one decreased, in fact, by 36.3% for unlisted versus 0.5% for listed, while the second decreased by 6.9% and 49.5% respectively.

Table 2.9: Deal multiples by target status

	EV/SALES			EV/EBITDA			EV/EBIT		
	2006	**2008**	**Δ**	**2006**	**2008**	**Δ**	**2006**	**2008**	**Δ**
Listed	1.02	1.01	−6.9%*	9.02	9.02	−0.4%	13.06	13.05	−0.5%
Unlisted	1.07	0.09	−49.5%***	9.03	6.07	−28.5%***	14.09	9.05	−36.3%***

***,**,*: *tests respectively significant at the 1%, 5%, 10% levels.*

The making of an investment banker

Share price performances can have a major impact on the wealth of investment bankers, many of whom have gained firsthand experience of this rather unpleasant fact as a result of the current economic crisis. But they can also have a long-term impact on their careers, and on the careers of students who are planning to enter the investment banking business. Paul Oyer (2008) of Stanford University has shown how market conditions over the period during which students are doing their MBAs modify the career decisions of those students. He has based his results on a survey of several thousand Stanford MBA graduates in the 1980s and 1990s.

Going straight into investment banking after completing an MBA has a long-term effect on the career of the young graduate. The probability of staying in investment banking is 73% higher than for a graduate who started his or her career in another business (consulting, entrepreneur, retail bank manager, etc.).

There are two possible explanations for this phenomenon:

- One is born an investment banker, i.e. some people are pre-disposed to investment banking and have a love and/or talent for it. Obviously, more natural-born investment bankers are likely to start out working in finance and will wish to stay in the business for as long as possible.
- One becomes an investment banker through experience. Good market conditions lead students to take more finance courses while they're at university or business school, and then to start their careers in investment banking, which means that early on, they develop the specific qualities that are needed to work in this field.

The results of Oyer's study argue in favor of the second explanation. When share prices are performing well, students who do not necessarily have a particular interest in or talent for finance are often attracted by the lure of money (investment bankers' earnings are far higher than average earnings in other sectors during such periods). If only natural-born investment bankers were to enter the field, such opportunistic students would switch fields as soon as there was a downturn in the cycle. Those who start out in investment banking when share prices are performing badly would be 'true' investment bankers, attached to their chosen field. Statistics show, however, that this is not the case. Those who start out in investment banking are just as likely to stay in the business, regardless of market conditions when they started their careers.

The study confirms that more students take finance courses when market conditions are favorable. Additionally, students who already have some experience of finance before starting their MBAs are more attached to the business than others. Oyer concludes that it is through experience that one becomes an investment banker. Initial choices made by students have long-term consequences on their careers, and these choices are influenced more by the economic situation at the time they are made than by any innate qualities.

Not only do market trends during the period that future investment bankers are studying have a lasting influence on their careers, they also have an impact on their discounted wealth. A Stanford MBA graduate working in finance for six to ten years was paid, over the period of the survey, \$15,814 per week, which is three times as much as Stanford MBA graduates working in other sectors earned. Oyer suggests that students beginning an MBA at a prestigious university or business school should hedge against a fall in share prices over the time it takes to complete their studies. Spoken like a true investment banker!

References and Further Reading

Oyer, P., The making of an investment banker: stock market shocks, career choice, and lifetime income, *Journal of Finance*, **63**, 2601–2628, 2008.

Corporate finance books

To improve your knowledge on the financial markets take a look at:

International Investments, B. Solnik and D. McLeavey, Addison Wesley, 2003.

A Random Walk Down Wall Street, B. Malkiel, Norton & Company, 2011.

Options, Futures, and Other Derivatives, J. Hull, 8th ed. Prentice Hall, 2011.

Corporate Financial Distress and Bankruptcy: Predict and Avoid Bankruptcy, Analyze and Invest in Distressed Debt, E. Altman and E. Hotchkiss, 3rd ed., John Wiley & Sons, 2005.

Triumph of the Optimists: 101 years of global investment returns, E. Dimson, P. Marsh and M. Staunton, Princeton University Press, 2002.

The Equity Risk Premium: The Long Run Future of the Stock Market, B. Cornell, John Wiley & Sons, 1999.

Discover the fundamentals of financial theory in:

Financial Theory and Corporate Policy, T. Copeland and F. Weston, 4th ed., Addison Wesley, 2004.

Capital Ideas: the improbable origins of modern Wall Street, P. L. Bernstein, John Wiley & Sons, 2005.

Beyond Greed and Fear: Understanding Behavioral Finance and the Psychology of Investing, H. Shefrin, Oxford University Press, 2007.

Value at Risk: The New Benchmark for Managing Financial Risk, P. Jorion, 3rd ed., McGraw Hill, 2006.

To perfectly master financial analysis, read:

Financial Accounting, D. Alexander and C. Nobes, 3rd ed., Prentice Hall, 2009.

Corporate Financial Reporting, H. Stolowy, M. Lebas and Y. Ding, 3rd ed., Cencage Learning, 2010.

IFRS 2010: Interpretation and Application of Internationl Accounting and Financial Reporting Standards, B. J. Epstein and A. Mirza, John Wiley & Sons, 2010.

Valuation: securities analysis for investment and corporate finance, A. Damodaran, 2nd ed., John Wiley & Sons, 2006.

Valuation: measuring and managing the value of companies, T. Koller, M. Goedhart and D. Wessels, 5th ed., John Wiley & Sons, 2010.

Discover the corporate finance strategy in:

Going Public: Everything You Need to Know to Take Your Company Public, J. Arkebauer, Dearborn financial publishing, 1998.

Takeovers, Restructuring, and Corporate Governance, F. Weston and M. Mithcell, 4th ed., Prentice Hall, 2003.

Real Options: A Practictioner's Guide, T. Copeland and V. Antikarov, Texere, 2003.

Creating Value from Mergers and Acquisitions, S. Sudarsanam, 2nd ed., Prentice Hall, 2010.

The Synergy Trap, M. L. Sirower, Free Press, 2007.

Dividend Policy: Its Impact on Firm Value, R. C. Lease et al., Oxford University Press, 2000.

The New Financial Capitalists: Kohlberg Kravis Roberts and the Creation of Corporate Value, G.P. Baker and G. Smith, Cambridge University Press, 1998.

Buyout: The Insider's Guide to Buying Your Own Company, R. Rickertsen, R.E. Gunther and M. Lewis, Amacom, 2001.

Or simply read research articles in finance:

Corporate Governance: An International Review

European Finance Review

European Financial Management

European Journal of Finance

Financial Analysts Journal

Journal of Accounting and Economics

Journal of Applied Corporate Finance

Journal of Business, Finance and Accounting

Journal of Corporate Finance

Journal of Finance

Journal of Financial Economics

Journal of Fixed Income

Review of Financial Studies

Brainteasers—PART I

1. The Dow Jones has got back to its historic highs of 2000 but the EuroStoxx 50 has not yet managed to do so because:
   - US firms are doing better than European firms
   - The Dow Jones does not reflect fluctuations in its market capitalization as accurately as the EuroStoxx 50 does
   - The Dow Jones does not include any technology, media and telecom (TMT) firms

2. SEPA stands for:
   - System for European Payment Advances
   - Société Européenne Par Action
   - Single Euro Payments Area

3. The net debt to EBITDA ratio at the start of an LBO is:
   - always below 5x
   - always above 6x
   - varies depending on the sector

4. The margin required by banks on the Tranche A of a senior debt in an LBO is generally:
   - between 175 and 225 basis points
   - above 250 basis points
   - below 150 basis points

5. To qualify for listing on the London Stock Exchange, a firm must:
   - be headquartered in the UK
   - have a share capital of at least €1,000,000
   - have financial records going back two years

6. When adjusting capital employed to equity, a firm's net debt on its seasonal activity corresponds to:
   - net debt on December 31
   - net debt on June 30
   - average net debt over the year

7. According to Modigliani and Miller, increasing the gearing ratio:
   - changes the WACC
   - does not change the WACC
   - increases the cost of equity and the WACC

8. Under IFRS, inventories should be valued:
   - using the LIFO method
   - using the FIFO method
   - using the identified purchase cost method

9. In Islamic finance:
   - in theory, interest at a fixed rate cannot be charged on a bank loan
   - in theory, the interest rate on a bank loan must be fixed
   - in theory, the duration of a bank loan should not exceed seven years

10. In the consolidated financial statements of a listed German company:
    - goodwill must be booked as a fixed asset and depreciated over a maximum of 40 years
    - goodwill must be booked as a fixed asset and written down if necessary
    - goodwill is systematically set off against shareholders' equity

11. The value of a put option rises:
    - if the exercise price is low
    - if the volatility of the underlying asset is low
    - if interest rates are low

12. What percentage of bank loans do banks in Europe sell on, directly or indirectly, to institutional investors?
- Less than 20%
- Around 40%
- Over 60%

13. EVA stands for:
- European Value Appraisal
- Enterprise Value Added
- Economic Value Added

14. Company A, with a P/E ratio of 12 acquires Company B on the basis of a P/E ratio of 25. The acquisition is fully financed using debt at 3% after tax.
- This acquisition will have no impact on Company A's EPS
- This acquisition will be accretive to Company A's EPS
- This acquisition will dilute Company A's EPS

15. A firm carrying debts with an overvalued share price can create value for its existing shareholders:
- by buying up its own shares at market price
- by carrying out a capital increase
- by buying up its own shares at a premium to the market price

Brainteasers—PART II

16. The weighted average cost of capital of a diversified company is:
- identical for each of its divisions
- specific to each division and each geographical region
- the same regardless of geographical region

17. An increase in the share of debt in the financing of a company:
- reduces the cost of equity
- raises the company's breakeven point
- lowers the beta coefficient of its shares

18. A company is more sensitive to changes in the economic situation if:
- it is a long way from breakeven
- its fixed costs (as a proportion of total costs) are high
- it is carrying little debt

19. Who said 'you can never spoil your shareholders enough'?
- John D. Rockefeller
- Albert Frère
- Warren Buffett

20. Which of the following shares do you expect to be more volatile?
- Cisco
- Imperial Tobacco
- BNP Paribas

21. The interest rate curve in the USA is currently:
- relatively flat
- sharp and rising
- sharp and falling

22. The vertical integration of a company within its sector:
- has no impact on its working capital requirements
- reduces its working capital requirements
- increases its working capital requirements in relation to sales

23. The yield to maturity on a loan with an interest rate of 6% paid quarterly will be:
- 6%
- 6.14%
- 6.66%

24. The leverage effect cannot be computed if the company has negative net debt.
- True
- False
- Partially false, because it depends on the level of interest rates

25. If the spot exchange rate is €1 = $1.2700, if the three-month interest rate on the dollar is 5.30% and if the three-month interest rate on the euro is 3.60, then the forward dollar/euro exchange rate is:
- 1.2647
- 1.2753
- 1.2725

26. A tag along clause enables:
- a lender to enjoy the same guarantees as those granted to another lender on a subsequent loan
- a minority shareholder to sell his or her shares at the same price as the majority shareholder
- a majority shareholder to force minority shareholders to sell their shares when he or she sells his or hers

27. The equity risk premium in Europe is around:
- 3%
- 4.5%
- 6%

28. In an LBO, the second lien is:
- more risky than the senior debt
- more risky than equity
- never used

Answers

Questions	Answers
1	*3*
2	*3*
3	*3*
4	*1*
5	*3*
6	*3*
7	*2*
8	*2*
9	*1*
10	*2*
11	*3*
12	*2*
13	*3*
14	*2*
15	*2*
16	*2*
17	*2*
18	*2*
19	*2*
20	*1*
21	*1*
22	*3*
23	*2*
24	*2*
25	*3*
26	*2*
27	*2*
28	*1*

True or false: test yourself

1. If there is no corporate income tax, cash flow depends on the depreciation policy. Why?
2. If corporate income tax is payable, cash flow depends on the depreciation policy? Why?
3. The ability of a firm to repay its debts is first of all measured by its ability to generate free cash flows. Why?
4. If the purchase of a 10% stake in another firm is financed by short-term bank borrowing, working capital will change.
5. The book value of a 100% fully consolidated subsidiary is equal to the book value of its equity plus goodwill not yet depreciated if any. Why?
6. The ratio financial debt/equity does not measure the liquidity a firm. Why?
7. If there is no corporate income tax, the leverage effect of debt does not exist. Why?
8. The closer the firm is to its breakeven point, the more sensitive are its profits to changes in sales.
9. Negative working capital and no cash or cash equivalent on the balance sheet means the firm is engaged in financial intermediation.
10. Profitability is equal to the income divided by the capital invested to produce this income.
11. An increase in value added does not affect working capital. Why?
12. A financial director does not create value. He or she just shares the wealth created by the firm among investors (shareholders and lenders) that provided the firm with its financial resources.
13. Higher indebtedness results in a ... beta coefficient? Why?
14. Higher fixed costs result in a ... beta coefficient? Why?
15. Are you speculating when you buy risk-free bonds?
16. Arbitrage is impossible without liquidity.

17. Diversification reduces risk but also eliminates the opportunity to cash in on a sudden rise in a share price.
18. Arbitrage serves no useful purpose.
19. If the required rate of return is met, the funds available to a firm are unlimited.
20. The risk of a well-diversified portfolio with a beta coefficient of 2 is twice as high as the market risk.
21. If the market capitalization of a firm is higher than the book value of its equity, can we say that the firm is overvalued? Why?
22. If the market capitalization of a firm is higher than the book value of its equity, can we say that its beta is higher than 1? Why?
23. If the market capitalization of a firm is higher than the book value of its equity, can we say that the firm is extremely profitable? Why?
24. If the market capitalization of a firm is higher than the book value of its equity, can we say that the accountants forgot something? Why?
25. If the market capitalization of a firm is higher than the book value of its equity, can we say that the markets are inefficient? Why?
26. In a securitization transaction, does a firm transferring its assets to an SPV run any risk should these assets be insufficient to cover the debts of the SPV?
27. In the area of off balance sheet financing, is the predominance of form over substance a feature of IAS or US GAAP?
28. Under IAS norms, can a firm consolidate another firm, in which it does not own a single share?
29. Should long-term debt and long-term rental contracts be treated the same way?
30. What do you think of the following: non-fraudulent off-balance sheet financing fools only those who want to be fooled?

Answers

1. If there is no corporate income tax, the depreciation policy does not influence the cash flow position, because the depreciation charge is just an accounting entry.
2. If corporate income tax is payable, cash flow is indirectly influenced by the depreciation policy, because the depreciation charge, a purely accounting entry, reduces the taxes due.
3. Even if the elements of working capital are short term (usually a few months, hence liquid), they are renewed permanently; hence, the working capital is permanent.
4. This operation is purely financial and it does not impact on operating activities. In particular, it has nothing to do with inventories, payables, and receivables.
5. True. By construction.
6. This ratio measures only the relative weight of debts in all sources of funds. Liquidity is best measured by the current ratio which is the ratio of short-term assets to short-term liabilities. It checks that short-term assets (less than one year) are bigger than short-term liabilities and hence allow debts to be paid off in due course, thanks to the progressive monetization of current assets.
7. The leverage effect exists whenever there is a difference between return on capital employed and the cost of debt. Taxation increases the leverage effect by reducing the cost of debt.
8. A firm close to its breakeven point shows very small profits. Hence, an increase in sales will translate in a considerable increase in profits. Profits being close to zero, any increase will seem considerable.
9. Financial intermediation consists of financing long-term investments with short-term borrowings. Negative working capital means that assets with maturities longer than one year are not fully covered by liabilities due in more than one year and are thus financed by short-term

liabilities, at least partially. This is financial intermediation.

10. Don't mix up margin with profitability. Margin is income divided by sales or production. Profitability is income divided by capital invested.
11. If the percentage of value added in sales increases, this means that the firm passes the product through more transformation stages, that it buys its raw materials at an earlier stage of the value chain and sells its goods at a later stage of the value chain. It means that inventories decrease, payables are smaller (the firm now buys less from its suppliers) and receivables are bigger (the firm now sells more to its clients). Hence, working capital increases.
12. The financial director cannot influence operating profits, which depend on the quality of assets only. His or her role is to distribute this profit among the various providers of funds, which financed these assets.
13. Higher indebtedness increases financial expenses and raises the firm's breakeven point. Profits will be less stable; hence, the share price will become more volatile (= increase in beta).
14. Higher fixed costs raise the firm's breakeven point. Profits will be less stable; hence, the share price will become more volatile (= increase in beta).
15. When you buy risk-free bonds (meaning there is no risk that the issuer will default), you are potentially speculating on a fall in interest rates. Such a fall would raise the price of your bonds.
16. An arbitrage is composed of several transactions that must be done simultaneously. Liquidity is thus necessary.
17. By diversifying your portfolio you eliminate the specific risks and run the market risk only. Therefore, profits from a sudden rise in a share price will be diluted in the overall performance of your portfolio.
18. It guarantees that the markets are always in equilibrium.

19. At least in theory. Still, it is necessary to have enough sufficiently profitable industrial projects to absorb all these funds!
20. The total risk breaks up into a market risk related to the beta coefficient and into a specific risk. This specific risk can be eliminated, especially in a well-diversified portfolio that we have here. Therefore, the only remaining risk is that of the market. This residual risk is twice as high as that of the market, since the beta coefficient of the portfolio is equal to 2.
21. It simply means that its return on equity is higher than the rate of return required by its shareholders.
22. It simply means that its return on equity is higher than the rate of return required by its shareholders. It has nothing to do with the beta.
23. It simply means that its return on equity is higher than the rate of return required by its shareholders.
24. It simply means that its return on equity is higher than the rate of return required by its shareholders.
25. It simply means that its return on equity is higher than the rate of return required by its shareholders. It has nothing to do with the efficiency of the financial markets. However, it shows that the industrial markets are less efficient than financial markets, because over certain periods, industrial markets can offer abnormally high returns.
26. No, the SPV is protected by insurance. In general an insurance technique is put in place to cover this risk.
27. US GAAP. American norms are based on rules, international norms (IAS) on principles.
28. Yes, if it exerts economic control.
29. Yes.
30. It is true. The notes to the accounts give enough information to avoid being fooled by non-fraudulent schemes. The notes are produced to be read!

Crossword

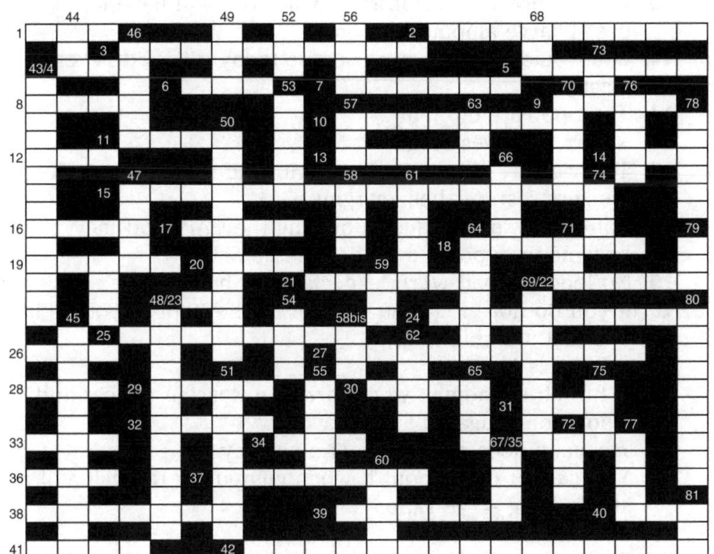

Horizontal

1. Difficult to keep them constant in the current environment.
2. Tours that take CEOs and CFOs of listed companies to London, Edinburgh, Geneva, Paris, Boston and New York once or twice a year.
3. Provided too much credit enhancement so that most of them are now bankrupt or in bad shape.
4. Only Fidel Castro believes it has a role in the current financial and economic turmoil.
5. Financial divisions that do not create value.
6. Weapon of mass destruction according to Warren Buffett.
7. Has lost his bonus and sometimes his job too.

8. Some countries are lamenting their failure to adopt it as their currency earlier but it's too late now!
9. If you were .... on real estate you will have lost a pretty large amount of money!
10. Life would be a lot more serene today if they'd never existed.
11. The opposite of unfair.
12. Return on investment.
13. The yield ..... is now steep, with the right slope to help bankers restore their margins.
14. Could have succeeded in ousting the CAPM but never became very popular with professionals.
15. No longer a bad word, especially in the UK.
16. If you do not ... .., you will not find, except of course if you just stumble onto it.
17. .... is king.
18. A British economist who married a Russian dancer and who is once again back in favor.
19. 7 usually does more than one per day.
20. You cannot do without it when computing the value of a share using a P/E ratio.
21. Same as definition 7.
22. Finance is all about it.
23. Has considerably increased for car manufacturers since the end of 2008.
24. We now know that it can be plentiful and then vanishes in a matter of days if not hours.
25. Until mid 2007, the sky seemed to be its only limit. Now people are treating it with more caution.
26. You should at least be able to keep it when your house is seized because you have stopped paying your monthly payments on your subprime loan.
27. Have plenty of work ahead of them.
28. Return on assets.
29. Sale of unexercised warrant
30. With 62, one of the two main culprits responsible for the current situation.
31. What most stock prices are now.

32. An option or a phone conversation.
33. Could it do a worse job?
34. They take place once a year, generally at this time of the year.
35. Single Euro Payment Area.
36. They are being progressively replaced by IFRS.
37. If you're on the dole then you're no longer on it.
38. This is what the Vernimmen is all about!
39. Earnings before interest, tax, depreciation and amortization.
40. Most non US groups are listed in the USA through them.
41. Adjusted Net Asset Value.
42. In three words; the best investment choice criteria.

Vertical

43. Will rise from the dead, just like Jesus did, but it will take more than three days!
44. Cannot go bankrupt but has clearly failed.
45. Was very much sought after when markets were up but proved to be illusory when markets turned down.
45. Same as 41.
46. A very regular guy who turned out to be a crook.
47. So are you if you have lost everything on the stock market including your shirt.
48. A booming area.
49. A barbarian relic according to 18.
50. They have so poorly performed recently, especially on structured products, that they have been deprived of their first N; two words.
51. The P/E ratio is one of them.
52. When I learned that most of my assets were placed with Madoff, I decided to drown my sorrows by drinking a whole bottle of it!
53. Useful for speculating, hedging or for arbitrages.
54. Widely used to compute the cost of equity or the cost of capital.

55. The one between Daimler and Chrysler was a disaster and ended up being unraveled.
56. A Spanish car trademark or the asset of a stockbroker.
57. The American equivalent of the AMF, CONSOB, CNMV or FSA.
58. If at end of the summer of 2008 you were …… on volatility you made a killing!
58. Enterprise Resources Planning.
59. Same as 14, created by Stephen Ross.
60. Computed in London and widely used in banking worldwide.
61. Has dramatically increased over the last 18 months but the impact of its increase on borrowers was mitigated by interest rate falls.
62. With 29, one of the two main culprits responsible for the current situation.
63. Cannot be increased forever without increasing risk taken.
64. A worthy successor to Nick Leeson even if he didn't bring his bank down.
65. Return on capital employed.
66. The option market in London.
67. Measure the market risk of an asset.
68. Companies are always reluctant to cut it but sometimes they simply have to in order to save cash.
69. Same as 51.
70. Has unwillingly illustrated that there may be exceptions to the 'too big to fail' rule even if everybody regrets it now.
71. Net Asset Value.
72. Same as 8.
73. No longer as popular with managers as before mid 2007.
74. Some companies are merging to achieve the right. …
75. A product that allows you to exchange a fixed rate for a floating one, a dollar for a euro, etc.
76. Net Operating Profit After Tax.
77. Most asset managers say they are pursuing it, very few deliver it constantly.

78. If you focus too much on this then you forget all about risk, and you are dead.
79. The missing brother of ROI, ROCE and ROA.
80. Can be normal, inverted or flat; two words.
81. Return On Equity.

Index